THE POWER
CENTRA

The Pilgrim's Guide

KEITH DOWMAN

Keith Dowman has spent the last twenty years in India and Nepal. He has been educated in the theory and practice of Tibetan Buddhism by eminent Lamas of several Tibetan schools, and has translated several major Tibetan texts into English. He now lives with his family in Kathmandu, where he continues to explore the Tibetan tradition and to interpret it for people in the West.

THE POWER-PLACES
OF CENTRAL TIBET:
The Pilgrim's Guide

KEITH DOWMAN

ROUTLEDGE & KEGAN PAUL
LONDON & NEW YORK

First published in 1988 by
Routledge & Kegan Paul Ltd
11 New Fetter Lane, London EC4P 4EE

Published in the USA by
Routledge & Kegan Paul Inc.
in association with Methuen Inc.
29 West 35th Street, New York, NY 10001

Set in 11/12 Garamond
by Columns of Reading
and printed in the British Isles
by The Guernsey Press Co Ltd
Guernsey, Channel Islands

Library of Congress Cataloguing in Publication Data

Dowman, Keith.
    The power-places of Central Tibet: the pilgrim's guide / Keith Dowman.
    p.   cm.
    Bibliography: p.
    Includes index.
    ISBN 0–7102–1370–0 (pbk.)
    1. Buddhist pilgrims and pilgrimages – China – Tibet – Guide-books.
2. Buddhist shrines – China – Tibet – Guide-books.   3. Tibet (China) –
Description and travel – Guide-books.   I. Title.
BQ6450.C62T533   1988
915.1'504–dc19   87–15757 CIP

British Library CIP Data also available
ISBN 0–7102–1370–0

CONTENTS

MAPS

PREFACE

This *Pilgrim's Guide* is based upon *Khyentse's Guide to the Holy Places of Central Tibet*. Jamyang Kyentse Wangpo (1820-92), a Khampa lama, made frequent, extended pilgrimages to Central Tibet and wrote his guide at the end of a long life as a contribution to the old and popular genre of Tibetan literature called *neyik*, guides to pilgrimage. Kyentse Rimpoche was no ordinary lama. One of the greatest figures in the eastern Tibetan eclectic renaissance of the last century, his scholarship and wisdom combined to give his work the highest mark of authority and integrity. His *Guide* was translated into English and partially annotated by the notable Italian scholar Alfonsa Ferrari, who never visited the East and who died before she could complete her work. The annotation was completed by another Italian scholar, Luciano Petech. His contribution was augmented by Hugh Richardson, the last British Resident in Lhasa. Richardson's clear, concise additions to the notes, detailing observations compiled during his wide travels in Central Tibet over several years, are of vital importance for information on the pre-1959 state of various monasteries. For their annotation, the Italian scholars relied heavily on the accounts of their master, Giuseppe Tucci, derived from his short journey to Central Tibet in 1948.

Khyentse's Guide covers Central, Southern and Western Tibet. The scope of this *Pilgrim's Guide* is limited to Central Tibet, the old province of U, which includes the Kyichu Valley system and the reaches of the Tsangpo (Brahmaputra) in its passage from Chaksam to Kongpo. Lhasa is the centre of the province and the places described herein are all within a radius of 250 km from Lhasa, except those listed in the chapter "Across Tsang to the Nepal Border". We visited most of the approximately 170 power-places in Central Tibet mentioned in *Khyentse's Guide* during the summers of 1985 and 1986. Information on the majority of his sites omitted from our itineraries (about thirteen) has been supplied by other pilgrims. Those very few places about which we have no contemporary information are so indicated in the text. Each entry in this *Pilgrim's Guide* enlarges upon the topics that concerned Kyentse Rimpoche: location and chief features of the site, cherished relics and treasures, and the history and importance of the place. Kyentse Rimpoche's description of the temples, images and treasures of the monasteries has permitted a useful comparison between what existed before 1959 and what now remains after the Cultural Revolution. Historical information about the power-places was derived from *Khyentse's Guide*, from various literary sources (see Bibliography) and from informants at the holy places.

Although Kyentse Rimpoche was involved in an eclectic renaissance, the gompas and shrines built by the Yellow Hats did not form any significant part of his pilgrimage itineraries. He was concerned mainly with the age-old power-places of the Red Hats, not with the relatively recent academies of the Gelukpa School. He mentions the great monastic foundations of Tsongkapa and his disciples – Ganden, Drepung, Sera, and also Chokorgyel for example – but he ignores most of the later Gelukpa monasteries. A few significant ancient power-places were unaccountably omitted from Kyentse's pilgrimages and these have been included here. The main inadequacy of *Khyentse's Guide* is its brevity. Its principal function was to locate and identify and merely to indicate historical associations and contemporary conditions, rather than to describe and comment upon them. In so far as space allows, that description and commentary has been added here.

The chief purpose of this work is identical to that of Kyentse Rimpoche – to indicate the location and significance of the principal power-places of Central Tibet in the hope that such information may be of practical use to pilgrims. Most of the valley sites are now accessible by jeep-road, although the cave

power-places can only be approached by foot. It is also intended
that this *Pilgrim's Guide* will complement studies in the historical
geography of Tibet and provide additional information and
correct old misconceptions.

In so far as this *Pilgrim's Guide* is based upon short visits to
each site, the information accrued is sometimes partial and
lacking corroboration, and in so far as rebuilding, restoration and
the gathering in of religious artefacts is still in process *The
Pilgrim's Guide* will require constant updating. We would be
grateful to receive corrections and any additional information,
particularly concerning those places that went unvisited, for
future editions. Please write to the author care of the publisher.

I would like to thank all the Tibetans who spontaneously
extended generous and gracious hospitality to us while on
pilgrimage, and also to thank the Tibetan guides and informants,
monks and laymen, who with great patience and generosity in
time and spirit gave us information. I have become indebted to a
host of people during the preparation of this book, so many that
it is impossible to mention them all by name. In particular,
however, I would like to thank Heather Stoddard-Karmay, A.
Bradley Rowe, Victor Chen, Steve McGuinness, Katie Hetts,
Brot Coburn and Edward Henning; *Stone Routes*, Raphaele
Demandre, Brian Beresford and Ian Baker for their black and
white photographs; Meryl White for the maps and line-drawings;
and Lokesh Chandra for use of selected line-drawings of Buddhas
and Lamas from the charts *Three Hundred Icons of Tibet*. Finally, I
acknowledge a deep debt of gratitude to my Lama, Dilgo Kyentse
Rimpoche, who supported this project.

Keith Dowman
Kathmandu
May 1987

INTRODUCTION

1 The Yoga of Pilgrimage

Pilgrimage as a devotional exercise and a yoga is as old as Buddhism itself. The Tibetan pilgrim may be a layman intent on accumulating merit to expedite a better rebirth or to obtain a mundane boon; he may be a yogin who has taken constant peregrination from power-place to power-place as his path to Buddhahood; in Central Tibet he may have come from the provinces to pay homage at the power-places associated with the founder of his lineage: there is a wide diversity of motivation, but pilgrimage in Tibet is as much a part of the Buddhist's lifestyle as summer vacation is in Europe. The karmically-blessed, committed yogin will find a cave or hermitage and spend as much as a lifetime in a single place to fulfil his destiny. The layman and the more restless yogin can aspire to the same end on pilgrimage. Thus the physical exertion and the sensual feast that is an integral part of pilgrimage in Tibet can become the mode and the means of attaining the Buddha's enlightenment. The rarity of the Tibetan atmosphere stretching the lungs to their limit; the sense of immense space and isolation; the unpolluted purity of the environment; and the unfiltered rays of the sun making a critical but undefined contribution: the body and mind are transformed and cleansed. As a support to meditation, physical exertion stimulates the senses to higher appreciation of sight, sound and smell, and the sparseness of human settlement gives a heightened awareness of the interdependent, holistic qualities of nature. In

the secluded valleys of hermits and herders, marmots, hares, rabbits, *lagomys*, antelopes and various deer, yaks and many birds are quite tame, evoking the Buddhist and the Franciscan vision of the lion lying down with the lamb. The pilgrim can be as much a yogin as the ascetic in his cave.

Nevertheless the most powerful places of pilgrimage in Tibet are certainly the cave-sites, and the most renowned cave-hermitages are associated with Guru Rimpoche, Padma Sambhava, Tibet's Great Guru. It is not coincidence that the locations where Guru Rimpoche is said to have meditated are age-old power-places of geomantic perfection. The Tibetans did not need the Chinese science of *feng-shui* to identify these sites. Just as the Druids in Europe and the Dravidian priests in India unerringly identified the sites of their temples and their cave-hermitages with focal points of natural energy, so did the Tibetans. In general, cave-sites are located high in the upper reaches of valleys, and frequently they are self-evident focal points, the topography leading naturally to them. They are found in phallic peaks with vistas pointing at every other significant point in the panorama; in scarps or crags at the very top of a valley with a vista overlooking the valley plain; on prominences at the confluence of rivers; on the top of large rocks in a valley plain; or at the centre of an amphitheatre of rolling hills. A sense of being at the centre of a mandala is frequently felt at such sites. The cave usually faces east or south. At least one vista will provide an impression of spaciousness. A spring or stream, the source of *drubchu*, meditation-water, will be found in the vicinity, and to find a tree nearby is auspicious. Guru Rimpoche's power-places are characterized by several of these features. Further, in every Guru Rimpoche cave-hermitage treasures were concealed by the Guru to be discovered by a fortunate "spiritual son" at a correct juncture. Thus the pilgrim's destination is always a special point of the earth's surface endowed with a powerful mystique.

Each principal valley possesses only a single Guru Rimpoche cave; but there are a variety of other power-places on the pilgrim's route. In this guide the largest category of power-place is the temple with a monastery built around it. The geomantic perfection of Guru Rimpoche cave-sites is not found at all

[1.] [above] RONGPAS: some village women watching clowns (photograph by I. Baker) [below] DROKPAS: yak-herdsmen and their black tents below the Gokar La (photograph by *Stone Routes*)

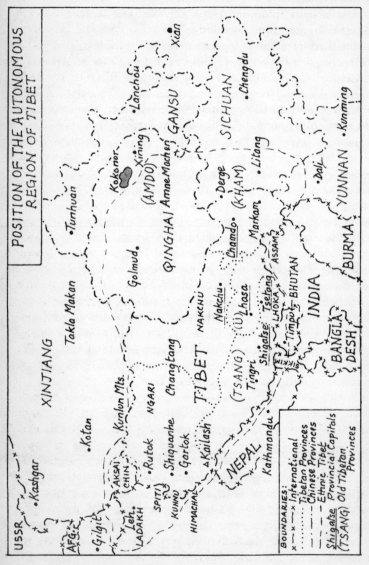

Map 1 Position of the Autonomous Region of Tibet

monasteries, although monastic establishments have often arisen around the hermitage of the founder. Also, the site of a monastery may have been the residence of an elemental spirit or a mountain deity propitiated by a yogin and bound to serve whoever invokes him. An Indian *siddha* or *pandita* may have taught there or a Tibetan yogin may have meditated there.

Another destination of the pilgrim is the *chorten* (see Glossary) that enshrines the relics of a saint or yogin, or which has been endowed by local tradition with some magical property. A rock or crag, often painted red, may be the residence of a local deity and the destination of a pilgrim with a connection to that deity.

As in so many aspects of the religious life Indian antecedents inspire the Tibetan yogin-pilgrim. Pilgrimage around the twenty-four pre-eminent tantric power-places of Buddhist India was a spiritual exercise that the *siddha*-Gurus included in their store of "skilful means of attaining the Buddha's enlightenment" At each of the twenty-four power-places the pilgrim recited the deity's mantra and performed the requisite devotions supported by the ecstatic vibration of like-minded pilgrims and the power emanating from the mystical forms impressed into the visible environment by generations of spiritually powerful masters. On a more esoteric level, the yogin could gather the sacred medicinal plants associated with the deity of the twenty-four places, and finally preparing an elixir from these herbs the resulting alchemical preparation would be the Nectar of Immortality. The Indian tradition of pilgrimage was adopted by the Tibetans and moulded by their specific cultural modes.

Circumambulation, prostration, offering, recitation of mantra, and meditation are the devotions performed by every pilgrim at the power-places on his route. Circumambulation, or *korra*, may appear to the western mind as a simplistic practice for a credulous devotee. To the pilgrim aware of the mandala principle and the calming and centreing of awareness that the exercise produces through identification of consciousness with the centre of a mandala circle and the symbolic modifications of its circum-ference, *korra* can be a potent method of heightening awareness. When *korra* is coupled with recitation of mantra its effects are increased. *Korra* is usually performed clockwise around an image, a chorten, a temple, a *gompa*, or a sacred mountain or lake, while some *korra* circuits embrace a unity of power-places that can take days or weeks to circumambulate.

The effect of prostration is self-evident: it induces a mindstate of devotion and receptivity to the deity or lama to whom prayers are addressed. The obeisance or prostration is performed before receptacles or symbols of one of the three existential modes, or "bodies", of the Buddha: an image represents the Buddha's form; books of scripture represent the Buddha's speech; and the chorten represents the Buddha's mind. Pilgrims prostrating from their home in eastern Tibet all the way to the Holy City of Lhasa, for instance, prostrate to a visualized image of a Buddha.

Offering, or ritual giving, is perhaps the most vital purpose of the pilgrim at the power-places he visits, but there is no one explanation of the purpose of this function. Offering is made as obeisance and as thanksgiving; as a token requiring reciprocal response from the deity; as propitiation averting hostile influences; as a means of accumulating merit towards a better rebirth; and as a symbolic gift of sensory pleasure. The meaning of the offering is determined by the giver and the object of the gift. The offering of a *katak*, a white flaxen scarf, is a token of respect; a butter lamp is the symbolic gift of light; incense gives pleasure to the deity; a piece of cloth or any personal effect left on an altar reminds the deity of the giver's prayer; food or drink offered to the deity pleases the deity and when returned to the giver contains the blessing of the deity. The prayer that accompanies the rite of offering is not to be confused with the mantra that is recited automatically by the pilgrim while walking from site to site, while performing *korra* and at every possible moment of the day. Pilgrimage, prostration and *korra* are exercises that purify the body; mantra purifies the voice and focuses the concentrated meditation that purifies mind. The Six Syllable Mantra, OM MANI PEME HUNG, the verbal symbols of the Protector of Tibet, Chenresik (Avalokitesvara), is recited by all devotees; the Twelve Syllable Mantra, OM AH HUNG VAJRA GURU PEME SIDDHI HUNG, evokes the blessing of Guru Rimpoche; and each initiate will recite the specific mantra of his *yidam*, his personal deity.

The pre-Buddhist and eternal Tibetan folk religion, a meld of animistic belief and quasi-Manichean Bon religion, quite naturally treats the lore of rocks. On the top of every Tibetan pass, high or low, a rock cairn is located that serves as an altar to the deity of the pass or the mountain god. Whoever crosses the pass either adds a stone to the *lhabtse*, the cairn, or builds a three stone pile himself, and he will also utter a prayer and end with "Lha sollo! Lha sollo! Lha gyello! Lha gyello! Kei kei! Ho Hoo!" As at any power-place he may also attach *lungta*, wind-horses or prayer-flags, singly or in a string. The symbols and prayers printed on prayer-flags purify the wind and please the gods. At other places of peculiar spiritual power conventionally designed altars with flat stones lodged on two side-stones are constructed. On the top of every significant hill a marker is erected, either a cairn, standing stone or a pole. The alignments which give certain prominences significance rather than others is a matter requiring study outside the field of Buddhist pilgrimage.

An indigenous Tibetan form of offering derived from pre-Buddhist tradition is the *sang* offering of juniper smoke. The chief sites of this offering are mountain peaks associated with mountain gods, but a *sangkang*, a white pot-bellied chimney containing the hearth, is to be found in the courtyards of most gompas. Large *sangkangs* located in the four cardinal directions of the Lhasa Jokang on the Barkor burn night and day. Although all the Buddhas and Guru Rimpoche are invoked in the prayer offered with the juniper twigs, the protecting deities are the main objects of worship.

Devotion is a necessary condition for the fulfilment of the pilgrim's purpose. Attitude distinguishes the pilgrim from the tourist, and in some places of pilgrimage it determines the style of welcome the western visitor receives. Generally photography will be welcomed, but courtesy is required in the act. Prejudice against smoking is inevitable. Unlike the "Southern" Buddhist monks of Sri Lanka and Thailand, the *mahayana* Tibetan monk is forbidden to touch tobacco, and little distinction is made between tobacco and opium because the smoke of both of them contaminates the air and poisons the spirits that live in it. The Tibetans, with their prayer-flags, their purifying incense and *sang* offerings, are highly aware of the spiritual presence in the air. The Tibetan conception that noxious smoke contracts, knots and degenerates the subtle energy-carrying channels of the body of the individual is of secondary import here; smoke pollutes the aerial environment for those who live permanently in it.

2 The Condition of the Gompas

For the first time in centuries it has now become possible for western pilgrims to visit the power-places of Central Tibet without great hardship. In the atmosphere of suspicion that pervaded Tibet in the late 1970s and early 1980s, when it became possible to visit selected sites under the rigorous guidance of couriers and guides, pilgrimage was impossible. Now, however, in this new era of liberal polity, now that the Tibetans possess a modicum of religious freedom that they are fully exploiting, now that the pilgrim finds a welcome at the shrines, sanctuaries, caves and hermitages, pilgrimage has become eminently desirable and a minimum of facilities are available to make it feasible. True, the depredations of Maoist policies from 1960-75 have left only a small fraction of Tibet's architectural heritage intact; but there are very few gompa sites in Central Tibet today where there is not some structure containing a shrine and at least one competent monk or lay initiate to tend it.

Only a few of the 3,000 monasteries that the Dalai Lama left behind him, when he embarked upon his self-initiated exile in 1959, now remain. A few shrines of great national significance in the Lhasa area, including the Jokang, the Potala, the principal temples of Sera and Drepung, and the Drolma Lhakang, were preserved at Premier Chou En-Lai's behest. At almost forty sites in Central Tibet the structure of at least one temple was saved from destruction, but after two decades as a granary, store-house, go-down or Party office, the temple murals are defaced and the sacred ornamentation of most of them destroyed. Most of these temples have been restored or are being restored. At a further forty sites mentioned by Kyentse Rimpoche where no roofed structure remained in 1980, new temples or chortens have been built. Another forty sites remained in ruins in 1985, but plans for rebuilding exist for many of them. Kyentse Rimpoche's 170 power-places in Central Tibet include some thirty cave-sites, and the majority of these shrines are intact and retain the qualities that have always given them importance. Where the power of a place was originally imbued by human activity, the pilgrim may sometimes be disappointed at a ruined site. But where man's attempts to improve upon nature's provision of natural power-places have finally been thwarted, the removal or reduction of structures in the vicinity of a cave or chorten has in some cases revealed the previously hidden geomantic perfection of a site and the pilgrim will be overwhelmed by the magnificence of the natural situation.

The Party authorities are subsidizing the rebuilding of at least one temple and limited monastic living quarters at each site with significance for the Tibetans. Further, it seems to be the authorities' rule to accede to a Lama's request for permission to rebuild his monastery, even when that Lama is returning from exile in Nepal or India. Support in the form of cash, materials and labour are generally provided by the local people, although the quality of a structure built with such limited resources may be little better than a peasant dwelling. The cost of large wooden beams imported to Central Tibet from the province of Kongpo is prohibitively expensive for the temple denied government funding. Cement is difficult to obtain and expensive. Otherwise, cut stone is usually available from the piles of rubble which are all that remains of the original buildings, unless a commune has utilized the stone to build a new village.

A thousand metres of tortuous incline that daunts pack animals was no obstacle to the Tibetans who built the mountain hermitages and monasteries above the valleys. Such inaccessibility was also no obstacle to the teams of Red Guards trained in use of explosives who, with a radically different form of religious zeal, followed the footsteps of the pious Tibetan contemplatives to destroy with modern explosives in a few hours what had been built with so much devotion over the centuries. But usually even the "eagle nests" have had a small temple rebuilt in their vicinity. It is unusual to find caves dynamited. The treatment that less important religious structures, such as hermitages, received was the removal of their roofs, leaving the elements to complete the destruction. Caves were immune to this method of vandalism. Thus at this most significant category of power-place, dwellings remain for those inclined to live there.

Who are the present inhabitants of Tibet's monasteries? The great monastery-towns outside Lhasa — Tashi Lhumpo at Shigatse, Pelkor Chode at Gyangtse, Pel Sakya and a few other vital tourist attractions – are administered directly by Communist Party authorities instituted for this task: an unsmiling political presence is evident around these monasteries which may be considered tainted to such a degree that the true pilgrim will wish to avoid them. The monks in robes who tend the shrines and live in the monasteries are mostly geriatrics, men of such an advanced age that they are of little use in the fields or for any other labour. Almost without exception they were ordained and trained in the monastery before 1959. Amongst them is found the monk who takes the western pilgrim aside to show him where the thumb with which he habitually told his beads has been amputated; the monk who was recently released from a re-education centre after twenty years of imprisonment; the monk who spent the period between 1960 and 1980 sweeping out latrines; the monk who watched his elderly Lama tied to the shafts of a cart to pull it around the yard before being interred alive; the monk who alone survived the genocide of his entire college of 800; the monks who watched or heard the destruction by hysterical Red Guards of the thousand-year-old temple-repository of sacred artefacts more dear to the monastic community than their mothers. Also, there are innumerable tales of the vicious brain-washing technique called *tamzing* or "self-criticism" that was applied to all those who remained devoted to traditional modes. The pilgrim will be informed that 500 monks now practice in Drepung, 250 in Sakya, and 200 in Gyangtse, and that many robes will be evident piled in the monks' seats in the assembly halls. These figures represent the number of individuals formally enrolled at the monastery who may be called upon on special occasions, but who were married, many forcibly, and are now prevented from practising any religious function by obligation to their families. However, the Party has permitted ordination of a limited number of boys for traditional religious instruction, and all these large monasteries have their complement of young students engaged in traditional studies.

Where there is reconstruction outside the centres of Party presence, there is a very different atmosphere. Tibetan labour gangs working on commune projects are habitually cheerful; but where we find them labouring to rebuild the monasteries, men and women, old and young, working voluntarily together, there is a veritable carnival in progress where CHINA RECON-STRUCTS could gather paradigmatic shots of happy workers reaping the fruit of honest physical labour. At Lhasa Ramoche, at Yarlung Trandruk, at Tolung Tsurpu, at Jang Reteng, one of the pilgrim's strongest impressions may be the songs and radiant faces of a gang of girls stomping the new floors of the temples. Tibet was slow to react to the new spirit abroad in China after the death of Mao and the fall of the Gang of Four, due to its isolation from the centre of power and to procrastination in the dismissal of hard-line officials. But the wariness with which the Tibetans greeted the change is gradually diminishing, and suspicion of a reversal of the new policies in the near future is slowly dissolving.

Today, evidence of the vitality of the Buddha-*dharma* in the Land of Snows is increasing like the spreading light of dawn. The Lamas see an historical parallel in the 10th century when nearly every monastery in Central Tibet had been destroyed and every Lama either killed or exiled by Tibet's last emperor, Langdarma. Some temples are being rebuilt or restored in faithful replica of the original buildings – when sufficient funds are available – by local Tibetan Party officials with no Lamas or educated monks in attendance. At other sites Lamas are building their own temples. These Lamas and monks may come from the local village; they may be the monastery's incarnate Lama whose birthplace is far away; some have returned from exile.

Many pilgrims will find that access to the spirit of the power-place they seek is accomplished in inverse proportion to the degree of institutionalization at the monastery on the site. Where Party money has been made available to rebuild a large temple requiring a work force of perhaps a hundred people, Party cadres are probably lurking in the vicinity overseeing the project, and devotees will be scarce. At another extreme, at the site of a small ruined temple founded in the 7th century near Gyangtse, a *tulku* from a neighbouring valley's devastated monastery, working with a single labourer, in five months built a small temple and four monks' cells in the temple's small walled compound. This fifty-year-old man embodied the faith and commitment that inevitably survived the persecution, and even because of persecution such qualities are now blossoming and bearing fruit at similar sites throughout Tibet.

The caves were always the preserves of the esoteric elite of Tibet's theocracy – the yogins – whose attainment included the control of their body-minds, enabling them to withstand exposure to the winter cold and summer heat. In Central Tibet there is a disproportionately large number of Khampas, men and women from the Eastern province of Kham, presently inhabiting the caves. In several of the Guru Rimpoche cave-sites we found Red Hat Khampa yogins who shamed the Central Tibetans with the intensity of their aspiration, depth of commitment and by their spiritual attainment. At Yarlung Shetak at over 5,000 m, at the base of the crowning phallic peak, where the monastery and every other dwelling but the Guru Rimpoche cave itself had been destroyed, a Khampa Lama had erected a lean-to on the roof of a temple filled up with rubble. He intended to re-establish the monastery there. At Drak Yerpa, a day's walk from Lhasa, in 1985 the only permanent inhabitant of the warren of caves high on a scarp at the top of the valley, was a Khampa yogin who had returned from a protracted pilgrimage in India and Nepal to install himself in a Guru Rimpoche cave. At Samye Chimpu, the most sacred of all the Red Hat hermitage sites, on the sharply rising scarp at the top of the valley a pyramidal crag 15 m high provides cave-hermitages for ascetics, a significant proportion of whom are nuns. Women possessing as great a sense of commitment as male yogins or monks comprise a much larger proportion of Buddhist practitioners than before 1959.

Thus, outside the large monastery-museums, the pilgrim will find the Buddha-*dharma* in Tibet flourishing and increasing. While those few pilgrims such as Alexandra David-Neel who penetrated Tibet at the beginning of the 20th century found an archaic religious culture in a state of stasis and ossification, today the pilgrim finds a youthful and resurgent culture relying on its own inner strength. In so far as teachers are scarce, men and women are found struggling in their yoga practice without guidance, in the same way that gnostics in Europe have done for centuries. If Chinese politics remain free of revolution for the coming generation, the lineages that were attenuated to breaking point by the disasters of the last twenty-five years may regain enough strength to initiate a small but sufficiently large Community born of "the lost generation" to survive the new official atheism and materialism, its utilitarian aesthetics, its foreign language and alien cultural ethos. Thus the lineages of tantric Buddhist initiates can instruct the common people in the traditional morality and world-view of Buddhism and in the language, the arts and traditional sciences that compose the unique and magnificent Buddhist culture that a few years ago appeared lost in its homeland.

3 "The Western Storehouse"

The quantity and quality and both the intrinsic and spiritual value of the treasure accumulated in pre-revolutionary Tibetan *gompas* is now difficult to credit. The Chinese call Tibet "The Western Storehouse". Evidence of the wealth accumulated by Tibetans during the Empire period (7th-9th centuries) could still be seen in Central Tibetan gompas in 1948. During the Chinese Mongol dynasty, when the priest-patron relationship between Tibet and China was established, gold intermittently poured into the Lamas' purses. The altars of "Glorious" Sakya still memorialize a period when trains of mules carried the Chinese Emperors' offerings to their Gurus in Western Tibet. The Karmapas of Tsurpu were also notable recipients of Mongol gold. Further, whatever wealth the obsessive traders of Tibet accumulated in their activity throughout Central Asia eventually found its way into the monasteries' coffers. The gompas were the national treasuries and banks.

The five precious metals and the five precious stones were offered to the Lamas and the Buddhas with ostentation to reap the psychotherapeutic benefits of giving, to improve fortune and prosperity in this life and to assure a better rebirth in the next. To lubricate and accelerate this process was a rudiment of priestcraft in which the Lamas were masters. Generous offerings indicated a healthy society and a healthy social psyche. Even the least educated members of society were aware of the inexorable laws of karma governing giving. There was not an inkling of suspicion in the minds of either priest or patron that there was any element of venality or self-service in their relationship — it was a law ordained by the disinterested mechanics of moral cause and effect. The Lamas' gold was ostentatiously displayed. Acres of gilt roofing covered the major gompas; and massive solid gold reliquary chortens, and immense gold images of Lamas, Buddhas and Bodhisattvas, were the gompas' most sacred icons.

In the 1950s, during the Han Chinese policy of Accommodation of the Minorities, an itinerary was compiled of all the valuable artefacts of Tibetan gompas. In the early 1960s, after the flight of the Dalai Lama, and as a precursor of the Red Guards, the most valuable of these artefacts were removed from the gompas and transported in fleets of trucks to the East. Shortly thereafter a period of years commenced during which the Red Guards, sometimes assisted by the artillery or demolition experts of the People's Liberation Army, demolished the fabric of the vast majority of the gompas. Thus was accomplished the policy of "liberation from feudalism", "freedom from the clutches of superstition and a venal priesthood", and "return of the wealth of the country to the masses", and so on. Respect for the sanctity of the gompas' contents and a watchful Party presence inhibited any desire for preservation that the Tibetans harboured, but with diverse motivation the Tibetans removed and concealed an unknown proportion of the gompas' remaining sacred artefacts before they were destroyed or buried in the Red Guards' destruction. With greater freedom of trade and a relaxation of anti-religious Marxist dogma, these concealed objects have reappeared to be reinstalled in the reconstructed temples or exported and sold on the international art market. Of the treasure that was removed to China, it appears that what could not be broken up or melted down into liquid assets was stored away, and although some of this has found its way to Hongkong part of it is now being returned to its original owners.

4 An Outline of the History of Central Tibet

Prehistory
Legends concerning the origins of Tibet's first line of kings, the Yarlung Dynasty, provide the earliest sources of information

about the Central Tibetan people. The story of the demoness mating with the monkey on Sodang Gangpo Ri in Yarlung to produce the six sons who became the original ancestors of the six original Tibetan clans, and the legends surrounding Wode Gungyel, have left orthodox Tibetans in no doubt that this stretch of the Tsangpo Valley was the cradle of their race. The story of their first king, Nyatri Tsenpo, further defines the source of Tibetan civilization. Descending from the sky to Yarlha Shampo, Nyatri Tsenpo was received by twelve local chieftains who carried him down the mountain on their shoulders and enthroned him as their king. This must have taken place some centuries before the Christian era, as several dynasties are listed previous to the historical Yarlung Dynasty. The earliest legends are bound up with Bon cosmological beliefs: from the time of Nyatri Tsenpo the kings ascended to heaven by means of a "sky-cord", until the ill-omened King Drigum was killed by a rival, and thereafter the kings were buried at Chongye. The country where these kings lived and died was called Pö; the Indians called it Bhot; and Europeans, courtesy of the Arabs, knew it as Thibet.

The Yarlung Dynasty and Empire

The way of life of the Yarlung people probably changed very little from the earliest times to the period when some credence can be given to Tibetan history. The settled people of the valleys lived by agriculture and the people of the uplands were nomads and pastoralists. Local chieftains ruled their clans from their forts located on high ground. Although Potang lays claim to have been the original seat of the Yarlung chieftains, or kings, the Yambu Lhakang is said to be the oldest building in Tibet. It was here that King Lhatotori is believed to have received Tibet's first knowledge of the Buddha-*dharma* in the 3rd century(?). However, the first Tibetan Buddhist converts were not made, and the first Buddhist temples were not constructed, until after the first emperor, Songtsen Gampo (r.627-50), was born in Gyama.

The Emperor Songtsen Gampo's father had consolidated his supremacy in Central Tibet, and his control of rival vassals, probably derived from the sacred character of his kingship, can be inferred from his military success. During Songtsen Gampo's reign the Tibetan cavalry gained victories over all Yarlung's surrounding kingdoms. Nepal was made to pay allegiance; the Bonpo kingdom of Shang-shung, with its capital city near Mt Kailash, was defeated and absorbed; and the northern tribes were subjected. The Tang Emperor of China was in such awe of Tibetan might that he acceded to the request of Songtsen Gampo's ambassador, Lompo Gar, that he send Songtsen Gampo a Chinese queen, who was known as Wencheng Kongjo, or Gyasa. The name of Songtsen Gampo's Nepali queen was Bhrikuti, known as Besa. During this springtime of Tibetan power foreign cultural influence flowed into Yarlung for the first time. The Chinese classics were imported and the sacred sciences of astrology, geomancy and medicine began to be assimilated as Tibetan nobles learned the Chinese language. Indian influence was felt primarily through Buddhism, although it is uncertain to what extent it penetrated at this time. The powerful and abiding influence that Sanskrit literature would assert in Tibet, however, was introduced at this time by Tonmi Sambhota, who devised the Tibetan alphabet from an Indian script and translated some basic Buddhist scriptures. Songtsen Gampo's construction of temples (p.287) and his propagation of a civil code based on Buddhist virtue indicates that Buddhism was regarded with the highest respect.

For 250 years the Tibetan kingdom and its empire flourished, developing the trends that had been initiated during the Emperor Songtsen Gampo's reign. The abiding strength of the kingdom's military mould was demonstrated by the passage of Tibetan arms to gather relics from Bodh Gaya in India, to confront the Muslim onslaught in Turkestan, to garrison Tibetan forts on the Silk Route in subjected Central Asia, and to plunder the Tang capital of Changan (Shian) itself and, briefly, to set up a puppet Emperor. The ancient tradition of sacred kingship continued as each king was succeeded by his son as he reached the horse-riding age of thirteen. The new king's maternal uncles governed during his minority. Although there were urban centres where artisans could produce their fine quality bronze, silver and gold artefacts, the court was nomadic, housed in a city of tents.

The three Great Buddhist Kings of Tibet were Songtsen Gampo, Trisong Detsen and Repachen. If Songtsen Gampo introduced Buddhism to Tibet then Trisong Detsen was responsible for its firm foundation and Repachen for its cultivation. During the Emperor Trisong Detsen's reign, which saw Tibet sure in its domination of all Central Asia, an Indian abbot and *pandita*, Santaraksita, was invited to establish Tibet's first monastery at Samye. At the same time the tantric master from the Swat Valley (Pakistan), Padma Sambhava, better known as Guru Rimpoche, was invited to convert the followers of the ancient Bonpo religion to Buddhism and to destroy their occult power. Although Trisong Detsen met determined opposition from his conservative nobles, at the end of his reign Samye Chokor had been built and a Tibetan abbot, Nyang Tingedzin, had been installed to govern the Tibetan monks ordained by Santaraksita.

King Repachen was responsible for inviting a large number of Indian *panditas*, learned monks, to Tibet to teach Buddhism and to translate the Indian Buddhist scriptures. However, Buddhism's success during the reign of this devout king led to intrigue by reactionary families supported by the Bonpo priests, and the king was assassinated by his brother Langdarma. After a few years of Langdarma's suppression, when books were burned, monks exiled or murdered, and temples destroyed, the king in his turn was killed, assassinated by a Buddhist monk, Lhalung Pelgyi Dorje. This unhappy period led to the decline of military and political cohesion, and the end of empire and of the Yarlung dynasty. For a century Tibet was in turmoil while Langdarma's descendants and powerful nobility fought to carve principalities out of the original imperial domain.

The Rise of the Monasteries (1000-1200)

By the beginning of the 11th century Tibet had attained stability under the noble families that ruled from their fortresses in every district of the country. Political stability permitted cultural resurgence under the patronage of wealthy families and the re-establishment of Buddhism was the chief result. Bearers of the lineage of Buddhist ordination that had been preserved in Eastern Tibet returned to Central Tibet; teachers such as Lume (p.295) constructed temples; and the trend towards travel to India for instruction commenced. Thus began the second period of propagation of the Buddha-*dharma* in Tibet. In Western Tibet the master Rinchen Sangpo (958-1055), whose studies led to prolonged residence in Buddhist Kashmir, was largely responsible for propagating the Buddha-*dharma* and the construction of temples. In 1045 the Indian abbot and *pandita* Jowo Atisha arrived in Central Tibet and taught the original masters of the Kadampa school of Tibetan Buddhism who founded important monasteries chiefly in the Kyichu Valley and in Penyul (p.295). The widely travelled southern Tibetan Guru Marpa the Translator (1012-96) began his instruction of the Tibetan disciples who would form the root of the prolific Kagyu lineages. Evidently the seeds shaken by Langdarma from the fallen tree of Buddhism had germinated. From this point until the advent of the Yellow Hats in the 17th century, political power in Tibet was to be shared between the ruling families and the temporal officials of the great monasteries. Hereafter the political history of Tibet becomes inseparable from religious history, and due to the increasing and eventually predominant wealth of the monasteries, temporal power becomes synonymous with spiritual authority: thus theocracy was born.

The seminal phase of Buddhism in the 11th century was followed by a century of almost obsessive preoccupation with religion. A flood of Buddhist aspirants travelled to India and Nepal to serve tantric Gurus and scholars both inside and outside the monastic academies. This was during the final blooming of Indian Buddhist civilization that occurred before the destructive Muslim invasions. During this period the bulk of important scriptures were translated and a wealth of Buddhist culture transported to Tibet. Almost without exception the monasteries that survived from this period grew up around the charismatic masters that have given the Tibetans their incomparable reputation for spiritual attainment, and undoubtedly this period produced innumerable masters of yoga and meditation who lacked the patronage and the disciples to perpetuate their teaching.

The first new religious school to be founded was the Sakya school, based at Sakya on the important Western Tibetan trade route from Shigatse to Nepal. A scion of the ancient land-owning Kon family, Konchok Gyelpo, a student of the scholar-traveller Drokmi, founded Sakya in 1073. His nephew Kunga Nyingpo gained a systematic mastery of the old *tantras* and the new Indian learning, and gaining an immense reputation he brought power and wealth to Sakya. Continuity of possession of the abbacy of the gompa at Sakya was maintained in the Kon family through the device of uncle to nephew succession, which was to be imitated at some later Kagyu foundations. The first 150 years of Sakya produced five extraordinary men – Konchok Gyelpo, Kunga Nyingpo, Sonam Tsemo, Sakya Pandita, and Pakpa – and the last two of these were the first Lamas to gain temporal authority over all of Tibet.

The founders of the first great monasteries in Central Tibet were the Kadampa disciples of Atisha. However, the Kadampas were monks and scholars first and foremost, and eschewing politics their chief contribution to Tibetan history was on the more subtle level of monastic discipline and scholarship. More significant in the political frame were the monasteries established by Kagyu masters, lamas of Milarepa's lineage. The monasteries of Densatil, Tse Gungtang, Tolung Tsurpu, Drigung and Taklung were all established by remarkable Kagyu yogins over a ten-year period at the end of the 12th century. However, although the spiritual attainment of their founders and of the lineal practitioners of their yogas is not in doubt, even within the arch-ascetic Milarepa's lifetime these institutions had accumulated wealth and ornamentation. Within a century all but the Taklung gompa had grown political wings supported by lay factions competing for temporal ascendancy of the country.

Sakya Ascendancy (1200-1350)

In the year 1207 Genghis Khan began his genocidal conquest of Central Asia, and in the same year his envoys arrived in Central Tibet demanding Tibetan submission. The arrangement that the Tibetan representative, the abbot of Tse Gungtang, was perceived to have made with the Mongols was the exchange of the Tibetan Lamas' religious guidance and magical power for political protection in the guise of suzerainty. Thus began the period of Tibet's priest-patron relationship with the Mongol emperors, who were to become the Emperors of China, and here were the beginnings of the lamas' reputation as the high-priests of Asia. Since Reteng was destroyed by a Mongol raiding party in 1239 the substance of the agreement was uncertain until Sakya Pandita answered the summons of Ogadai Khan's son Godan to send a Tibetan representative to his court in 1244. The Sakya accounts of their lama's success in his role of priest to the Khan would seem to be substantiated by his achievement, for he returned as the effective regent of Tibet. After his nephew and successor, Pakpa, imitated his success, this time at Kublai Khan's court, Sakya ascendancy in Tibet was consolidated. Pakpa gained Kublai's confidence and with it the title of Tishi, Viceroy.

With the advantages to be gained at the Mongol court now evident the Lamas of Drigung and Tse and the Karmapa of Tsurpu all made the journey to the Mongol court, which had become the court of the Yuan Dynasty at Peking. The Lamas undoubtedly outshone the missionaries of all faiths gathered there, and their success was manifest in the immense hordes of treasure that they brought back to enrich their gompas. But jealous of Sakya power the Drigungpas became aggressive and during armed conflict in 1290 Drigung Til was burned down. The waning power of the short-lived Yuan Dynasty (1280-1368) was accompanied by loss of Sakya influence.

Kagyu Ascendancy (1350-1550)

One of the administrative reforms instituted in Tibet by the Mongols was division of the country into so-called myriarchies, which appear to have been based upon pre-existing districts dominated by the old clans. In the middle of the 14th century the Yarlung myriarchy was in the hands of a member of the Pakmodrupa family whose power had been gained through the wealth and influence of Drogon Pakmodrupa's Kagyu gompa of Densatil. Pakmodrupa Jangchub Gyeltsen was one of Tibet's most remarkable men. In a very short period, by diplomacy and armed conflict, he succeeded in wresting political power from the hands of the Sakyas and establishing an independent Tibet with its capital in the Yarlung Valley at Neudong. Although Jangchub Gyeltsen obtained the title of Tai Situ from the Yuan court, when the new Chinese Ming dynasty ousted the Mongols in 1368 he was quick to disavow Chinese overlordship and to sweep away all evidence of Mongol intervention in Tibet. Under his leadership resurgent Tibetan nationalism reverting to the ethos of the Empire period re-established the country's independence at the beginning of the Ming dynasty.

Jangchub Gyeltsen took the Tibetan title of Desi, or "Ruler", governing free of the influence of any particular monastery. He initiated various civil works and reforms that benefited the entire country. The Nyingma school, the Old School, experienced a resurgence in the 14th century with the revelation of numerous treasure-texts, particularly in the valleys close to Yarlung. These revelations stressed the nature of the Buddha-*dharma* during the first period of propagation of Buddhism in Tibet in the Empire period. However, it was the Karma Kagyu school at Tsurpu that prospered most during this period of peace, prosperity and stability, allowing the monastic, religious innovations of the previous centuries to become hallowed tradition. At the close of the 15th century the power of the Pakmodrupa rulers of Neudong, who had changed their allegiance to the Yellow Hats, had been usurped by the Princes of Rinpung who had been their prime ministers. But this movement in the centre of political power up the Tsangpo River was attended by little change — except that the Karmapas at Tsurpu were the rulers' lamas. The Rinpung chieftains in turn were succeeded at the seat of power by their ministers, the Depas, or Governors, of Western Tibet at Shigatse. These Depas were conservative laymen at the helm of a ship of state that was sailing with the wind. But by the end of the 16th century their imperviousness to the dissatisfaction of families excluded from power and their opposition to a rising tide of reformist sentiment was to cause a storm that they could not survive. The complacent and devitalized Kagyu schools, particularly the Karma Kagyupas, whom they patronized and with whom they were identified, were to share in their shipwreck.

Yellow Hat Victory and Hegemony (1642-1951)

The Yellow Hats had not begun as a politically conscious school. Je Tsongkapa, born in Amdo in 1357 and taught by the great Gurus of the day in Central Tibet, founded the Ganden Namgyeling gompa which quickly gained a high reputation for its instruction of both *sutras* and *tantras* within the framework of the strict monastic discipline of the Kadampas. The master's own aspiration was purely religious, but patronized by powerful families, attuned to the mood of the times, his ambitious disciples established gompas – Sera and Drepung in Central Tibet and Tashi Lhumpo in Tsang – that quickly became politicized. As it grew in the 15th century the Gelukpa or Virtuous School, as it was known, became highly centralized, every monastery acknowledging the Dalai Lama's authority, while the Red Hats' power was dispersed amongst the various monasteries' heads. However, the Red Hats were entrenched amongst the old nobility and particularly were identified with the Princes of Tsang who in the late 16th century were virtually Kings of Tibet. Thus the Karma Kagyu school's jealousy of the rising political power of the Gelukpas translated into military force would probably have been successful had not the Great Fifth Dalai Lama invited a foreign army to achieve Gelukpa supremacy. Although the Karmapas' monastery of Tsurpu was in Central Tibet, the conflict between the Yellow Hat and Red Hat schools can also be seen in terms of a continuing rivalry between Central Tibet and Tsang. The Pakmodrupas had ruled for a century from Yarlung, but by the end of the 16th century power had again moved to Shigatse. The victory of the Gelukpas was to finally establish Tibet's centre of power at Lhasa in Central Tibet.

Sonam Gyatso (1543-88), abbot of Drepung, had successfully converted the Qosot Mongols to the Geluk school's Buddhist view. Altan Khan, the Qosot leader, bestowed the title of Dalai Lama upon him, retrospectively exalting his two predecessors, Gendun Drub of Tashi Lhumpo and Gendun Gyatso, abbot of Drepung, to the same rank. Thus Sonam Gyatso became the third Dalai Lama. The fourth Dalai Lama was discovered as a grandson of Altan Khan, and the political die was cast that would bring Tibet again under the sway of the Mongols and eventually the Chinese. The fifth Dalai Lama invited the Qosot Mongol general Gusri Khan to invade Tibet and subject the Gelukpas' enemies. In 1642 the King of Tsang was defeated and slain by the Mongols at Shigatse and in the same year the Karma Kagyu gompa at Tsurpu was sacked and many monks were killed. Ranging from Kham to Ladakh the Mongols defeated every opponent of the Gelukpas with the exception of the Drukpas (Bhutanese), who alone amongst the Tibetan peoples retain their independence today. Gusri Khan gave ultimate authority over the realm to the Great Fifth, but imposed a lay regent as his representative. In 1679 the Dalai Lama elected his spiritual son, Sangye Gyatso, to the position of Regent.

Lobsang Gyatso, the Great Fifth Dalai Lama, born in Chongye in 1617, was undoubtedly one of the most competent Lamas in Tibetan history. A highly learned man, prolific in his writing on sacred topics and conscientious in his religious duties, history moulded him into a giant on the political stage. He reformed the reintegrated state and its finances; with tact he expropriated run-down monastic foundations of the Red Hats and restored them; a census was taken, penal laws were promulgated and trade prospered. His death in 1682 was concealed by the Regent Sangye Gyatso to avoid a hiatus in government, but in the absence of a genius at the helm of Tibetan affairs even Sangye Gyatso could not prevent the repercussions of Mongol intervention in Tibet. The untimely recognition of the sixth Dalai Lama, a poet and sensualist, was the signal for renewed invasion. Lhazang Khan, the Qosot ally of the Chinese Manchu Emperor, invaded Lhasa in 1706, killed the Regent, burnt many gompas, kidnapped and assassinated the sixth Dalai Lama and installed his son in his stead. In 1717 the Qosots' rival Mongol clan, the Dzungars, took advantage of the Tibetans' disaffection for Lazang Khan and after killing him in his defence of Lhasa plundered and terrorized Central Tibet for five years. Peace was restored by a Manchu army that brought the new incarnation of the Dalai Lama to Lhasa in 1723. The lay-regency was abolished, future Regents being monks responsible for government only during the Dalai Lama's minority, and thereafter for twenty years a capable Tibetan minister, Polhane, successfully arbitrated between the Manchu Emperor's stranglehold on the country and the Tibetans' animosity against this new army of occupation.

The Chinese Emperor's representatives, the Ambans, maintained an influential presence in Lhasa during the 150 years after Polhane's death. Their influence gave Tibet peace and prosperity, but the seclusion imposed on the country by the Manchus, supported by various conservative factions in the large Geluk foundations in and around Lhasa, became the means by which Tibet was maintained within the Chinese sphere. In Lhasa a succession of Regents favourable to the Ambans' dictates retained power through the expediency of murdering the Dalai Lamas by poison before they attained their majority. Further, during this period when the eighth to twelfth Dalai Lamas died young, the Panchen Lamas of Tashi Lhumpo at Shigatse, who were equal or even superior to the Dalai Lamas in spiritual status, were played off against the Lhasa Geluk establishment, thus exploiting the old rivalry between Central Tibet and Tsang.

The increasing weakness of the Manchu Qing dynasty in Beijing, and also Lhasa, at the end of the 19th century was accompanied by the installation of the first Dalai Lama to attain his majority since the beginning of the Chinese occupation. In breadth and depth of vision the thirteenth Dalai Lama (1876-1933) stood head and shoulders above his monastic contemporaries. The Geluk establishments in the great Lhasa gompas had atrophied in a pro-Chinese stance, ignorant of and uninterested in world developments, particularly in the western influence in Asia led by the British in India. Colonel Younghusband's military expedition to Lhasa in 1904, designed to open Tibet to trade and to exclude both Russian and Chinese influence from the country, gave the Tibetans a glimpse of the European culture that by way of Marxism was finally to swallow their ancient traditions and politically engulf them. The thirteenth Dalai Lama proclaimed his country's independence and took refuge in Darjeeling in India during the last, failed attempt of the Chinese to regain authority in Lhasa. After the ousting of Chinese troops from Lhasa, upon his return he turned his own troops on the conservative monasteries that had supported the Chinese. However, his attempts at modernization of the country were foiled by the continuing strength of isolationist and traditionalist sentiment, and it is possible that at his end he was poisoned by the powerful opposition.

Integration with China

With the death of the Great Thirteenth in 1933 at the early age of fifty-seven, Tibet's opportunity to enter the world stage as an independent political and cultural entity was lost. Although British influence in Lhasa was consolidated by a series of sympathetic and able Residents, the regency of the young Reteng Rimpoche merely maintained the status quo. When Reteng resigned to return to spiritual retreat a successful conspiracy led to his death in prison and thereafter no strong or even competent hand was available to defend Tibet against the Maoist invasion that followed the defeat of the Chinese Republic. With British withdrawal from India in 1947 Tibet lost its only friend. In 1951 an unfortunate choice of general led to the surrender of the flower of the Tibetan army at an unassailable position near Chamdo in Eastern Tibet, and the People's Army, at the height of its power and self-confidence, flooded across the Tibetan plateau. An indication of the confusion existing in Lhasa was the directive of the State Oracle to install the fifteen-year-old fourteenth Dalai Lama as head of government. By 1959 Tibetan indignation at the humiliation suffered during eight years of Chinese rule on May 10th led to a spontaneous popular revolt known as the Lhasa Uprising. This resulted in the Dalai Lama's flight to India and reduction to the status of refugees of the 100,000 Tibetans who followed him.

The merciless suppression of the Lhasa Uprising by Chinese artillery positioned on the flanks of the valley was merely a foretaste of the suffering that Tibet was to endure in the following fifteen years. First the monasteries were forcibly dissolved and agriculture was communalized. Later, with the advent of the Red Guards, with the exception of monuments of historical importance specifically named by Prime Minister Chou En-Lai, every defensible building in Central Tibet above the level of the valley bottom, every religious building, every building with more than two storeys, were destroyed. Dissenters against Maoist thought were executed, imprisoned or brainwashed by means of the infamous *tamzing* system, as indeed was the case throughout China. Artificially aggravated famine, loss of menfolk to enforced labour camps and the futile attempt at Mao's order to turn grazing land into wheat fields and to replace barley and wheat by rice cultivation, led to widespread death from starvation in conditions in the villages unprecedented in Tibetan history. Guerilla activity throughout Tibet, chiefly carried out by the proud individualistic Khampa warrior-people, kept Tibetan nationalism alive but provoked the Chinese to even harsher policies of suppression.

Relief, indeed reprieve, came with the death of Mao, the

disgrace of the Gang of Four and liberalization under the present enlightened leadership of Deng Zhao Ping. Although in 1986 there was no Tibetan in a decision-making capacity in Lhasa, the Communist cadres in the valleys were often generous nationalistic Tibetans intent upon developing the country economically. These officials oversee the reconstruction of the gompas and, except in a few communes such as Sakya, where reactionary Maoist cadres were still in power in 1985, they institute the new freedoms permitted under the liberal regime. Like a phoenix rising out of the ashes, the Buddha-*dharma* in Tibet is being resuscitated. Lineages of ordination and yoga-practice, lost in Tibet, have been reintroduced from India, where the exiled Lamas have re-established their gompas and teach their students in the traditional manner. The Dalai Lama, Chenresik, may never again rule Tibet, but the age-old spirit of the Tibetan people is alive and well on the Sino-Tibetan plateau.

5 The Schools of Tibetan Buddhism

The Indian Mahayana Tradition is the essence of Tibetan Buddhism. However the overt forms of the Tibetan religious tradition are indigenous developments and provide its unique flavour. All the four chief Tibetan schools are based in physical and moral discipline, the philosophy and metaphysics, and the yoga and meditation, that were developments of the Buddha Sakyamuni's teaching in India. The distinctive qualities of Tibetan Buddhism were derived from elements of the indigenous pre-Buddhist Bon tradition that were assimilated by the adaptable medium of *tantra*. The tantric phase of Indian Buddhism evolved during the period of India's major impact on Tibet (8th-12th centuries), when Indian Buddhist missionaries were teaching in Tibet and when Tibetan aspirants were studying in Indian *viharas*. Each country where Buddhism took root adapted the external Indian forms to its unique needs and conditions.

The four schools of Tibetan Buddhism were established at different periods with different Indian lineages as their antecedents.

These Indian lineages were the original sources of the schools' diverse paths of metaphysics and yoga that are said to lead to one end — the Buddha's enlightenment. Thus each school is characterized by the distinct path that its initiates follow. Although monastic organization and similar Tibetan exegetical minds have blurred the original distinctions to some extent, still the four schools mentioned below are quite separate.

The Nyingmapa School, the Old School, was founded during the first period of propagation of the *dharma* in Tibet (8th-9th centuries) by Guru Rimpoche. Guru Rimpoche converted the Bon priests to Buddhism by assimilating the animistic Bon deities as Protectors of the Dharma. The Nyingmapas became the agents and custodians of the means whereby the powers of these ferocious gods could be harnessed for the benefit of all sentient beings. During the 9th-century period of suppression the Nyingma lineages became attenuated, and with the later, new schools' monopolization of wealth and political power the Nyingma tradition tended to be transmitted in family lineages and practised in small village gompas and mountain caves. This tendency has persisted, but after the ascendancy of the reformed Geluk school and during the rule of the Great Fifth Dalai Lama who came from a Nyingma family, two important Nyingma gompas — Mindroling and Dorje Drak — were developed in Central Tibet. Thereafter Nyingma monasticism was brought in line with the other schools. However, Nyingma mysticism was never grounded by political preoccupations, and significant evidence of this is provided by the tradition of revelation of treasures concealed by Guru Rimpoche (p.290). Most of the important Nyingma Lamas were discoverers (*tertons*) of treasures (*termas*), the majority of which were treasure-texts. The tradition of revelation gave the Nyingmapas the means by which didactic innovation could be introduced for a particular purpose at a specific time and place. Orgyen Lingpa, Longchempa (Longchen Rabjampa), Godemchen, Jigme Lingpa and Minling Terchen were some of the great treasure-finders associated with resurgences of Nyingma spiritual influence in Central Tibet. The *summum bonum* of Nyingma spiritual paths which these Lamas taught is called Dzokchen, which provides particularly efficacious meditation practices on a short-cut path to Buddhahood in a "rainbow body".

The Sakya School was the first school founded during the second period of propagation of the *dharma* in Tibet (11th-12th centuries). The school's Indian lineage was derived from the *mahasiddha* Birwapa (Virupa), an enlightened *tantrika*, and transmitted to Tibet by Drokmi Lotsawa. Konchok Gyelpo who had also been schooled by Nyingma teachers was the first Sakya Guru, and his successor, Kunga Nyingpo, developed a mix of old and new *tantra* and also the systematic philosophical and logical analysis that more than any other feature was to characterize the school. It is not unusual to discover old deities such as Dorje Purba and Dorje Lekpa guarding Sakya gompas. The academy at Sangpu Neutok called "the source of Tibetan learning" became dominated by the Sakyapas during its heyday, and the most revered Sakya Lamas were some of Tibet's most learned scholars. Lama Dampa Sonam Gyeltsen, Rendawa and Rongtonpa are some of these famous names. But Sakya Pandita and Pakpa who both held the position of Grand Lama of Sakya during the period of political ascendancy are probably the most renowned of the Sakya Lamas, and they are remembered for their abilities in magical power as much as for their scholarship. With some justification the Sakyapas claim that all succeeding Tibetan schools depended heavily upon their methods and analysis. The Sakya school is primarily a monastic school with accent on intellectual achievement, but the *summum bonum* of Sakya practice is the mystical path called *lamdre*, a quintessential tantric path that leads quickly to the Buddha's incomparable enlightenment.

The Kagyu School (*kagyu* means "lineal oral instruction") has a strong unbroken lineage originating with the Indian *mahasiddha* Tilopa. The lineage descended from Tilopa to Naropa, to Marpa and then Milarepa. Milarepa's two chief students were the yogin Rechungpa and the scholar Je Gampopa who transmitted the oral instruction governing uncompromising ascetic yoga to two extraordinary students — Drogon Pakmodrupa of Densatil and Karmapa Dusum Kyempa of Tsurpu. The former taught Drigung Kyapgon of Drigung, Taklung Tashi Pel of Taklung and Tsangpa Gyare of Ralung in Tsang. These five important, independent gompas became the seats of the five Kagyu schools that have survived to this day. With the astonishing growth of these gompas and with increasing Kagyu political preoccupation, the spirit of Naropa and Milarepa was diluted by monasticism, but the ideal of retreat to a cave on the snowline robed in cotton cloth and subsisting on nettle soup survived the tendency towards academic study, and the Kagyu tradition continued to produce yogins of remarkable calibre. The ascetic Drogon Pakmodrupa's great achievement was to produce three masters of status equal to himself; but his lineage at Densatil became mired in a political swamp. The Karmapas' Karma Kagyu school became the most successful Kagyu school in the political arena but still maintained its yoga traditions. It instituted the system of consecutive incarnation of its chief hierarch as the means to assure continuity of authority. Both the Drigung Kagyupas and Drukpa Kagyupas assimilated much of the Nyingma tradition and maintained a strong inclination for the hermitage. The Taklung Kagyu, strongly influenced by Kadampa monastic discipline, became renowned for its monastic purity but was a casualty of the Great Fifth's reorganization. All these lineages transmitting Milarepa's instruction concentrate upon yogas of control and manipulation of the subtle energies of the spiritual "body" in order to resolve its inherent dualities and to attain *mahamudra*, where the oneness of the Buddha's enlightenment is achieved.

The Kadampa School was the fruit of the visit of the Indian abbot and *pandita* Jowo Atisha to Central Tibet (1047-54). He was the first master to fill the cultural and religious vacuum existing after Tibet had recovered from the disastrous end to the Tibetan Empire. During this interim period tantric practice in Tibet had become corrupted, lacking the foundation of discipline and study that is necessary for an understanding of tantric methods. Students poured into Penyul and the Kyichu Valley area from all over Tibet to study with Atisha's root disciples. Dromton, Sharapa, Potowa, Neuzurpa and Puchungwa were some of the masters to found gompas where, according to Atisha's precepts, the *tantras* were given a secondary role and study of the *mahayana sutras* in a strictly disciplined monastic environment became the path to the Buddha's enlightenment. Perhaps it was the Kadampas' purity of living that excluded them from the wealth and political power that led to the Sakya and Kagyu schools' success, or perhaps it was an innate Tibetan need for involvement with the powers of the gods that tantric ritual

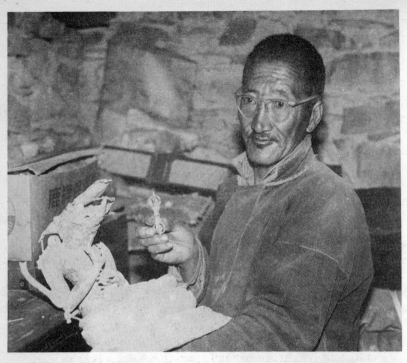

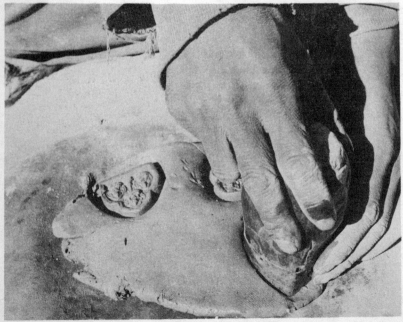

provided. Despite an enormous contribution to Tibet's religious life provided by academies such as Sangpu, and also Reteng and Langtang, to aspiring yogins and scholars of all schools, the Kadampa school itself lacked a quality that would have assured its survival.

Some Kadampa gompas were assimilated by the Sakya school, but the vast majority were transformed into Yellow Hat establishments after the unimpeded popular success of Je Tsongkapa's school founded at Ganden in 1409. Originally this school was called Gandenpa after its first monastery; later it became known as *the Gelukpa School*, or the Virtuous School, stressing monastic and moral discipline. The Chinese distinguished it from the earlier "Red Hat" schools by the term "Yellow Hat". The brilliant scholar and adept Je Tsongkapa, born in Amdo and taught by Kadampa, Sakya and Kagyu masters, applied the Kadampa ethos and method not only to study of the *sutras* but also to four of the principle *tantras* – the Jigche (Bhairava), Demchok (Samvara), Sangdu (Guhyasamaja) and Dukor (Kalacakra) *tantras*. Besides, his own *magnum opus*, the *Lamrim Chempo*, The Stages of the Path, provided perhaps the clearest and most inclusive analysis of the Buddhist path that had yet been written. Tsongkapa's voluminous commentaries on every imaginable topic related to the path provided the largest and most integrated corpus of scripture written by a Tibetan mind. This Geluk tendency towards study and scholarship was established at the school's inception and since no greater mind than its founder's has been produced by the Gelukpas, subsequent practice has been a constant reworking of Tsongkapa's own ideas. Twenty years of study leading to the academic degree and title of *geshe* is required of Geluk monks before yoga and meditation practice in the tantric tradition is permitted. The Gelukpas developed the monastic system, devoted chiefly to study, to new heights in Tibet. Further, the centralization of authority over all Geluk monasteries in the hands of the Dalai Lamas was to lead to integrated theocracy after the Great Fifth gained political control of the country.

[2.] [above] RELICS: a Drukpa Kagyu *ngakpa* holding a dorje and a bronze image unearthed at Ralung (photograph by *Stone Routes*)
[below] RELICS: *tsatsa* (votive offerings) stamped from a bronze mould (photograph *Stone Routes*)

Central Tibet gave birth to almost all the schools of Tibetan Buddhism and during the period of the rise of the monasteries (11th-14th centuries) the energies of the Tibetan people were concentrated here. However, many of the individuals responsible for founding great gompas were eastern Tibetans who had come to Central Tibet to study. After the establishment of the Yellow Hat sect as the dominant school, the centre of vitality and innovation appeared to move to the East, and although Central Tibet is still revered as the original source of spiritual power, the monasteries of Kham and Amdo and their Lamas dominate the Tibetan religious scene. Perhaps the most important development to arise in Kham was the eclectic *rime* movement which united the Red Hat sects in a renaissance of aspiration and systematization in the 19th century. The Jamyang Kyentse Wangpo who wrote *Khyentse's Guide*, Lodro Taye, Mipam Namgyel and Choling Rimpoche are only a few of the extraordinary Lamas who participated in this upsurge of activity in Kham.

Notes on Pronunciation and Tibetan Names

No standard system for reducing the complex Tibetan language to roman phonetics has yet been produced. In *The Pilgrim's Guide* a highly simplified system of phoneticization has been adopted in the text, and transliterated equivalents are given in the index. No distinction is made between unaspirated and aspirated consonants, between *k* and *kh*, *t* and *th*, *p* and *ph*, *ts* and *tsh*, *s* and *z*, *sh* and *zh*, or between the vowels modified by a final consonant.

The Tibetan letter *r* in a compound consonant (not as a final consonant) is barely articulated. It is sometimes phoneticized as an aspiration (e.g. Drigung = Dhigung). In rendering the compound consonants *kr*, *tr* and *pr* the *r* is omitted herein.

In general each syllable of a multi-syllabic phoneticized word must be pronounced separately. The vowels are pronounced as in Italian and a final *e* should be pronounced *é* (e.g. Lume = Lu-mé).

In rendering the principal place-names an attempt has been made to follow local pronunciation (e.g. 'On = Yon). In some cases the conventional English form of a place-name is used. Unavoidably, consistency has not been fully achieved.

Early European and Indian travellers and map-makers found great difficulty in romanizing Tibetan place-names and there is little agreement amongst them. The forms of important place-names used on the early maps (usually erroneous), and those which have entered common usage, are given in the notes.

An asterisk (*) in front of a place-name indicates that the Tibetan spelling could not be obtained and that the name approximates local pronunciation.

Tibetan place-names are conventionally preceded by the locality or district in which the place is located (e.g. Tolung Tsurpu, Yarlung Shetak). This method is most often used to distinguish between places of identical or similar name (e.g. Tsang Cholung, Woka Cholung).

The paucity of consonants in the Chinese language presented grave problems for Chinese geographers when transliterating Tibetan place-names into Chinese. The names of important places have been given in transliterated Chinese in the notes.

In China the metric system is in use. All distances and measurements in this guide are given in kilometres, metres and centimetres. Kilometre milestone numbers are sometimes given in parenthesis.

Note on Cartography

No maps are available that show the majority of sites mentioned in this guide. Indeed, accurate maps of Tibet have yet to be made. The difficulties of judging distances in Tibet, caused particularly by the peculiar foreshortening phenomenon on the Tibetan plateau, has resulted in only approximate locations of sites and their relative positions on the maps included herein. The relief data is derived from the most accurate maps available, but contour lines should be regarded only as a guide to relief rather than as a definitive index. It will be noted that the contour intervals and spot heights unavoidably are given in feet rather than metres. It would be appreciated if travellers in Tibet who discover any errors or important additions to the maps would communicate them to the author to increase the reliability of future editions of this guide.

Glossary of Geographical Terms

chu (*chu*): river, stream
chumik (*chu mig*): spring
da (*mda'*): "arrow", the lower, flat part of a valley
gang (*gangs*): snow- or ice- field
gangri (*gangs ri*): snow mountain
la (*la*): pass
lhari (*lha ri*): divine peak
pu (*phu*): the upper part of a valley
ri (*ri*): mountain
tang (*thang*): plain, pasture-land
tsangpo (*gtsang po*): major river, particularly the Brahmaputra
tso (*mtsho*): lake

Qu (Chinese): district sub-centre
Xian (Chinese): administrative centre of district

Key to Maps

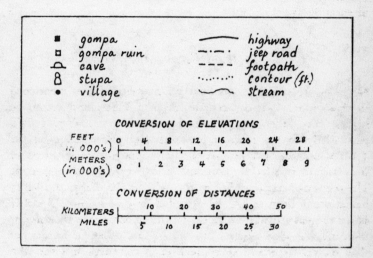

- ■ gompa
- □ gompa ruin
- cave
- stupa
- • village

——— highway
—·—· jeep road
– – – footpath
.... contour (ft.)
～～ stream

CONVERSION OF ELEVATIONS

FEET (in 000's)	0	4	8	12	16	20	24	28
METERS (in 000's)	0	1	2	3	4	5	6	7	8	9

CONVERSION OF DISTANCES

KILOMETERS		10	20	30	40	50
MILES	5	10	15	20	25	30

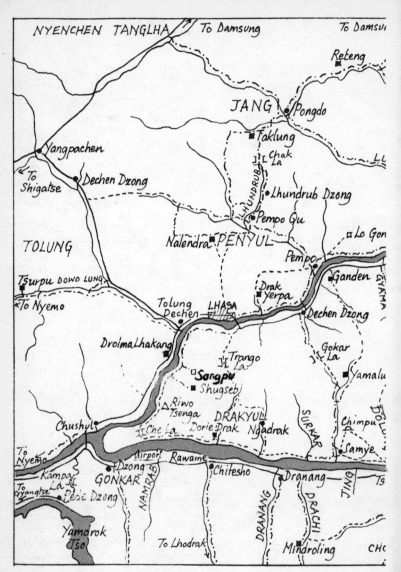

Map 2 The Valleys of Central Tibet

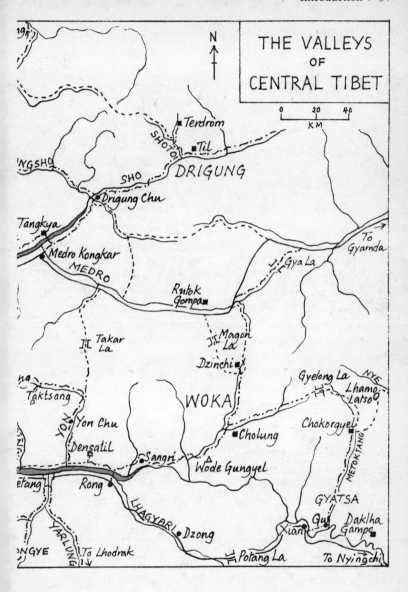

THE VALLEYS
OF
CENTRAL TIBET

N

0   20   40
KM

Terdrom

SHOTO

Til

NGSHO

SHO

DRIGUNG

Drigung Chu

Tangkya

To Gyamda

Medro Kongkar

MEDRO

Gya La

Rutok
Gompa

Takar
La

Magon
La

Dzinchi

Gyelong La

NYE

na

Taktsang

WOKA

Lhamo
Latso

YON

Yon Chu

Cholung

Chokorgyel

Densatil

Sangri

Wode Gungyel

METOKTANG

etang

Rong

GYATSA

LHAGYARI

Gui

Daklha
Gampo

NGYE

YARLUNG

To Lhodrak

Dzong

Xian

Potang La

To Nyingchi

1

THE HOLY CITY OF LHASA

Lhasa was founded by the Emperor Songtsen Gampo as a principal centre of the Tibetan Empire in the 7th century. Since the beginning of the Dalai Lamas' temporal ascendancy in the 17th century, the Holy City of Lhasa has had no rival in the domination of Tibet's spiritual and political life. Today the Lhasa Jokang, called the Lhasa Cathedral by early western travellers, focuses Tibetan national consciousness and the recently redis-covered religious freedom as no other place of pilgrimage in Tibet. It is here that Tibetan spirituality is seen to be alive and well. Unfortunately the same cannot be said of the Potala Palace and the great Yellow Hat monasteries of Drepung and Sera, which are monuments to the past. However, within these vast monastic museums and throughout the Lhasa area are shrines as vital and significant as anywhere in Central Tibet.

Lhasa straddles the Kyichu Valley, here four kilometres wide, above its confluence with the equally fertile Tolung valley. At Lhasa the Kyichu flows on the southern side of its valley, leaving considerable width on the north side for the city's growth. The topographical features that made this spot most desirable for settlement were the easily defensible rocks, or hills, protruding out of the valley floor. Marpo Ri, the hill that the Potala Palace rides and probably the site of the earliest settlement at Lhasa, is the most prominent. From Lhasa communication with the entire country is facilitated by the valley-spokes radiating from this hub. The Tsangpo Valley gives access to Tsang and Ngari in the west, and in the east to the heartland of Yarlung and to the provinces of Dakpo, Kongpo, Kham and Amdo beyond it. To the north-east the Kyichu gives access to Drigung which provides an alternative route to Kongpo and the far east of Tibet. The chief route to the north led directly north of Lhasa to Penyul, Jang and Namtso. The new highway to the north runs up the Tolung valley to Yangpachen and then north-east, eventually to Golmud.

In 1959 Lhasa was a town of some 10,000 inhabitants, although another 10,000 lived at Drepung and Sera monasteries as monks. To the east and south-east of the Potala were several large monastic foundations – Tsomon Ling, Tengye Ling, Gyuto Dratsang, Shide Dratsang, Gyume Dratsang, Muru Sarpa and others. Around the Barkor were the Lhasa houses of the nobility and the dwellings of lay Tibetans. Today the much enlarged city, with its broad tree-lined boulevards, can be divided by a north-south line drawn to the east of the Jokang. West of this line is Chinese-Lhasa with its large enclosed commune compounds, while to the east is the old city of paved alleys, tourist hotels, Muslim restaurants, bazaars and innumerable pilgrims. Most of the rebuilding and restoration of Lhasa was accomplished during 1984 to 1986.

Until 1959 Lhasa demonstrated in timber and stone what was obvious to every visitor to Tibet: monks and monasteries dominated life in that country in the same way that commerce and industry dominates life in Europe. The Potala Palace of Gyelwa Rimpoche, the Dalai Lama, is still the massive obtrusive presence it always has been, and as Chenresik's Pure Land it still represents the overwhelming moral authority and respect that the exiled Dalai Lama commands. In 1959 a fifth of the country's males were ordained Buddhist monks. Today only a token number of monks have returned to the monasteries and only a small number of acolytes are permitted. These monks are frequently dressed in lay clothes, Mao suits perhaps, and although the religious freedoms granted to all Tibetans have evidently been received with enthusiasm there is still some reluctance to demonstrate overtly the old forms of worship. The Jokang is governed by Chinese officials who open and close it for their own benefit and for that of western tourists rather than for Tibetan pilgrims. But although an attempt was made to create a museum of it, that attempt has noticeably failed. Greater success in creating monastic museums was achieved in the case of the Potala, and the monasteries of Drepung and Sera. In these great shrines to the spiritual and temporal power of the Dalai Lamas and their Yellow Hat school the pilgrim may find a hostile environment. The atmosphere of a deconsecrated, dead temple-museum, locked grids across altars covered with dust, and dismally cared-for icons that have sometimes been overturned and confused as in an uncatalogued gallery, is not always conducive to an attitude of devotion. However, despite the depredations of the Cultural Revolution, the visitor with a taste for art, history and beautiful objects will not be disappointed.

So large are the monastery-museums of the Lhasa area, and so great in number the smaller shrines, that there is no space here to give them the same detailed coverage as the power-places outside Lhasa. Following Kyentse Rimpoche's guide, disproportionate space has been given here to the more ancient and vital power-places of Lhasa.

Circumambulation: Nangkor, Barkor, and Lingkor

Lhasa is the centre of the Tibetan mandala and the Jokang is the centre of the Lhasa mandala. The Jokang's inner *korsa*, the innermost path of circumambulation, called the Nangkor, lies within the precincts of the temple complex and encompasses only the inner Jokang.

The famous Barkor, the most popular circumambulatory devotion of pilgrims and the people of Lhasa, encircles the entire Jokang complex, the Muru Nyingba (the Lhasa seat of the former State Oracle), and several erstwhile noble houses, in a rectangular, kilometre walk. Four *sangkangs*, the large pot-bellied incense-burners, where perfumed smoke constantly rises to please the Jokang's protecting gods, stand in the four cardinal directions around the Barkor. In front of the Jokang is a walled enclosure containing a tree grown from a cutting of willows that stood nearby, called the Jowo Utra, The Hair of the Jowo. Also in the enclosure is a *doring* pillar inscribed with the terms of the Sino-Tibetan treaty of 822 which was enforced by the Emperor

Repachen. The inscription records China and Tibet's vow of eternal peace and mutual respect of the borders of their independent states. The stele in the enclosure was erected by the Chinese in 1793 during a smallpox epidemic, and moved to its present prominent position in 1983. It gives instruction to the Tibetans on anti-smallpox hygiene, although the concavities in the stone were formed by Tibetans rubbing their heads on it in the hope of magical intervention. On the northern side of the Barkor stand the old residences and shops of the *katsaras*, Tibetans of Nepali extract, and behind the northern *sangkang* is the old Lhasa Magistrates court. Within the Barkor to the south of the Jokang is an open space dominated by the Dalai Lama's Shuktri, his preaching-throne.

The Lingkor originally encircled the old city of Lhasa in its entirety. Today's Lingkor lies within the new, enlarged city, and although new roads have modified the route it still surrounds every shrine of importance (see map p.42-3) with the exception of Bompo Ri and the site of Kundu Ling to the west of Chakpo Ri. Pilgrims still use this important circumambulatory path, walking or prostrating around it, and worshipping at the shrines *en route*.

The Jokang (Jo khang) *or* Tsuklakang (gTsug lag khang)

The importance of the Jokang in contemporary Tibet cannot be exaggerated. It is the focal point of all lay Tibetans' religious and national aspirations. Not only has it an historical significance greater than most other power-places in Tibet, but it survived the Cultural Revolution with only minor damage, though substantial loss, and in the absence of the fourteenth Dalai Lama, in a reawakened vitality and intensity of religious feeling, it is to the Jokang that the people look for succour.

The original Jokang was built by the Emperor Songtsen Gampo, probably in 642. His Nepali and Chinese queens, Bhrikuti (Besa) and Wencheng Kongjo (Gyasa), had brought important Buddha images as dowry from their Buddhist homelands, and the provision of suitable temples as symbols of this desirable foreign religious culture and of the King's

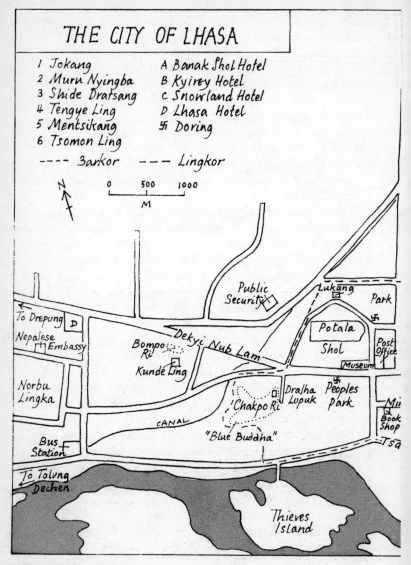

Map 3 The City of Lhasa

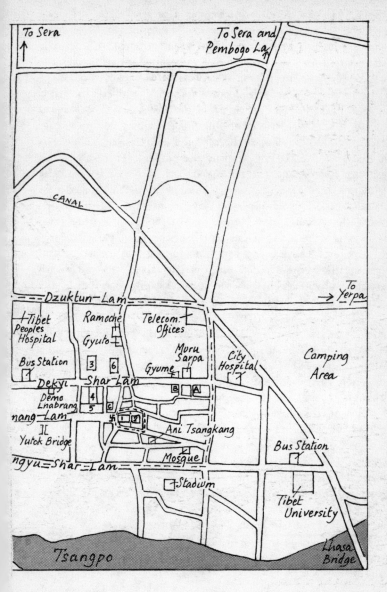

To Sera

To Sera and
Pembogo La

CANAL

To Yerpa

Dzuktun-Lam

Tibet Peoples Hospital

Ramoche

Telecom Offices

Gyuto

Bus Station

3   6

Muru Sarpa

Gyume

City Hospital

Camping Area

Dekyi

Shar-Lam

Demo Lnabrang

4

5   C

B   A

nang-Lam

Yutok Bridge

1   2

Ani Tsangkang

Mosque

Bus Station

ngyu=Shar-Lam

Stadium

Tibet University

Tsangpo

Lhasa Bridge

conversion to the Buddha-*dharma* was a priority. The site upon which the Jokang was to be built was determined by Wencheng Kongjo, who had brought texts on geomancy from China. The marsh that covered the site had first to be filled in with stone: the water underlying the Jokang is said to lie at the bottom of the well within it. The temple was originally called the Rasa Tulnang Tsuklakang, The House of the Mysteries, The Magical Emanation at Rasa. Rasa, The Place of the Goat, became Lhasa, the Seat of God, soon after the temple's completion. Today it is still known as Tsuklakang. During the Emperor Trisong Detsen's reign the Jokang and the hermitage site at Yerpa (p.74) were one of the three earliest pairs of Buddhist monastic foundations. During the period of suppression by Langdarma and the Bonpo faction, the Jokang was boarded up. In the 11th century Jowo Atisha taught here and it has remained the principal monastery and temple of Lhasa ever since. The Jokang was sacked several times during Mongol incursions, but its fabric survived. With the establishment of Lhasa as the political capital of Tibet by the Great Fifth Dalai Lama in the 17th century, the building was at last restored, and as the heart of the sacred city the Jokang became renowned as the most significant shrine in the entire country for the majority of Tibetans. And so it has remained.

Approach to the Jokang

Although a new square has opened a vista across the Barkor in front of the Jokang complex's façade and doorway, the plethora of buildings around the actual temple prevent a clear vision of its design. Likewise, the profusion of pillars, images, offerings, dark passageways and lattice screens within the temple obscure the simple interior layout. The design of the central Chokang or Offering Hall, which the Nangkor circumambulates, is similar to that of Ramoche (p.59) except that the sides of the Hall are filled with separate Ihakangs (shrine-rooms).

The three-story buildings to the right and left of the entrance-way and down the sides of the Jokang were originally government buildings: (on the right) the *silon* or prime minister's rooms, and the *kashak* or cabinet's chamber, and the foreign office; and (on the left) the Dalai Lama's and guest chambers. The pillared area open to the sky that is enclosed by these buildings is the Dukang or Kyangra, where monks of Sera, Drepung and Ganden still assemble at Monlam, the New-year Festival of Prayer. The Dalai Lama's throne is on the left side of this Dukang. Passages to the north-east and south-east of the Dukang give access to the Nangkor.

Inside the Jokang

Just inside the main door that opens upon a passage to the Jokang's Chokang hung the Great Bell of Jesus taken from Lhasa's Capuchin monastery when it was destroyed in 1745. The passage contains images of protecting spirits, spirits of water, mountains and the ether (*lu, nojin* and *drisa*). The Chokang is divided into two parts, Kawa Tungtung and Kawa Ringpo, the areas whose roofs are supported by short and long pillars respectively. Many of these pillars have remarkable carved capitals. Twenty-four shrines open onto this central area. At the back is the *sanctum sanctorum* in which the Jowo is located.

The Four Deities Emanating Light

Kyentse Rimpoche's list of power-objects in the Jokang contains four images: Jowo Chempo (Sakyamuni), the Buddha of our age; Tujechempo (Mahakarunika), the Bodhisattva of Great Compassion; Jampa (Maitreya), the Future Buddha of Loving Kindness; and Drolma (Tara), the Goddess of Devotion. These are the Four Deities Emanating Light.

The Jowo Chempo, the Great Lord, is called Yishinorbu, the Wish-fulfilling Gem. The image depicts the Buddha Sakyamuni at the age of twelve sitting in lotus posture and in meditation mudra. Although Queen Bhrikuti's dowry image of Mikyo Dorje was originally housed in the Jokang, probably in the period following the great Emperor Songtsen Gampo's death it was exchanged for Wencheng's Jowo Chempo dowry image, which had been lodged in Ramoche. Thus, it is the Indian image said to have been made in the time of Sakyamuni Buddha, given to the Chinese Emperor by a Bengali King, and brought to Lhasa from the Tang Emperor's capital city at Changan, that was the Great Jowo of Lhasa. The original image would have survived two centuries of sometimes harsh opposition to Buddhism in order to have reached the early 18th century, when it is thought that the

Dzungar invaders stole it during the 1717 sack of Lhasa. The Chinese artistic influences that some can see in the present image's casting suggest an 18th-century origin; but others believe the present Jowo to have its origin in Pala Bengal. The absence of a known date of manufacture for this sublime artefact does not reduce its ancient significance or sacred power, and its survival through the Cultural Revolution has recently magnified that power. The intricate repousse aureole that stood behind the Jowo is believed to have been made by the renowned 13th-century Nepali artist Aniko, who introduced the Nepali style pagoda to China. The authenticity of the present aureole is in doubt.

The image of Tujechempo, Mahakarunika, called Rangjon Ngaden, the Fivefold Self-manifest Lord (incorporating the spirits of Amritakundala, Tamdrin, Songtsen Gampo, Bhrikuti and Wencheng) that stood on the north side of the Chokang in the central lhakang with the golden roof, we know was destroyed during the Cultural Revolution. A new image has replaced it. The original Tujechempo, the Eleven-headed Chenresik, was the first image to have been consecrated in the Jokang. Another image of Tujechempo (said to have been brought from Drepung) stands next to Guru Rimpoche in the Kawa Ringpo.

The image of Jampa, Maitreya, called Chokorma, the Wheel of Dharma, also known as Mipam Gompo, Invulnerable Lord, stands in the lhakang to the south of the Jowo. It is believed to have been the receptacle of the deity of King Tritri, a contemporary of Sakyamuni, and to have been brought to Tibet from Nepal as part of Bhrikuti's dowry. In front of this lhakang in the Kawa Ringpo is another image of the Future Buddha called Miwang Jampa. Further, in the lhakang to the west of Tujechempo, is Jampa Trudze, Cleansing Jampa, and in the central lhakang on the south side are the Four Jampa Brothers. In the latter lhakang is also the stone head of the goat that carried the rocks that give the Jokang its firm foundations.

The image of Drolma, Tara, called Darlenma, Recipient of the Scarf, stood in the passage to the Jowo's left. She gained her name by asking the Sakya Pakpa Rimpoche for an offering scarf. This image seems to have disappeared. The more famous image of Drolma originally installed in the Jokang was a small sandalwood image brought by Bhrikuti from Nepal; but this is believed to have vanished by the 18th century.

Also of significance amongst the lhakangs on the ground floor of the Jokang, to the east of Tujechempo's chamber, is the lhakang containing the image of Tsongkapa called Ngadrama, a likeness of the Yellow Hat master that he verified as resembling himself. It is uncertain whether the present image is the original. Behind this lhakang is the chamber that gives intimation of the lake that survived the draining of the marsh upon which the Jokang was built. The lhakang of Wopame, Amitabha, Boundless Light, lies on the Jowo's right-hand side.

The Upper Storeys

The first storey consists of seventeen lhakangs opening onto the four sides of the gallery that overlooks the Chokang. The chief lhakang, the Chogyel Lhakang on the west side, is covered by a golden roof. Images of the Emperor Songtsen Gampo with his Nepali and Chinese queens and his ministers are worshipped here. Inside this lhakang between the doors is a silver jar with a long neck surmounted by a horse's head and with drinking scenes carved on its pot-belly. The Chinese noted the Tibetans' skill in making animal figures in precious metals in the 7th and 8th centuries, and it is a credible belief that asserts that this Horse-headed Chang Container (*Chang snod rta mgo can*) dates from the Empire period.[1]

The chief lhakang in the Jokang dedicated to Guru Rimpoche, called the Guru Tsengye Lhakang, lies to the south of the space above the Jowo. Next to it is a lhakang containing an image of Demchok Yabyum (Samvara). In the south-west corner is the Jatri Chokyong *gomkang* where four Protectors of the Jokang are propitiated, and also the gomkang of the Ku-nga Protectors led by Pehar.

At the turn of the stairs to the second storey is a gomkang containing images of both wrathful and peaceful forms of the Protectress Pelden Lhamo. It is said that souls of the dead would be brought here by the Goddess' retinue for her judgement and retribution. At the top of the stairs is a large room called the Pelden Lhamo Dukang, where monks assemble for worship of the

Protectors. There are interesting murals on the rear and northern walls. Most of the other chambers in the second storey are used for accommodation.

The Roof

The gilded roofs, called *gyapip*, are the crowning glory of the Jokang. The origin of such gilt, beaten copper work was certainty Nepal, but this particular form became uniquely Tibetan. The gyapips that cover the Jowo and Tujechempo are said to have been the gifts of Kings of Western Tibet in the 14th century. In the corners on the south side are turrets that contained the lhakangs of the Protectresses Maksorma (p.260)(S.E.), who turns back aggressors, and the Tsering Chenga (S.W.), the Five Long-life Sisters. The turret in the north-west corner covers a treasury building.

Muru Nyingba (rMe ru snying pa): The State Oracle's Lhasa Seat

The ancient foundation of Muru[2] lies immediately behind and to the east of the Jokang. It is accessible from the north side of the Barkor. This temple is built on the Indian *vihara* plan with the lhakang on the north side of a courtyard and monks' quarters on the other three sides. The first building on this site is said to have been built by the Emperor Songtsen Gampo and it was here that Tonmi Sambhota, the formulator of the Tibetan alphabet, finalized his work in the 7th century. In the 17th century the Muru Nyingba became the Lhasa seat of the Nechung Oracle (p.66), who is possessed by Pehar in his trances, and this explains why the entire lhakang has the appearance of a gomkang.

The fine murals in the dukang depict the Protectors of the Dharma. At the front of the dukang is an image of Pehar, and it is Pehar's mask kept in the glass case to its right. Within the inner lhakang, the central image is of Guru Rimpoche and in the glass cases around the walls are fine images of the five Nyingma Yidam-Protectors of the five directions and also images of Tseumar and Tamdrin.

On the first storey of the western side of the surrounding gallery is a gomkang dedicated to Bramze, the Sadhu-Protector of Muru Nyingba. His image is located to the right of the doorway.

Chakpo Ri (lCags po ri): Medical College Hill

To the south of the Potala, Chakpo Ri[3] is now easily identified by the steel telecommunication transmission tower on its bare summit. This hill is sacred to Chagna Dorje (Vajrapani), and legend has it that the Master-Doctor Yutokpa Yonten Gompo, the Emperor Trisong Detsen's doctor, had a residence here. This was the location of the famous medical college, or Mentsikang, called Rikche Dropenling, which was conceived by the Great Fifth Dalai Lama in 1413 and completed by Sangye Gyatso. It adorned this ridge until its destruction by artillery fire during the 1959 Lhasa Uprising. Also destroyed was its temple containing, most notably, a coral image of Tsepame made by Tangton Gyelpo (p. 137), a mother-of-pearl image of Tujechempo, and a turquoise statue of Drolma. In 1913 the thirteenth Dalai Lama built another Mentsikang. This was built on the site of the post-revolutionary traditional hospital near the Jokang. The present impressive modern building houses some of the treasures of the old, particularly a set of *tankas* depicting human anatomy that is used as a teaching aid.

On its south-west side Chakpo Ri terminates in a spinal ridge, and here sculptors took advantage of a sheer rock wall to carve every square metre of rock surface to form a mosaic of engraved Buddhas and Bodhisattvas. Tsepame, the so-called Blue Buddha, is the outstanding figure. Previously these figures were painted immaculately with a considerable amount of gold; today the painting is crude but still effective.

Dralha Lupuk (Brag lha klu phug): The Serpents' Cave

The Dralha Lupuk[4] is located on the north-eastern side of Chakpo Ri. In this cave of the *lu*, the Serpent Protectors of the lake that once covered the site of the Jokang were imprisoned after they had attempted to prevent the work of drainage. The Emperor Songtsen Gampo meditated in this power-place; Guru Rimpoche stayed here; Nyang Tingedzin (p.111) achieved rainbow body here; and Pakpa Chegom Sherab Dorje, who in this cave realized the nature of Tujechempo, the Bodhisattva of Compassion, is one of many *gomchen* who have lived here.

The entrance of the Dralha Lupuk is found in the upper storey of a small reconstructed lhakang. Within the cave a *korsa* circumambulates a large central pillar of rock out of which images of the Five Dhyani Buddhas are said to have self-manifested on all of its four sides. Notable images on the outer walls of the *korsa* are of the *siddha* Birwapa (Virupa) (south side), Pelden Lhamo (west side) and the Emperor Songtsen Gampo and his Queens (north side). Shelves of old bronze images can also be seen here. All of this remarkable sculpture, said to have appeared magically from the rock, was damaged during the Cultural Revolution, but excellent work has restored it.

Further up Chakpo Ri from Dralha Lupuk a new dukang is under construction. To the right of the gateway into the Dralha Lupuk compound is the cavernous cave of the Neten Chodruk, the Sixteen Arhats, with a central altar featuring Sakyamuni. Also in the compound is the residence of the Yellow Hat abbot-instructor of several young students.

Bompo Ri (dBong po ri): Gesar's Temple

The Bompo Ri,[5] or Barma Ri, is located a few hundred metres to the west of Chakpo Ri. It is sacred to Jamyang, being his *lari* or life-power mountain, and like Chakpo Ri and the Potala Hill it is said to represent one of the glands of the Supine Demoness that is Tibet (p.284). The hill is said to have been built upon originally by the Emperor Trisong Detsen, and Guru Rimpoche is believed to have meditated here, concealing various caches of treasure. But the present remarkable temple dates only from 1793 when the Chinese had it built to commemorate their victory over the Gorkhalis of Nepal. The lhakang has been gutted, but the simple, light wooden structure stands undamaged. The compound is now inhabited by several *anis*.

The temple is dedicated to Gesar of Ling, the mythical Tibetan hero-king whose saga is described in a forty-volume epic and who figures frequently in folk drama, bards' epic songs and in popular literature. But here Gesar is identified with the Chinese god of war, Kuan Yu.

The Glorious Potala Palace

The Potala Palace, known locally as Tse, the Peak, or Tse Potang, the Peak Palace, was the residence of the Yellow Hat hierarch, known to the Chinese as the Dalai Lama, "Ocean Lama", and to the Tibetans as Yishinorbu, Wish-fulfilling Gem, or Gyelwa Rimpoche, the Precious Victorious Buddha, in whose name Tibet has been ruled for the last 300 years. The location of the Potala is evident to anyone who scans the horizon anywhere near the Lhasa stretch of the Kyichu, as this architectural gem, built in the colossal monastic style of Central Tibet by Gyelwa Ngapa, the Great Fifth Dalai Lama, in the 17th century, stands 300 m above the valley atop the hill called Marpo Ri.

The Emperor Songtsen Gampo is believed to have built the first palace on Marpo Ri in the year 637. It is generally believed that his eleven-storey construction called the Potang Karpo, the White Palace, that became the residence of the Tibetan emperors, still stands on Marpo Ri, distinguished from later additions by its white colour. However, it seems most probable that the 7th-century construction was smaller in size, that lightning, fire, and time wreaked irreparable damage, and that if Songtsen Gampo's structure still stood in the 17th century it was demolished to its foundations and rebuilt by Gyelwa Ngapa, the Great Fifth Dalai Lama. After establishing control of Tibet, Gyelwa Ngapa laid the foundations of his nine-storey palace in 1645. The Regent Desi Sangye Gyatso, who succeeded him, completed the work by building the Potang Marpo, The Red Palace. The murals in the gallery above Gyelwa Ngapa's Throne Room, graphically illustrate the enormous expenditure of energy involved in this construction. The thirteenth Dalai Lama added the top two storeys and on the upper of these the light and airy apartments of the fourteenth Dalai Lama can be seen. From at least the 11th century the palace was called "Potala", after the mythic Indian residence of the Bodhisattva Protector of Tibet, Chenresik (Avalokitesvara) – the Emperor Songtsen Gampo was regarded as an incarnation of Chenresik as were the Dalai Lamas themselves.

The chambers certainly attributable to the Emperor Songtsen Gampo are the Chogyel Drupuk (The Emperor's Meditation Cave), the adjoining treasury room and the Pakpa Lhakang above. The Pakpa Lhakang, containing the Potala Jowo Lokeswara, is considered to be the most sacred shrine in the Potala, an opinion supported by its wealth of ancient, revered images, many of Indian and Nepali origin. The Regent's Potang Marpo, completed in 1694, contains the majority of the principal lhakangs. The Potang Karpo of Gyelwa Ngapa contains living quarters, the Namgyel Dratsang (the Dalai Lamas' own monastery), government offices, fortifications, and other ancillary buildings.

Gyelwa Ngapa, the Great Fifth Dalai Lama, Ngawang Lobsang Gyatso, was born in Chongye (p.198) in 1617. He was the first Dalai Lama to exercise temporal power in Tibet, receiving his investiture as ruler of Tibet from Gusri Khan, the Mongol general who defeated the princes of Tsang in 1642. One of the most powerful personalities in Tibetan history, his energy was felt in all political and cultural fields. Besides constructing the Potala, he caused many gompas to be rebuilt and many more to be restored. Although he sustained the traditions of Tsongkapa, he was also a Dzokchempa with a *purba* in his belt, and he supported the work of Minling Terchen (p.167). He was a scholar and a prolific writer. He died in 1682, but his death was concealed by the Regent until 1697.

The Regent, Desi Sangye Gyatso, continued the work of his master, Gyelwa Ngapa, during an effective period of regency from 1679-1705. He concealed Gyelwa Ngapa's death during a period of political uncertainty while he was attempting to secure all power to himself at the expense of the Qosot Mongols, who had been Gyelwa Ngapa's instruments. He failed in this attempt and was killed during the Qosot Mongol's subsequent invasion of

[3.] [above] LHASA: the Potala from Drala Lupuk (photograph by *Stone Routes*). [below] LHASA: Ramoche, founded in the 7th century by Princess Wencheng (photograph by K. Dowman)

Lhasa. Soon thereafter, the Chinese Qing emperors replaced the Mongol influence in Lhasa, and not until the accession of the thirteenth Dalai Lama was there to be a Yellow Hat ruler in the Potala with power of independent action. The rule of the Yellow Hat Lamas from the Potala, therefore, was to undermine Tibetan sovereignty and pave the way for the final 20th-century disaster of foreign domination.

Lhasa was sacked by the Dzungar Mongols in 1705 and 1717 and the Potala also fell victim. What was lost is not known. During the Cultural Revolution the Potala was protected by the Chinese Prime Minister Chou En-Lai. Thus the fabric suffered no damage and the priceless relics of its lhakangs were preserved. However, there was considerable displacement of movable items, and there is no longer the symbolic and systematic ordering of artefacts that existed previously. Besides, the Potala is now a state museum, albeit a museum of incredible proportions, and the vibration of sanctity that pervaded it previous to 1959 has been lost.

Kyentse Rimpoche mentions specifically only the Dalai Lamas' golden reliquary chortens and particularly that of Gyelwa Ngapa; the Jowo Lokeswara and several other images in the Pakpa Lhakang; the three-dimensional mandalas of the Lolang Lhakang; and the Chogyel Drupuk. Only the principal artefacts of the chief lhakangs, in the order visited after entering from the north door, are detailed below.

Dungrab Lhakang (gDung rabs lha khang)
In the Lhakang of Lineal Succession, in front of the shelves bearing the Kanjur and Tenjur canon, are notable images of Sakyamuni and Gyelwa Ngapa (in the centre); the Guru Tsengye, the Eight forms of Guru Rimpoche; and small images of Tsangpa Choje and Dromton. The *serdung* (golden reliquary chorten) of the eleventh Dalai Lama, a Jangchub Chorten, is on the far left with the Menlha Gye, the Eight Medicine Buddhas. Remarkable Chinese brocade covers the ceiling above the corridor.

Tse Dungkang (Tshe gdung khang): The Great Fifth's Kudung
The reliquary chorten of Gyelwa Ngapa is called the Dzamling Gyenchik, Unique Ornament of the Universe. Built by Sangye

Gyatso, 14.8 m high, it is said to have been gilded with an incredible 3,700 kg of gold. It is studded with diamonds and sapphires, etc. The tusk of the elephant that was Sakyamuni's previous birth, which stood before the chorten, has vanished. The *serdungs* of the tenth and twelfth Dalai Lamas stand to both left and right, with the Chorten Gye, the Eight Forms of Votive Chorten.

Nyingma Lhakang (sNying ma lha khang)

At the centre of the Lhakang of the Old School is an image of Guru Rimpoche with his consorts Yeshe Tsogyel (right) and Mandarava (left). In front of them is a small but remarkable image of Tangton Gyelpo, whose image in found in many lhakangs. Also: the Guru Tsengye, the Chorten Gye, and the Lopon Gye (the Eight Teachers of Guru Rimpoche).

Geluk Lhakang (dGe lugs lha khang)

The Yellow Hat Lhakang has Tsongkapa and his disciples in the centre and Gyelwa Ngapa and the Emperor Songtsen Gampo to their left; also the Twenty-one Tara *tankas* painted black on gold.

Throne Room

The walls of the Great Hall of Gyelwa Ngapa with its eight pillars are covered with murals depicting his life.

Gallery above Throne Room

This gallery contains fine murals typical of the 17th-century Central Tibetan style depicting contemporary scenes: construction of the Potala, invasion, the Monlam Prayer Festival, Gyelwa Ngapa's funeral procession, Samye Chokor, and also portraits of Desi Sangye Gyatso, Gusri Khan (the Qosot Mongol general) and Gyelwa Ngapa himself.

Chogyel Drupuk (Chos rgyal sgrub phug): The Emperor's Cave

In the 7th century this meditation cave of the Emperor Songtsen Gampo is said to have stood alone by a chorten on the summit of Marpo Ri. It contains images of the Emperor and his son; his ministers Tonmi Sambhota and Lompo Gar Tongtsen Yulsung; his Chinese, Nepali and Monpa consorts – Wencheng, Bhrikuti and Monsa Tricham; Je Tsongkapa; and also the Bodhisattvas Jampa, Drolma and a self-manifest Lokeswara as Padmapani.

Treasury

The locked and sealed chamber within the Chogyel Drupuk contains many old *tankas* (painted scrolls) collected and stored there after 1959.

Tsepak Lhakang (Tshe dpag lha khang)

The Lhakang of Tsepame contains the Nine Buddhas of Long-life, and Drolkar and Droljang (White and Green Drolmas). In a mural by the left-hand window Tangton Gyelpo is depicted with the Chuwori Chaksam gompa (p.137).

Drubwang Lhakang (Grub dbang lha khang)

This lhakang contains the *serdung* of the seventh Dalai Lama together with images of Sakyamuni and the Eight Bodhisattvas.

Dukor Lhakang (Dus 'khor lha khang): Kalacakra Lhakang

A three-dimensional gilt brass mandala *(lolang)* of Dukor (Kalacakra), The Wheel of Time, is the centre piece. An image of Dukor stands by the window, and small statues of lineage Lamas line the walls. Tribute silks cover the ceiling.

Pakpa Lhakang ('Phags pa lha khang): Lhakang of Pakpa Lokeswara

The Pakpa Lhakang is said to have been the upper storey of the Emperor Songtsen Gampo's Meditation Cave and it is the oldest lhakang in the Potala. It contains the Potala's most sacred image – Pakpa Lokeswara or Jowo Lokeswara – which is a standing image of Padmapani made of sandalwood. It gives the chamber its name. This image, brought from India, was the receptacle of the Emperor Songtsen Gampo's personal deity. The Pakpa Lhakang altars are a treasury of sacred art in bronze and wood. Kyentse Rimpoche mentions the following: an image of Jetsun Drakpa Gyeltsen (1147-1216 – the successor to Sonam Tsemo as Abbot of Sakya) called Dsetoma, Leper Skull; a small terracotta statue of Kache Panchen (p.161); an image of Tangton Gyelpo called Jatsonma, The Rainbow; and the footprints of Guru

Rimpoche taken from the Gungtang La, where the Guru finally left for Sangdok Peri.

Lama Lhakang (bLa ma lha khang)
The Protectress Pelden Lhamo and Gyelwa Ngapa are the chief images.

Thirteenth Dalai Lama's Serdung
The thirteenth Dalai Lama's *serdung* standing 14 m high is only slightly smaller than that of Gyelwa Ngapa. The chorten is surrounded by offerings, including a pagoda made of 200,000 pearls. Murals depicting this great Dalai Lama's life decorate the walls.

Drukpa Lhakang (Drug pa lha khang)
The Lhakang of the Sixth Dalai Lama, whose relics are missing from the Potala due to his assassination by the Chinese, contains a fine statue of the Protectress Relchikma (Ekajati), and 1000 images of Tsepame, The Buddha of Long-life.

Lolang Lhakang (bLos bslangs lha khang)
The Chamber of Three-dimensional Mandalas contains the Demchok (Samvara), Sangdu (Guhyasamaja) and Jigche (Yamantaka) mandalas in gilt metal. The Dukor Lhakang contains the *lolang* of the fourth Geluk *tantra*.

Jampa Lhakang (Byams pa lha khang)
The Jampa Lhakang was restored after a fire damaged it in 1984. It contains images of Miyowa, Dondrupa Drolma, Misum Gompo, Dukor and a Namgyel Chorten.

The basements of the palace contained the State and Dalai Lamas' treasuries, granaries, storerooms containing pilgrims' offerings, innumerable cells of monks and servants, and at the bottom were dungeons.

Shol
At the base of the Potala on its south side was the village of Shol. Shol was the village that serviced the Potala; it was also Lhasa's

traditional red-light area. The Parkang, the printing house where the woodblocks of the Lhasa Kanjur and Tenjur were stored, lay on the western side. The Kashak Building, Tibet's cabinet meeting house, lay in the centre, near a notorious jail. The People's Museum, on Dekyi Nub Lam, has been built over the site of the Potala's main gateway.

In a small enclosure on the south side of the Dekyi Nub Lam stands the Doring Chima, the famous Shol Pillar, erected (c.764) during the reign of the Emperor Trisong Detsen. It proclaims the virtues and rewards of the successful general and minister Takdra Lukong. The lower part of the inscription has been rendered indecipherable and piles of rock further obscure the lower parts of the pillar. The Doring Nangma stood in the centre of Shol, below the stairway to the Potala.

Lukang (kLu Khang): Temple of the Lu Protectors

The Lukang is a lhakang on a circular island in the lake excavated during the building of the Potala, located on the Potala's northern side. It was built under Chinese architectural influence by the pleasure-loving poet, the sixth Dalai Lama (1683-1706), in a charming setting consisting of water, island and trees and the presence of animistic powers secured to work for the benefit of man and The Law.

If indeed the sixth Dalai Lama pursued his pleasure in the Lukang, it did not remain a pleasure house for long, as the fine murals on three walls of the upper-storey lhakang indicate. The murals on the west and north walls describe Dzokchen yogas resulting in Rainbow Body. Indian *mahasiddhas* are depicted on the eastern wall. These fine murals, probably dating from the 18th century, no doubt indicate the Yellow Hat Dalai Lamas' secret practice of Dzokchen. The Lukang is now a residence of Yellow Hat monks and a school of yoga-practice for Lhasa laymen.

Ramoche (Ra mo che): Wencheng's Temple

Ramoche, located to the east of the Potala and to the north of the Jokang, is the most important lhakang in Lhasa after the Jokang itself. Built at the same time as the Jokang by the Emperor Songtsen Gampo's Chinese wife, Wencheng Kongjo, it housed the Jowo Chempo image of Sakyamuni Buddha that she had brought from China as part of her dowry. But probably immediately after Songtsen Gampo's death this image was exchanged with the Jowo of the Jokang, and it has taken pride of place in the Jokang ever since.

The Ramoche Jowo, also known as the Jowo Chungwa, the Small Jowo, is an image of Mikyo Dorje (Manjuvajra), and it was brought to Tibet as part of the dowry of Bhrikuti, the Emperor Songtsen Gampo's Nepali wife. However this sacred treasure of 7th-century Nepali workmanship cannot be identified with the image that was consecrated in Ramoche in 1986. Ramoche was gutted in the 1960s and the Jowo vanished, and when search was made for it in 1983 it is said that the lower half was discovered on a Lhasa rubbish tip and the upper half found unmarked in Peking. The two parts were uncomfortably joined. However, there is no certainty that the 7th-century image existed in 1959, as the Ramoche suffered the same fate as other Lhasa shrines during the Mongol invasions. Today the Jowo is surrounded by the Eight Bodhisattvas, with the Protectors Chagna Dorje and Tamdrin standing just within the lhakang. The Dalai Lama's throne and images of Je Tsongkapa and his two chief disciples, Kedrub Je and Gyeltseb Je, stand in front of the Jowo. On the left between the entrance and the dukang is an area utilized as a gomkang. The protective relics and images are found in a glass case just beyond this area.

Restoration of the dukang was completed and the first storey of the temple was in process of restoration in 1986. The monks' quarters are located in the first storey. Only the second-storey lhakang remained in a state of disrepair. On the walls of the *korsa* around the building, fine murals of Tsepame, Drolkar and Namgyelma have been painted in gold on a red background.

Until 1986 married Nyingma monks were the caretakers of this shrine. Now Gyuto monks live here, and Ganden Tri and

Ling Rimpoches, the Dalai Lama's late tutors and Gyuto abbots, are Ramoche's spiritual heirs. There are now two *geshe* instructors and fifty monks attached to Ramoche.

Shide Dratsang (bZhi sde grwa tshang)

To the south-west of Ramoche, and accessible from Dekyi Shar Lam (Happiness Road), was a college associated with Ramoche called the Shide Dratsang. This college was founded in the 14th century during the ascendancy of the Tsepa clan (p.98) by four monks originating in four different areas of Tibet. The buildings of the *dratsang* have now been destroyed or transformed into residences.

Gyuto Dratsang (rGyud stod grwa tshang): The Upper Tantric College

The buildings of the Gyuto Dratsang were located to the east of Ramoche in the Ramoche Chora, and also to the south of Ramoche. The Gyuto College was attached to Ramoche. Its buildings have been converted into residences, but Gyuto monks again officiate at Ramoche. Gyuto was renowned as the superior tantric college of the Geluk school, known particularly for its initiates' skill in chanting.

Tengye Ling Lhakang (bsTan rgyas gling lha Khang)

Tengye Ling[6] was located to the north of the new Mentsikang and west of the new Snowlands Hotel. Its sole surviving temple is found in the upper storey of a building on the north side of the Tengye Ling compound. Other buildings have been transformed into residences. This Tengye Ling Lhakang contains a large altar with a new image of Guru Rimpoche at its centre. To the right, in a glass case, is an old mask of the Protector Tseumar and a new image of Tseumar. The arrow on the altar is carried by the bride in wedding processions.

The Ling Shi (gLing bzhi): The Four Royal Colleges
The Tengye Ling Lhakang is the only temple belonging to any of the Four Royal Colleges of Lhasa (Ling Shi) to have been restored in 1985. The Four Lings were Tengye Ling; Kunde Ling, located to the south and east of Chakpo Ri, within the old Lingkor, now destroyed; Tsomon Ling, located south of Ramoche on the corner of Dekyi Shar Lam, its dukang — still one of the tallest buildings in Lhasa — and surrounding monks' quarters all converted into residences; and Drib Tsemchok Ling, located on the south bank of the Tsangpo west of the Lhasa Bridge, now vanished. These Yellow Hat colleges were established by the Dalai Lamas' Regents under Chinese patronage in the 18th century. The Lama-Regent who ruled during the Dalai Lama's minority could be chosen from the abbots of these colleges.

The most important of the Four Lings was Tengye Ling, the seat of the Demo Qutuqtus, who dominated the position of Regent during the 18th and 19th centuries, when a series of Dalai Lamas was assassinated before they reached their majority. Tengye Ling represented the most conservative and pro-Chinese monastic forces during the thirteenth Dalai Lama's attempts at reform. In 1901 the college was suppressed, and in 1912 attacked and ravaged due to its anti-government policies. Thereafter the Demo Qutuqtu took up residence in the Tsomon Ling. The old Demo Labrang, now residences, is located to the east of the Refugee Reception Centre on Dekyi Shar Lam.

Gyume Dratsang (rGyud smad): The Lower Tantric College

The second of the tantric colleges of Lhasa is located directly opposite the Kyirey Hotel on Dekyi Shar Lam, Happiness Road. The fine structure of this very large college complex is undoubtedly old, but it contains no artistic remains of merit. The monks' quarters have become residential accommodation; the dukang is now a workshop printing the Lhasa Kanjur woodblocks; while in the upper storey is a lhakang where the original, aging monks of Gyume practice their ritual worship. The Gyume College was renowned for the strict discipline of its Yellow Hat monks, who studied the four Geluk *tantras*, and also for their high level of learning. All monks were required to spend a part of the year on pilgrimage carrying their own luggage. The abbot of Gyume was a candidate for the office of Ganden Throne Holder (p.100).

Muru Sarpa (rMe ru gsar pa)

The Muru Sarpa is located immediately to the east of Gyume on Dekyi Shar Lam. It is no longer functioning as a monastery and it is used by the Lhasa Modern Drama group. Although this monastery is called the "New Muru" its foundation is said to date from the reign of the Emperor Repachen, who built lhakangs at the cardinal directions of Lhasa. After the 9th-century period of suppression it was rebuilt on the site of a chorten and a *dundro*. However, there is nothing of great age remaining in the Muru Sarpa. This community changed to the Yellow Hat school at the time of the third Dalai Lama (1543-89).

Ani *Tsungkang Gompa

A Yellow Hat Ani Gompa stands to the north of the path leading west from the Lhasa Mosque. This secluded shrine is remarkable for two reasons. Firstly in a basement at the rear is a spot where the Emperor Songtsen Gampo meditated and where he left his footprint; and secondly, by 1986 some seventy *anis* had made this an exemplary nunnery, fully functional in a beautifully restored building.

Norbu Lingka (Nor bu gling kha): The Dalai Lamas' Summer Residence

The Norbu Lingka is located to the south-west of the city outside the Lingkor. This was the summer residence of the Dalai Lamas from the mid-18th century. The old palaces were looted during the Cultural Revolution, but the New Palace of the fourteenth Dalai Lama, built in 1956, remains as he left it, and the Tibetans' extraordinary devotion to the embodiment of Chenresik can be seen by the quantity of offerings deposited by his throne and his bed. The seventh Dalai Lama's Kalsang Potang finished in 1755 and located to the west of the compound is a beautiful example of Yellow Hat architecture. Its fully restored throne room is also of interest.

Sera Tekchenling (Se ra Theng chen gling)

Sera gompa was one of the four great Yellow Hat monasteries in Tibet (with Drepung, Ganden and Tashi Lhumpo). It housed more than 5000 monks in 1959. Much of the original complex was destroyed during the Cultural Revolution, but the chief colleges and lhakangs along with their images and relics were preserved. Some 300 monks are now associated with Sera, but it presents a sorry reflection of its former glory, and apart from two or three small lhakangs where especially sacred relics are preserved it is to be considered more a museum than a place of power. For this reason it has not been given the amount of space that its past reputation requires.

Sera lies some 5 km north of the Jokang in the lee of Purbu Chok Ri.[7] It was founded in 1419 by Jamchen Choje Sakya Yeshe of Tse Gungtang, who was one of Tsongkapa's chief disciples. The number of its colleges has fluctuated over the centuries. Its original four *dratsangs* became five in its heyday, but in 1959 there were only three: Sera Me which gave fundamental instruction to the monks; Sera Je, the largest, reserved for wandering monks, particularly Mongols; and the Ngakpa Dratsang, a school for teaching the Geluk *tantras*. The meaning of the name "Sera" is Enclosure of Roses, but it is commonly given as Beneficent Hail, a name that indicates the rivalry, often less than friendly, that existed between Sera and Drepung, since hail (*ser*) destroys rice (*dre*).

Tsokchen (Tshogs chen)

The common assembly hall, the Tsokchen, is built against the rock on the eastern side of Sera's central road. The principal image is a colossal Jampa (Maitreya). But in the upper storey, in the lhakang to the west side of the gallery overlooking the Jampa, is the Tujechempo Lhakang containing the image of Tujechempo (Mahakarunika), considered to be Sera's most beneficent, blessing-bestowing image. Its blessing may be received by means of a stick, one end placed on the deity's heart-chakra and the other on the devotee's head-chakra. It was the personal deity of the Gelongma Pelmo, probably Srimati Laksmi of Kashmir, who initiated a tradition of fasting for Tujechempo in the 11th century. It was concealed at Pabongka and recovered later to be installed at Sera.

Jepa Duchen (Byas pa 'dus chen)

The great assembly hall of the Jepa Dratsang is located in the middle of the Sera complex to the west of the central road. Beside it is a garden where the monks practice debate. The Duchen was built by the Dzungar Prince Lhazang Khan, who ruled Lhasa from 1705-17 after executing the Regent Sangye Gyatso.

The fine murals that have been restored in the portico of this magnificent building are typical of paintings found on the outer walls of all Tibetan gompas: on the left side wall is the Wheel of Life illustrating the three passions that cause the wheel to turn, the six realms of sentient beings' potential rebirth, and the twelve interdependent elements of karmic causality; the mural on the right side wall depicts the mandala of Mt Meru and the Indian-derived Buddhist cosmos; in the middle are the Four Guardian Kings, of Chinese origin.

At the north-western corner of the Jepa Duchen is the Tamdrin Lhakang, and this remarkable chamber is undoubtedly the most powerful place in the entire Sera complex. Within a copper-gilt shrine in the centre of the lhakang is an image of the Wrathful Deity and Protector Tamdrin, Hayagriva, the Horse-necked. This statue is known as Pema Yangsang Drakpo, the Lotus of Hidden Wrath, a name that indicates his symbolic representation of the negative energy that emanates from Divine Being in order to destroy obstacles to enlightenment. This image is said to speak to warn of forthcoming disaster. Further, a compartment on the upper left-hand side of the shrine contains the *purba* (ritual dagger) of the 13th-century *siddha* Darchar. This *purba* is also said to be the original *purba* of Dorje Shonnu (Vajrakumara), the Deity that embodies the *purba*. Tradition has it that this *purba* came flying from India to land on the hill behind Sera. Previously it was revealed only during Monlam. Nowadays its blessings can be received on the 15th day of the 12th lunar month. The walls of the Tamdrin Lhakang are decorated with masks, weapons of war and suits of armour.

Pabongka (Pha bong kha): The Emperor Songtsen Gampo's Hermitage

Pabongka is one of Central Tibet's most ancient power-places. It is located on the hillside some distance to the west of Sera, built upon an immense flat-topped boulder. Only the foundations of the principal lhakang survived the Cultural Revolution, but restoration was in progress in 1986. The chief image in the main lhakang was Avalokitesvara Karsapani. Hugh Richardson described a small lhakang built by the Emperor Songtsen Gampo where the images of the Rigsum Gompo are carved in the rock. This must be identified with the walled-in overhang beneath and on the west side of the rock.

History
In the 7th century a nine-storey place of retreat was built on the great flat rock of Pabongka by the Emperor Songtsen Gampo for his own use. It is said that on this spot, gazing at Marpo Ri, he conceived the plan to build his Potala Palace. In the 9th century the first seven Tibetan monks, the Misedun, ordained by the Samye abbot Santaraksita, lived at Pabongka. Destroyed by Langdarma in the 9th century it was rebuilt during Pakpa's rule in the 13th century and again destroyed (14th century?). The recently-destroyed building was completed at the beginning of the 17th century.

Pabongka is the Tibetan equivalent of the Indian tantric

pithasthana in northern Bengal called Devikotta, which was one of the Twenty-four Power-places associated with the Mother-*tantras*. Thus Kyentse Rimpoche calls it the Second Devikotta.

Hermitages

There are several hermitages located in the vicinity of Sera. SERA TSE or DRUBKANG TSE is a hermitage older than Sera, but now attached to it, located on the mountain directly behind the gompa. Some monks were in residence in 1985. PURBU CHOK was a small gompa built on the spot where Sera's Darchar *purba* fell on the mountain called Purbu Chok behind the monastery. KARDO RITRO was located to the east of Sera. It has been destroyed. DRAKRI RITRO, or *Bari Gompa, was located on a spur about 1.5 km west of Sera; its present condition is unknown.

Nechung Chok (gNas chung lcog): The State Oracle's Seat

To the east of the track that leads from the highway to Drepung stands the monastery which was the residence of the Yellow Hats' chief Protector, Pehar, and the State Oracle, the Nechung Chokyong. It is also called Sungi Gyelpoi Tsenkar, the Demon Fortress of the Oracle King. Nechung was gutted and converted into a farmyard during the Cultural Revolution, but in 1986 restoration was advanced and the art that had invested the place with its special quality of pre-Buddhist magic was again in evidence. To the east of Nechung is a college of debate, now attended by more than 130 young students.

The main doors, which lead into the gompa's large courtyard, are painted with the motifs associated with the doors of gomkangs, and the rings on the outside of the doors are let into intricate gilt copper-work in the form of skulls. On the east side of the courtyard are remarkable murals depicting protecting deities. In the courtyard stands the tree in which Pehar, the deity whose seat this is, resides. The gompa's dukang, lhakang and the Oracle's residence stand at the north side of the courtyard. In 1986 the dukang was still empty and the Jowo Lhakang awaited its new Sakyamuni and Eight Bodhisattvas, but the gomkang to the left of the Jokang contained new images of two aspects of Pehar, and the gomkang to its right contained images of Pelden Lhamo and the Dzokchen Protectress Nyima Shonnu. Behind the empty central room in the first storey is the restored 10 m image of Guru Rimpoche Sinon, Overwhelming Splendour.

Nechung is essentially the residence of the Protector Pehar. Pehar was originally the deity of the Horpas who lived to the east of Lake Kokonor, but seeking a Protector for the new Samye gompa Guru Rimpoche invoked him and bound him at Samye to serve the *dharma*. During the reorganization under the Great Fifth Dalai Lama, Pehar was moved first from Samye to Tse Gungtang and then, due to conflict with the ethos of that gompa, Pehar was caught in a box and expelled. Curiosity caused the box to be opened near Drepung and Pehar escaped, taking the form of a dove that lodged in the tree that is now his residence at Nechung. The medium of Pehar's prophecy and instruction, the Nechung Oracle, was adopted by the Geluk school and became the Great Fifth's State Oracle, an institution that has flourished since that time. The Nechung Rimpoches continued in their Nyingma practice while the State Oracle, now in exile, was chosen independently by the Yellow Hats for his receptivity to possession by Pehar. It was the Nechung Oracle who directed the decisions of the Regent and the Dalai Lama in the last years of theocracy.

Drepung ('Bras spungs)

Pelden Drepung,[8] Glorious Drepung gompa, the largest of Tibet's monastic cities, is located 8 km to the west of Lhasa, built below the valley wall. This was the principal seat of the Yellow Hats before the Great Fifth Dalai Lama constructed the Potala. Thereafter, it retained its premier place amongst the four great Geluk monasteries, housing more than 7,000 monks. About forty percent of the old monastic town has been destroyed, but Drepung's chief buildings – the four colleges, the Tsokchen, and the Dalai Lamas' residence – have been preserved. It was one

of the richest foundations in Tibet and its wealth is reflected in the decoration of these buildings. However, founded in 1416 Drepung became the centre of the Yellow Hats' webs of political intrigue, and it was destroyed and rebuilt at least three times, the last time in the early 18th century, and little has survived from earlier periods. – During the third Dalai Lama's period there were seven *dratsangs* at Drepung, but by the 18th century these had been consolidated into four: Ngakpa, Gomang, Deyang and Losel Dratsangs. The buildings of these four colleges, each with its own abbot and syllabus, surround the Tsokchen. Some 400 monks are now attached to Drepung, but the overall feeling of the gompa is of a monastic museum. Most of the monks in evidence in 1985 were those aged *gelongs* who had remained in the Drepung Commune to farm the orchards that lie below the temples and who were working as caretakers.

Tsokchen (Tshogs chen)

The great communal assembly hall was rebuilt by the Regent after it had collapsed in 1735. It is also known as the Jamkang Sarpa, as its most powerful image is of Jampa, the Lord of Drepung, called Jampa Tongdrol, which liberates the faithful from samsara merely by sight of it. This image of the Bodhisattva Jampa at the age of twelve is found in the first storey of the building and to the left of the stairway.

Ngakpa Dratsang (sNgags pa grwa tshang)

The tantric college called Ngakpa Dratsang was consecrated by Tsongkapa himself. It contains the most powerful of Drepung's images, the statue of Dorje Jigche, Vajra Bhairava, called Chogyel Chaktakma, the King with the Iron Rope. This buffalo-headed deity is the Geluk school's principal tutelary deity and protector. Added sanctity is given to this image by the relics of Ralo Dorje Drak. Ra Lotsawa, or Lama Ralo (b.11th century), was born in Nyelam and studied in Nepal with the teacher Mahakaruna of Naropa's lineage. He learned the Yamantaka, Vajrabhairava, Samvara and Vajrayogini *tantras*, and his transla-

[4.] [above] PABONG TANG: Reteng *gelongs* performing rite in front of the Dakini's Rock (photograph by K. Dowman)
[below] DREPUNG: *gelongs* chanting in the Assembly Hall (photograph by R. Demandre)

tions are considered second to none. He attended the national Buddhist council of the King of Guge in 1076. This image containing his relics "radiates a lustre which gives blessing".[9] It is found in one of the side lhakangs of the Ngakpa Dratsang's assembly hall. The images on the central altar of this assembly hall are the Buddhas of the Three Times and also the Eight Bodhisattvas. The founder's reliquary chorten was originally located in this dukang.

Loseling Dratsang (bLo gsal gling grwa tshang)
Loseling was a school of logic. Jampa is the chief image. A mural of Sonam Drakpa, one of the greatest Geluk scholars and abbot of Loseling in the early 17th century, is found in the assembly hall. Sonam Drakpa, through pressure of political intrigue, was forced to commit suicide, but his spirit returned as the narrow Yellow Hat Protector Dorje Shukden, carrying sword, human heart and riding a snowlion.

Tashi Gomang Dratsang (bKra shis sgo mang grwa tshang)
Murals depicting 108 scenes in the life of the Buddha Sakyamuni are found in the assembly hall. On the west side is the lhakang of the chief Geluk Protectress Pelden Lhamo.

Deyang Dratsang (bDe yangs grwa tshang)
This college was dedicated to Menlha, the Medicine Buddha.

Ganden Potang (dGa' ldan Pho brang)
Located to the south-west of the Drepung compound, the Ganden Potang was built by the second Dalai Lama, Gendun Gyatso, c.1530, as his residence. As the inscriptions on Tibetan coins bear witness, it is the Ganden Potang rather than the Potala that is the symbol of Yellow Hat government in Tibet. This political association begun by Gendun Gyatso continued in concrete form until the Great Fifth moved to the Potala in 1655. However, the Dalai Lamas maintained quarters here until 1959. Two important images are to be found in the assembly hall: the Talking Drolma that was Jowo Atisha's tutelary deity and the Tujechempo that was the Indian metaphysician Candragomin's tutelary deity.

Jamyang Choje's Hermitage ('Jam dbyangs chos rje'i gzim phug)

The founder of Drepung, Jamyang Choje (1397-1449), meditated in the hermitage located behind the Tsokchen when Drepung was a bare hillside. Born at Samye, Jamyang Choje was an important disciple of Tsongkapa, and then Drepung's founder and first abbot. His faith and knowledge have been overshadowed by the power-politics that later became associated with his gompa. The meditation cell now contains a self-manifest, blessing-bestowing image of Tsongkapa, and Jamyang Choje's staff.

History

Jamyang Choje Tashi Pelden founded Drepung in 1416 on the model of the famous South Indian *vihara* called Sri Dhanyakataka where Sakyamuni Buddha is said to have taught the *Kalacakratantra*. The Depa of Neudzong (p.140) patronized the establishment. In 1419 Tsongkapa, then in his sixty-second year, gave instruction to the monks of Drepung, and consecrated the Ngakpa Dratsang. The second Dalai Lama, Gendun Gyatso (1475-1542), second abbot of Tashi Lhumpo, became abbot of Drepung in 1526 and built the Ganden Potang. Thereafter, Drepung was the principal political centre of the Yellow Hats. In 1578 the Qosot Mongol Emperor Altan Khan bestowed the title Dalai Lama (*Ta-la'i bla ma*) upon Sonam Gyatso who became the third Dalai Lama, his predecessors retroactively receiving the same title. In 1618 Drepung was destroyed by the King of Tsang in his anti-Geluk campaign, and many thousands of monks were slaughtered. In 1635 the gompa was burnt down by invading Mongols. Around 1655 the Great Fifth moved from the Ganden Potang to the Potala. In 1706 Drepung was sacked by the Dzungars of Lhazang Khan after the gompa had persisted in its support of the Regent Sangye Gyatso.

In the 20th century, Drepung became associated with the conservative and Chinese faction in Yellow Hat politics. It opposed the great thirteenth Dalai Lama's attempts at reform and was involved in the dispute over the Regency after his death. This resulted in the confused political conditions that the invading Communists used to great advantage.

Gepel Ritro (dGe 'phel ri khrod)

This hermitage, visible high on Gepel Ri above Drepung, has been partially restored and several monks are in residence. These monks look after the herd of yaks that graze on the medicinal plants that grow on the mountain side. Previously the curd produced from their milk was reserved for the Dalai Lama. The hermitage was founded by Tsepa Drungchen Kunga Dorje in the 14th century.

The summit of Gepel Ri is one of the auspicious mountain peaks around Lhasa where the *sang* offering is performed for the mountain gods. On Saga Dawa, the Buddha's birthday, it is an auspicious site for lay celebration. The most popular site for the offering of *sang* to Lhasa's protecting deities is *BUMPA RI, which rises to the south of the Lhasa Bridge. On top of the southern end of the ridge that is Bumpa Ri are natural pillars shaped like vases, and it is on top of these that the fragrant twigs are burnt.

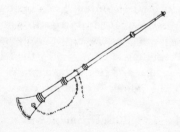

2

THE CAVES OF DRAK YERPA

Within easy access of Lhasa is one of Central Tibet's outstanding hermitage power-places. In a spectacular limestone scarp, high above the Yerpa Valley, from pre-Buddhist times cave-hermitages have been excavated from the rock. The history of Drak Yerpa[1] includes many of the great names responsible for the establishment of Buddhism in Tibet and many master yogins who have meditated there down the centuries. The Emperor Songtsen Gampo meditated in seclusion here; Guru Rimpoche and several of his disciples also meditated here; and here Jowo Atisha chose to preach extensively. Although the ancient Kadampa gompa has been destroyed, the geomantic qualities that made Drak Yerpa a major power-place still remain and still attract hermits to its caves.

Access

The road to Yerpa runs east-north-east from Lhasa for about 10 km along the northern bank of the Kyichu. At the village of *Kawa the road turns north over a low pass and down into Yerpa Da at the foot of the Yerpa Valley. Below the village is the confluence of the Yerpa Chu and the Kyichu, 16 km to the north-east of Lhasa. From Yerpa Da the river runs north for some 10 km before turning north-west, and Drak Yerpa is located above the north-east side of this bend. From Lhasa it can be reached in less than a day by foot or in two hours by jeep.

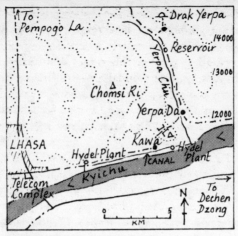

Map 4 The Yerpa Valley

The Amphitheatre

The Yerpa Valley is fertile and well-watered, and the jeep-road climbs steadily through terraced barley fields supporting a number of prosperous villages. Finally, above the fold of a ridge the white cliff of Drak Yerpa becomes visible some 300 m above the river. Climbing up to the typical chorten that guards the entrance to the Drak Yerpa complex, and crossing a small lateral valley, the pilgrim reaches the site of the Yerpa Drubde gompa. The ruins are perched on a belt of flat land at the base of a high cliff. From the vantage of Yerpa Drubde the many black holes, seemingly natural caves in the white cliff above, are seen to have possessed walled facades that have been blown away. This makes for difficult access to some caves. Below the gompa ruins is a perennial spring.

Climbing 100 m up to the restored Dawa Puk, the Cave of Guru Rimpoche, a magnificent 180-degree vista opens up and the paradigm of geomantic perfection that is Drak Yerpa is revealed. The ridges to east and west form a vast amphitheatre and directly to the south the Yerpa Valley winds its way between interlocking spurs down to the Kyichu. Beyond, on the horizon, are the snow-covered peaks of the massif between the Kyichu and Tsangpo Valleys, a central phallic peak cast as Mount Meru.

Immediately to the east, across the shallow valley with a seasonal stream running through it, is a ridge that rolls away to the higher ridges forming the eastern circumference of the amphitheatre. The highest peak in this ridge, dominating the skyline to the south-east, is a pyramidal peak called Yerpa Lhari, the residence of the protecting mountain deity of Yerpa. To the west the cliff curves to the south-west to form a spur blocking further view up the Yerpa Valley. The principal caves lie in an arc mostly to the west of Dawa Puk.

In 1948 Tucci found Drak Yerpa remarkable in that its flora was most similar to the vegetation on the south side of the Himalayas. "Giant junipers and tufts of rhododendron topped a thick tangle of undergrowth, brushwood and grass victoriously fighting the barrenness of the rocks. We were greeted by a warbling of birds conferring upon the hermitage an air of unexpected merriment."[2] The victory of the barren rock at today's Yerpa is indicative of the Tibetans' struggle for survival during the last decades.

Dawa Puk (Zla ba phug): Guru Rimpoche's Cave

Guru Rimpoche lived in the Dawa Puk, the Moon Cave. This large rock overhang has now been restored as a lhakang, and an altar has been built against the back wall with an image of Guru Rimpoche as the central object of worship. A footprint of Guru Rimpoche is visible by the altar. The original statue of Guru Rimpoche and other self-manifest images were not in evidence. The offering accepted by Guru Rimpoche in this cave is a draught of *chang* to be drunk by the worshipper from a skull-cup. Both the Guru and his consort Yeshe Tsogyel hid "profound" treasure (*zapter*) here, but no prophecy was given concerning it and no specific *tertons* are related to Dawa Puk.

Dorje Puk (rDo rje phug): Pelgyi Dorje's Cave

To the west, below Chogyel Puk, is Dorje Puk. According to legend this is the cave in which the monk Lhalung Pelgyi Dorje hid himself after assassinating the Bonpo Emperor Langdarma in 842. Pelgyi Dorje's hat was kept here until 1959. This cave is now inhabited.

Lhakang

Beneath the Dawa Puk is an important lhakang that has been rebuilt. Its inner sanctum consists of a central free-standing plinth with four ovoid aureoles, one on each side, that once haloed images of the Four Dhyani Buddhas. The *korsa* around this altar is cut into the rock that forms the lhakang's rear wall. This altar is probably the oldest at Drak Yerpa. Originally the outer rooms of the lhakang contained the image-receptacle of Yerpa's Protectors.

Chogyel Puk (Chos rgyal phug): Songtsen Gampo's Cave

Above and to the west of Dawa Puk is the Chogyel Puk, the cave of the Emperor Songtsen Gampo, the 7th-century emperor who introduced worship of Chenresik into Tibet and who meditated here after his conversion to the Buddha-*dharma*. The emperor's own deity, Chaktong Chentong, the Thousand-armed Thousand-eyed Chenresik, from whose finger-tips nectar dripped for his devotees, dominated this cave. In 1986 the Chogyel Puk was a large empty cave with remnants of murals in which Gompo (Mahakala) was prominent.

Drubtob Puk (Grub thob phug): The Siddhas' Cave

To the west of the Chogyel Puk is the Cave of the Eighty Siddhas of Yerpa. Legend has it that this grotto, which has several small meditation caves inside it, was the retreat of the eighty yogins associated with Yerpa in the 9th century. Their achievement was the *siddhi* of flying in the sky. "It is well known that many of the inmates of Yerpa possessed the faculty of soaring in the air."[3]

Jampa Lhakang (Byams pa lha khang)

In 1986 the interior of this large excavated cave, west of the Siddhas' Cave, was in the same trashed state as the Red Guards left it. Large leaves of handmade-paper manuscripts were scattered about, or buried beneath the wreckage of the giant image of Jampa, the Future Buddha Maitreya, who took pride of place on a central, free-standing altar. Only Jampa's legs and feet survive. This grotto had a square structure, now partially destroyed, built within it. The Jampa Lhakang housed one of Tibet's four most powerful statues of Jampa, an image commissioned by Marton in the 13th century. Nectar once flowed from the aureole of light that haloed the image. Images of Jampa's father and mother, Namse and Drolma, were also lodged here.

Chagna Dorje Puk (Phyag na rdo rje'i phug): Meditation Caves
About 200 m to the west of the Jampa Lhakang, and somewhat below it, is a terrace of four small meditation caves. These ideally situated, south-facing caves with small terraces in front of them, have low platforms for beds and higher shelves for altars carved out of the living rock, as in the Indian cave-monasteries. Replete with the vibrations of centuries of occupation, it is natural that the first yogins and yoginis to return to Yerpa should choose these caves to live in. The Chagna Dorje Puk has a rough self-manifest image of Chagna Dorje, the Body's Protector, emerging from a wall.

Atisha's Simpuk (Atisa'i gzim phug): Jowo Atisha's Hermitage
Beyond the Chagna Dorje Puk is a large cave leading to Jowo Atisha's Sleeping Cave. Access to the Sleeping Cave can be gained by a 2 m tunnel from within the grotto or by a narrow path around its western end. This was one of Atisha's favorite hermitages. Jowo Atisha, the renowned Bengali teacher from Vikramasila, taught and meditated at Drak Yerpa c.1057. His image was once found in the cave he lived in.

Utse Puk and Pukar Rabsel (dBu rtse phug dang Phug dkar rab gsal)
Two significant caves at Drak Yerpa that we failed to locate are the Utse Puk, the Peak Cave, a cave of difficult access at the top of the cliff, and a cave called Pukar Rabsel, the All-illuminating White Cave, in the central area of the cliff. There are many other caves in the cliff that remain unidentified and which were never named.

Neten Lhakang (gNas rten lha khang): The Temple of the Arhats
The oldest original temple structure at Drak Yerpa in 1959 and one of the oldest in Tibet was the Neten Lhakang, the Lhakang of

the Sixteen Arhats. This was located below and to the east of Dawa Puk, and its ruins still remain. This lhakang is said to have been built by Lume at the beginning of the 11th century when Buddhist practice was re-established at Drak Yerpa. The images of the Sixteen Arhats that were to be found here in 1959 were either made in China or copied from Chinese models and probably dated from the 11th or 12th centuries. Worship of the Sixteen Arhats originated in China. One of the *arhats* was the Chinese Hwashang Mahayana, who brought the Taoist-influenced doctrine of *chan* to Tibet in the 9th century. It is believed that this temple was instrumental in initiating worship of the Sixteen Arhats in Tibet. A most remarkable set of images of the Sixteen Arhats can be found today in the second-storey lhakang of the main temple at Gyangtse.

Atisha's Throne
An artefact relating to Jowo Je is the stone seat in the meadow below the site of the Neten Lhakang. It was here that Atisha would preach, and he is reputed to have given a complete exposition of the *sutras* to his disciples at Yerpa.

The Protectors
The Geluk protecting-deities of Drak Yerpa are Pelden Lhamo, Begtse, and also Treumar Serpo. An unusual, peaceful form of Pelden Lhamo (the Tibetan Kali), called Machik Pelha Shiwai Nyamchen, is peculiar to Drak Yerpa.

Lama Tsenpo
The 19th-century Tibetan geographer Lama Tsenpo[4] mentions two notable boulders which may have survived the holocaust, although we failed to locate them in 1985. The first is a black stone in which a self-manifest Six-syllable Mantra (OM MANI PADME HUNG) appeared in white; and the second is a large blue rock in which images of Drolma, Dzambhala (Kubera) – the Buddha-Deity of wealth, Rigjema (Kurukulla), and Birwapa – the Root Guru of the Sakya sect, are self-manifest in white. He also mentions the existence of many *chakje*: "the footprints and handprints of many holy ones are to be found in the rock".

History

There is no reference to Drak Yerpa before the time of the Emperor Songtsen Gampo, but to assume that it was a Bonpo site is not unreasonable. In the 7th century the Emperor Songtsen Gampo's queen, Mon Tricham, had a temple built here, and the Emperor meditated in Chogyel Puk. During the Emperor Trisong Detsen's reign Guru Rimpoche meditated here and hid a lode of treasure. Thereafter Drak Yerpa became one of the three principal centres of meditation retreat in Central Tibet: Yerpa was to the Lhasa Jokang as Chimpu was to Samye. "Three thousand monks were ordained in Lhasa and five hundred hermits took up residence at Yerpa";[5] perhaps these figures are somewhat hyperbolic, but they establish Yerpa as a focal point of the *dharma* during the first period of its propagation in Tibet. Kapa Peltsek, one of the early translators, and Wodren Shonnu, practised the propitiation of the Mamo Goddesses here after their initiation with others of the Twenty-five disciples at Chimpu. The hermits of Yerpa who lived at this time created the legend of the Eight or Eighty-four Adepts (*siddhas*) of Yerpa. The Indian master Padampa Sangye stayed here and meditated in the Dawa Puk in the 11th century. After the confusion of the period of Langdarma's suppression, Lume (p.295), with his disciple Ngok Jangchub Dorje, built the Neten Lhakang at Drak Yerpa (c.1012) after he had returned from taking orders in Kham where the old tradition of ordination had survived. When Jowo Atisha and Dromton were invited here by Ngok (c.1047) Drak Yerpa was a flourishing sanctuary. Yerpa was one of four places where Jowo Je preached extensively. A Kadampa gompa, Yerpa Drubde, the second largest Kadampa gompa of the time, was established here. This passed to Geluk control after Tsongkapa's reformation. At the beginning of the 19th century there were some 300 monks living in the gompa and that number was sustained until 1959. It was the summer residence of the Gyuto Lhasa Tantric College.

NORTH OF LHASA TO RETENG

There is a unity and continuity in the religious history of the two valleys to the north of Lhasa – Penyul and Jang – that is not to be found elsewhere in Central Tibet. Although Guru Rimpoche is said to have visited this area in the 8th century to subdue demons, no power-places relating to the first period of propagation of the *dharma* in Tibet are located here. However, when Jowo Atisha visited Tibet in the 11th century it was the people of these valleys who responded most immediately to his teaching and it was to Penyul and Jang that innumerable disciples flocked to be instructed by the Kadampa school masters at their many Kadampa gompas. The Kadampa monks were strong in monastic discipline and in study of the *sutras* and, unusual amongst Tibetan monastic schools, had no time for politics. Eventually, after the rise of the later schools, their gompas were to be adopted either by the Sakyapas or the Gelukpas. In Penyul, in 1959, the principal gompas of Nalendra and Langtang were Sakya establishments, and in Jang Reteng was one of the most important Geluk gompas. The exception was the gompa of Taklung Tang, which indeed began as a Kadampa hermitage but was chosen by a disciple of Je Gampopa as the site of the Kagyu gompa that became the seat of the Taklung Kagyu, one of the major Kagyu schools. Otherwise, as Kyentse Rimpoche remarked in the 19th century, most of the gompas founded by the early Kadampa lamas such as Potowa, Neuzurpa and Puchungwa, decayed long ago, so that even their locations are lost.

Perhaps due to their proximity to Lhasa, Penyul and Jang suffered much destruction during the Cultural Revolution. The large complexes of Nalendra, Reteng and Taklung were all devastated. However, rebuilding has begun at all these sites, and the historical emphasis on scholarship and monastic discipline that characterized them as important monastic academies endows them with particular importance in the Tibetan tradition. The beauty of their sites also gives them a vital attraction.

Access

The main caravan route from the Holy City to the North left Lhasa by way of the valley to the east of Sera Gompa, passed over the Pempogo La, The Gate to Pempo, into Penyul, and then continued directly north to Chomdo over Chak La (5,300 m) into Jang. The jeep-road up the Kyichu Valley from Drigung Qu provides alternative access to Jang, to Taklung and Reteng. The old caravan route continues from Chomdo to Reteng and then over to Damsung.[1] Further, there is a new jeep-road that leaves the Lhasa-Ganden highway beyond Dechen Dzong, and crossing the Kyichu bridge it ascends the long Penyul Valley up to Pempo Qu for 20 km before following the caravan route for a further 25 km over the Chak La and down to Taklung. From Lhasa to Reteng via the Chak La is approximately 100 km.

Bomto ('Brom stod)

The village of Bomto[2] is located just beyond the Kyichu bridge on the jeep-road from Dechen Dzong to Penyul. Its significance lies in the cave of Nyen Lotsawa Darma Drak called Nyen Gompuk, which is located above the road. The hermitage is deserted but a new chorten has been built on the side of the road in the village. Nyen Darma Drak accompanied Ra Lotsawa to India and Nepal in the late 11th century to learn Sanskrit and to translate several major texts.

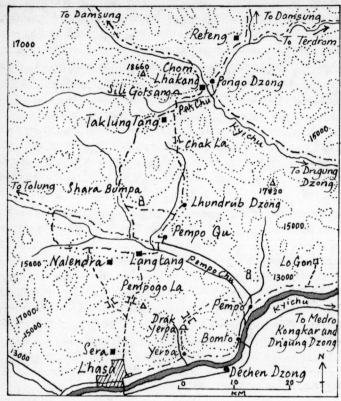

Map 5 North of Lhasa: Penyul and Jang

Lo gon (Lo dgon)

Lo Gompa is located on the northern side of the Kyichu some 20 km north-east of the entrance to the Penyul Valley. It is included in this chapter because it was an important Kadampa gompa founded in the 11th century by a disciple of Dromton and its history is connected to Penyul. We were unable to visit Lo and thus have no contemporary information about the gompa.

History

The Kadampa gompa of Lo was founded in 1095 by Chenga Tsultrim Bar (1038-1103). Chenga was a disciple of Dromton at Reteng and was an important teacher of Jayulpa and many other Kadampa luminaries. Jayulpa helped Chenga build Lo Gompa, and after his teacher's death he visited it frequently. Kache Panchen visited Lo in 1212. As a Jayulpa establishment it thrived, so that in an early 14th-century armed conflict it could successfully thwart the powerful Drigungpas. After passing into the hands of the Gelukpas, Lo Tsetang, as it became known, was the seat of the influential Gelukpa incarnation Lo Sempa Chempo. In the 18th century Sempa Chempo played a considerable part in the court of the seventh Dalai Lama.

Penyul

The Pempo Chu waters the broad, fertile Penyul Valley for 30 km before joining the Kyichu. Rich in agriculture it is also renowned for the glazed pots that it produces for the Lhasa market.

Langtang (gLang thang)

Langtang[3] gompa was founded in 1093 on the flat plain on the south side of the Pempo Chu and close to the old Lhasa caravan route. During the Kadampa period it was a large and vital gompa. That Langtang survived when many other Kadampa gompas of equal original vitality did not, is due to its association with Nalendra and its conversion to the Sakya school.

In the middle of the old Langtang monastic complex, which has been converted into part of a farming commune, a single building has survived. Reached by stone steps the old *labrang* dating from the 15th century has been restored as a small dukang and lhakang where some twenty monks now worship. The surviving relics of the gompa are now found in this lhakang. In the centre of the altar is a new image of the founder, Langtangpa;

to the right is an old Buddha image and the small, original image of Drolma Sungjonma, Talking Drolma, that was the principal relic of the old gompa; to the left are shelves of lineage lamas. In the contiguous, unrestored dukang, either side of the doorway, on the rear wall, are old murals depicting the Sakya protecting-deities. In so far as these Protectors are also the deities of the Nyingma school, Old School origins of the Sakya tradition are demonstrated here. Below the courtyard in front of the dukang are the ruins of the old Lhakang Chempo. On this site the founder of Langtang built his hermitage. Behind the dukang is a chorten, rebuilt in the Kadampa style, that previously enshrined relics of Langtangpa.

History

Dromton gathered Atisha's disciples around him at Reteng, but the number of students seeking instruction became too many for Reteng to hold, and the principal Kadampa masters began to establish their own gompas. Potowa and Neuzurpa were two such adepts, and the founder of Langtang was one of their disciples. Langri Tangpa Dorje Senge (1054-1123) founded this Kadampa gompa in 1093 and gathered 2,000 disciples around him. This large number is more readily accepted when it is remembered that at this time the entire country was eagerly sending its sons to absorb the doctrines and practices of the lineages founded by Atisha. It is unclear when Langtang was absorbed by the Sakyapas, but a renowned succession of abbots includes Geshe Nyen and Sangye Won of Gyama (p.104). In the 15th century the gompa was restored by Panchen Sakya Chokden, an abbot of Nalendra and a disciple of Rongtonpa, but it must have been adopted by the Sakya school long before this. The renown of this place was enhanced by the legend that part of the Indian master Padampa Sangye's relics were enshrined here (see also p.281).

Pel Nalendra (dPal Nalendra)

Glorious Nalendra, named after the ancient Buddhist academy of Nalanda near Bodh Gaya (Bihar, India), is located to the south-west of Langtang, built across the entrance to a side-valley.

Behind it a path climbs to the Pempogo La. Nalendra was founded by Rongtonpa, a contemporary of Tsongkapa, in the early 15th century, and it has been a major centre of the Sakya school ever since.

The extensive ruins of the walled monastic complex of Nalendra comprises one of the most melancholy sights the pilgrim encounters in Central Tibet. The ruins, largely deserted, are much as the destroyers left them. The newly built lhakang and *labrang* residence of the Nalendra abbots, and another larger *labrang* in process of restoration, are dwarfed by the devastation. Kyentse Rimpoche mentions the Choje Labrang and Rongton's hermitage, together with the enormous Tsokchen, as buildings of importance. A college of debate and the tantric college lie in ruins as do the five monks' dormitories and another *labrang*. In the new lhakang the image of the founder, Rongtonpa, takes pride of place. Other relics, such as Rongtonpa's faeces transformed into jewelry, and his chair, have disappeared. A large reliquary chorten, built in the Kadampa style like that at Langtang, has been rebuilt outside the compound's walls.

History

Rongton Chempo Mawai Senge (1367-1449) was born in Gyelpo Rong in Western Sichuan into a Bonpo family. He travelled to Central Tibet to study and practice the pure doctrines being taught at the academy of Sangpu Neutok (p.140). His scholarship, particularly in the *sutras*, and his debating skill, were legendary, earning him the epithet Omniscient (*kunkyen*), and he sustained the ethos of the Kadampas. He was a polymath who composed more than 300 works, and he was included amongst the Sakya school's Six Jewels of Tibet. His skill in dialectics was peerless, and his irrefutable works of criticism of Tsongkapa's treatises were proscribed by the Gelukpas. Before his death at the age of eighty-four it was said that he could fly like a bird and resurrect the dead. He founded Nalendra in 1435 and his principal disciple was Tashi Namgyel, the founder of Dakpo Dratsang (p.153).

As in many Kadampa gompas, after the death of the founder the number of monks at Nalendra diminished rapidly. By the end of the 15th century Nalendra had formally become a Sakya establishment, Rongtonpa claimed as an initiate of that school, and the noble Che family had gained control of the appointment of abbots. Nevertheless, until 1959 Nalendra was considered one of the principle seats of learning in Tibet.

Shara Bumpa (Sha ra 'bum pa): Sharapa's Chortens

Shara Bumpa is located on the mountainside to the north of the Pempo Chu and to the west of the Lhundrub Valley. It is accessible from the south by way of a track turning off the jeep-road serving the upper part of the Pempo Chu valley, or from the east by way of a turning off the jeep-road ascending the Lhundrub Valley from Pempo Qu.

As its name implies it is the site of an important chorten, and circumambulation of it is reputed to cure blindness. Many lesser chortens, all built in the ancient style typical of these Kadampa sites, surround it. An Ani Gompa, now in ruins, is located nearby, and a small rebuilt lhakang containing only a few modern icons serves the two or three devoted *anis* who stay at Shara Bumpa. Restoration, which began in 1985, found the chortens dilapidated and the relics that had been enshrined at their centres rifled, but with the structures still standing. Several have now been restored and production of the clay *tsatsa* images that fill the chortens is in process.

History

The founder of this Bumpa, Sharapa Yonten Drak (1070-1141), was another of the 11th-century Kadampa masters, a pupil of Potowa for eighteen years. He was considered an incarnation of Jamyang (Manjughosa), possessing the Bodhisattva's skill in memorization of the entire Kanjur – the *sutras* and *tantras*.

[5.] [below right] SHARA BUMPA: the 12th century Kadampa chorten with gallery, built by Geshe Sharapa (photograph by K. Dowman) [below left] DRIGUNG: the Namgyel Chorten east of Katse (photograph by K. Dowman) [above] SILI GOTSANG: the chorten below the 13th century hermitage of Sangye Yarjon (photograph by K. Dowman)

Jang

Jang means "The North", and refers to the upper part of the Kyichu river system, which includes the Pak Chu valley of Taklung and the *Rong Chu valley of Reteng. From Pembo Qu a jeep-road ascends the Lhundrub Valley to Lhundrub[4] Qu, previously Lhundrub Dzong, and then climbs over the Chak La and down to the Pak Chu.

Pel Taklung Tang (dPal sTag lung thang): Seat of the Taklung Kagyu

The monastery that gave its name to one of the four chief Kagyu schools, the Taklung Kagyu, is located in the western part of Jang. The new jeep-road descends from the Chak La to the Pak Chu, turns west for 2 km, and Taklung[5] is discovered in a small side-valley to the south.

The site of Taklung gompa is still dominated by the Lhakang Chempo, although this immense assembly hall, called the Taklung Tsuklakang, and also the Markang, the Red Temple, now lies in ruins. This 13th-century building was one of the architectural wonders of Tibet. In the three-storey building, twenty-four of its eighty pillars supported the first storey, and thirty-two pillars supported the second storey. Its enormous walls still stand, but the wooden pillars have vanished. It is intended to rebuild this Tsokchen. The ruins of Taklung's two *dratsangs* are located one above and the other below the Lhakang Chempo.

In 1986 the site was alive with workers clearing rubble and putting the finishing touches to a lhakang rebuilt against the cliff on the western side of the complex. Beside it were small buildings, one containing an altar on which are found the relics of Taklung, a statue of the founder, Taklung Tangpa, taking pride of place. The Drolma Sungjonma that was kept previously in the founder's cell is one of the chief relics of Taklung. Next to the altar room is the residence of a most venerable, aging abbot trained in the gompa before 1959 and now presiding over the instruction of a number of young neophytes. Below the Lhakang Chempo, closer to the river, is the farming commune that utilizes the monks' old quarters as dwellings. A *labrang* is situated on the west side of the village. The Protector of Taklung is Taklung Genyen, a form of Chingkarwa (p.94).

History

The existence of a chamber that Jowo Atisha's chief disciple Dromton occupied, plus references to the hermitage-residence of Dromton's disciple Potowa at Taklung, attest to the existence of a gompa on the site in the mid-11th century. Kyentse mentions the hair of Dromton, which continued to grow, kept in the Lhakang Chempo, and it is said that the actual reliquary of Dromton (1005-64) was located here. However, the Kagyu gompa was founded in 1180 by Taklung Tangpa Tashi Pel (1142-1210). He was born in Kham, and against the wishes of his family he became a monk and then spent many years wandering from place to place in Central Tibet and Tsang engrossed in meditation. Particularly, he spent six years with Pakmodrupa Dorje Gyelpo in Densatil, although the Drigung Kagyupas were to have the strongest influence on his school. He received Kadampa precepts from Medro Chekawa and Potowa before settling at Taklung and founding his own monastery at the age of thirty-eight. He stayed there for the next thirty years. As a fully ordained *gelong* he gave special attention to the vows concerning meat, alcohol, women and laymen, and Taklung became renowned for the exceptional purity of its monks' discipline. In the year of his death, 1210, Taklung Tangpa had 3,000 disciples.

The lineage of the Taklung Rimpoches descended through suitable candidates born into Taklung Tangpa's Ragasha family. The founder's nephew was the most active builder of Taklung. Particularly, he was responsible for the Taklung Tsuklakang, finished in 1228, and also a *kumbum* and various statues and reliquaries. The continuing wealth and power of the gompa is demonstrated by continued building and embellishment through the 15th century. The first 300 years of Taklung were its glorious age: discipline was good; it was spared the Mongols' depredations; disputes with the rival Drigungpas were won; and an apolitical stance held the gompa in good stead. In the 16th century, when the Red Hats were in conflict with the rising Geluk power, Taklung gave refuge to retreating monks from Sera and Drepung. In the 17th century there were several disputes over the abbots' succession and Taklung's estates were confiscated by the Yellow Hats, who gained control of the appointment of Taklung's abbots. An incarnate line of *tulkus* was initiated. With the Ragasha family ensconced in Lhasa, and the gompa having little independence, the recent history of Taklung has been anti-climactic. The real centres of Taklung Kagyu teaching and practice became Riwoche in Amdo, a gompa established by the fourth abbot of Taklung in the 13th century, and also Lho Taklung, near the Yamdrok Tso. The throne-holder at Taklung was the senior of the three incarnate lamas – Shabdrung, Matrul, and Tsetrul.

Sili Gotsang (Si li rgod tshang): Sangye Yarjon's Cave

A large rebuilt chorten is located on the jeep-road 5 km east of Taklung and on the north side of the Pak Chu. As much as 300 m above the chorten, in the crags of the precipitous mountainside, is the Sili Eagle's Nest.[6] Despite the vision of towering walls visible from the road the lhakang was destroyed during the Cultural Revolution. However, the meditation cave (*drupuk*), which is the principal place of power on the mountain, has been maintained and a small new lhakang constructed adjacent to it. The chief object of worship on the cave's altar is an image of Taklung Tangpa. Several other images from the past are preserved here.

History
Sili Gotsang was the hermitage of Sangye Yarjon Sherab Lama (1203-72), the third of the abbots of Taklung, and a scion of Taklung Tangpa's clan. Sangye Yarjon continued the strict tradition of solitary meditation for which the Taklung Kagyupas were noted. Sili Gotsang is also reputed to have been the seat of Gotsangpa Gompo Dorje (1189-1258), the Drukpa Kagyu disciple of Tsangpa Gyare.

Chom Lhakang Dong (bCom lha khang gdong)

Chom Lhakang[7] is located in the old section of Pongdo Xian, previously Pongdo[8] Dzong, 8 km south-west of Reteng. This temple was built at the geomantically significant position of a crossroads, where the path from Dam in the north to Drigung Dzong in the south-east crosses the road from Taklung to Reteng. It is now in the process of restoration. It was built by the highly astute 18th-century nobleman and political intriguer Polhane, who served the Chinese cause in Lhasa and ruled Tibet from 1728-47.

Reteng Gompa (Rwa sgreng): The First Kadampa Gompa

The famous name of Reteng[9] belongs to the gompa founded in the 11th century by Jowo Atisha's chief disciple, Dromton, in fulfilment of an ancient vow. To Reteng Dromton brought the relics of Atisha after his death at Netang. Thus it became the first of the Kadampa gompas.

Reteng Gompa is in the far north of Central Tibet, located in the *Rong Chu valley in the old district of Jang. The forest of juniper trees, some of which are 20 m high, and which are said to have grown from the hairs of Dromton, planted by himself, form the backdrop to the extensive ruins of Reteng. Thus despite the gompa's complete destruction, Reteng still resembles "a heavenly garden with its great divine trees", as Kyentse Rimpoche described it. The principal buildings were built half way up the valley side, and behind these extended the secondary monastic construction.

Never again will Reteng Gompa spread across the hillside like a small city, yet restoration has been more extensive here than at many other major sites. The enormous Tsokang has been reconstructed to the extent of half its previous size and the important lhakang within it contains the remaining relics of the dozen lhakangs that have been destroyed. Perhaps its most revered object of worship is the statue of Jowo Jampai Dorje

(Manjuvajra), a 45 cm image said to be made of solid gold and brought from India. It was "generated from the seed of pure awareness of Dorjechang Yabyum" where Dorjechang is the Kadampa *adibuddha*, and his consort is Yumchenmo (Prajnaparamitama). It is a relic that grants the prayers of its devotees (*yishinorbu*). Another sacred relic on the altar of the inner lhakang is the Drolma Sungjonma, the Talking Drolma. Besides new statues of Lamas of the lineage there are also small images of Jigche and Sangdu. Several old and important *tankas* have been preserved for Reteng and now hang in the lhakang and the dukang; but the unique collection of books written by Atisha and Sharapa, together with Indian palm-leaf manuscripts, are amongst the treasured relics of Reteng that have disappeared. Close to the Tsokang are the decayed reliquary chortens of Jowo Atisha, Dromton and Geshe Serlingpa. Beyond the restored buildings containing Dromton's meditation chamber is the tree which is identified with his life-spirit (*lashing*) and the spring which he conjured called the Dutsi Chumik Ringmo, the Everlasting Spring of Ambrosia.

History

This first Kadampa gompa in Central Tibet was founded in 1056 by Dromton Gyelwai Jungne (1005-64). This master was born in upper Tolung at the beginning of the period of the second propagation of Buddhism in Tibet. When Jowo Atisha was about to leave Western Tibet to return to Vikramasila in Bengal, Dromton approached him and invited him to visit Central Tibet. Atisha toured the sanctuaries of the region before settling at Netang, where he died in 1054 after charging Dromton with the task of sustaining his *dharma*. Dromton brought part of Atisha's relics to Reteng where he remained to teach for the remaining nine years of his life. His enduring fame is largely due to his achievement in retaining unity amongst the disciples of Atisha and establishing a school and a method of analysis that has affected the spiritual life of Tibet through all its Buddhist

[6] {above} RETENG: the juniper forest with gompa ruins (centre) (photograph by K. Dowman) [below] PABONG TANG: the Dakini's Residence in a circle of boulders (photograph by K. Dowman)

schools. Dromton is considered an incarnation of Chenresik, and as such a forerunner of the Dalai Lamas. Amongst his disciples were Potowa, Puchungwa and Chenga, who became known as The Three Brothers.

Reteng was expanded by Dromton's disciple and successor as abbot, Neljorpa Chempo, but in 1240 this work on the plane of material illusion was undone by the Mongol Genghis Khan's general Dorta, who invaded Tibet and marched as far as Reteng, where the gompa was ravaged and 500 Tibetans killed.

Serlingpa Tashipel (1292-1365) lived and died at Reteng, and his remains were entombed there in a reliquary chorten. He was an initiate of the Tsepa Kagyu lineage. The relics of Nyenton, a master of the same school, were also kept here.

When Tsongkapa reformed the Kadampa school, which then became known as the New Kadampa, or the Geluk sect of the Dalai Lamas, Reteng became a major Geluk establishment. The Reteng Rimpoches became one of the candidates for Regent during a Dalai Lama's minority. Thus the Reteng Lama was Regent from 1845 to 1855, and again in the crucial period from 1933 to 1947. The political confusion resulting from this Reteng Regent's abdication may be considered one of the chief causes of the collapse of Tibet in the face of Chinese aggression.

Yangon (Yang dgon): Je Tsongkapa's Hermitage

The hermitage of Yangon is located behind Reteng Gompa. It was built amidst juniper trees at the base of rising crags that give the impression of a lion's head and are therefore named Senge Drak, Lion Rock. Further to the north is the red-painted rock that is the residence of the Protectors of Reteng. The principal Protector of Reteng, Chingkarwa, called the Reteng Jowo, is said to have been brought to Tibet by Jowo Atisha from Nalanda. The hermitage is now in picturesque ruin, but the spot on which Tsongkapa composed his *magnum opus*, the *Lamrim Chenmo*, in the 15th century, can still be seen. In the 11th century Dromton preferred to live here, and after Taklung Tangpa was attracted to it in the 13th century it belonged to the Taklung Kagyupas for a

hundred years. It became the principal site of retreat for the
Reteng monks.

Tsongkapa Lobsang Drakpa (1357-1419), born in Tsongka in
Amdo, was the brilliant scholar and organizer who reformed the
Kadampa school founded by Dromton 350 years before. He is
better known simply as Je Rimpoche. Amongst his voluminous
writing the *Lamrim Chenmo* has had most impact and is most
widely known. It provides instruction in detail on the stages of
the path to enlightenment, but the purpose of the work was also
to synthesize various *mahayana* doctrines within the framework
established by Atisha. The *Guyhasamaja*, *Hevajra* and *Kalacakra-*
tantras were the subject of Je Rimpoche's tantric practice and
commentary.

Pabong Tang (Pha bong thang): The Dakini's Residence

To the south-west of Reteng, between road and river, is Pabong
Tang, Boulder Field. The single large boulder on these flat
meadows is the Palace of the Kandro Sangwai Yeshe, the
Protectress and female principle of gnostic awareness. She belongs
to the mandala of the *Samvara-tantra*. A circle of smaller boulders
surrounds her residence, and walking anti-clockwise around it
while reciting the Samvara mantra leads to certain rebirth in the
Orgyen Kandroma Paradise. Circumambulation to the left is the
rite of the *yogini-tantra*.

To the North of Jang

To the North of Jang is the vast mountainous plateau of the
Drokpas. These nomadic yak-herders are called Horpas, Norther-
ners, but although they probably migrated from the far north-
east of Tibet many centuries ago they are now assuredly Tibetans.
Their four communities are called Naktsang, Namru, Nakchu
and Yangpachen. (See also p.131.)

4

TO GANDEN AND BEYOND

The highway from Lhasa to Eastern Tibet follows the left bank of the Kyichu to Medro Kongkar,[1] and then turns south-east towards the Gya La. The principal place of pilgrimage along this stretch of the Kyichu, one that every pilgrim to Lhasa must make, is the great monastery of Ganden Namgyeling. Founded by Je Tsongkapa in the 14th century, Ganden became the most renowned repository of Yellow Hat learning and integrity, and today its ruins remain a potent symbol of traditional Tibetan aspirations. It occupies a magnificent position across an amphitheatre on the south side of a ridge that dominates the Kyichu Valley.

Other gompas along this route have played important roles in the past, although they have had little influence in recent centuries. Tse Gungtang was the seat of Lama Shang of the Tsepa Kagyu school, and the Tsepa clan played a dominant role in Tibetan affairs during the period of priest/patron relationship with the Mongols. The gompas of the Gyama Valley were important Kadampa establishments from the 12th to 14th centuries.

Tse Gungtang (Tshal Gung thang): Seat of the Tsepa Kagyupas

Less than 10 km from Lhasa, south of the highway, stood the once important monastery of Tse Gungtang. The complex had

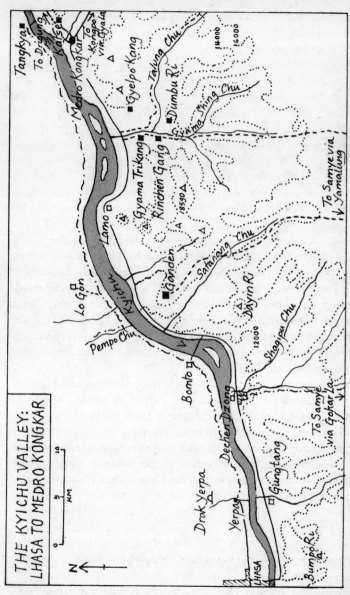

Map 6 The Kyichu Valley: Lhasa to Medro Kongkar

three parts: Tse Gungtang, the oldest, consisting of three buildings (*lhakang, simkang* and *chokang*); Gungtang, a later addition of a single large *tsuklakang*; and the chortens, of which the Kumbum founded by Shang Rimpoche has always remained an important object of worship and pilgrimage. The Kumbum was the most important place of pilgrimage at Tse. The entire complex has been destroyed and no restoration has begun.

History

Originally Tse Gungtang[3] was the seat of the Tsepa Kagyupas, founded in 1175 by Lama Shang[4] (1123-93) of the Tsepa clan. Lama Shang, known as one of the Three Jewels of Tibet (with Pakmodrupa and Tsongkapa) was taught by many Lamas, but his principal teacher was Gompa, a successor of Je Gampopa. Tse Gungtang's power grew with the protection extended by Kublai Khan and his bequest of the lordship of Central Tibet and Tsang to the Abbot Ponchen Ringyel. For 200 years thereafter the Gungtang abbots possessed a strong voice in Tibetan affairs. By the 16th century Tse had changed its allegiance to the Yellow Hats, for in 1546 it was burnt down by the Gelukpas' Kagyu adversaries. Although rebuilt it had lost its importance and its days of influence were over. In the 17th century it became a temporary residence of the Protector Pehar, who was moved there from Samye.

Dechen Dzong (bDe chen rdzong)

On the left bank of the Kyichu, 21 km from Lhasa, is an isolated hill guarding the entrance to the rich valleys to the south. On the hill are the old ruins of the large Dechen Dzong that was once the seat of the Kyisho Depa, the name of the ancient ruler of the Lhasa district. There was a Yellow Hat college within the confines of the fortifications called Sangnak Kar, where Tsongkapa and his disciple Kedrub Je stayed for some time. A lhakang has been restored and a few monks are in residence on the hill.

The Taktse[5] Xian, the modern centre of the district, is situated below the *dzong*. A jeep-road proceeds south from here towards the Gokar La (p.234).

Ganden Namgyeling (dGa' Idan rNam rgyal gling): Je Tsongkapa's Gompa

Founded by Je Tsongkapa himself, Ganden[6] was the first of the three great Geluk monasteries (Ganden, Drepung and Sera) to be established. 40 km along the highway to the north-east of Lhasa, a jeep-road turns south and climbs a switch-back track up the south-facing slope of the ridge called Drok Ri, or Wangkur Ri, where the gompa is situated at an altitude of some 4,750 m. Crowning the ridge with a spectacular view of the Kyichu Valley, most of Ganden's structures were built in an impressive south-facing, natural amphitheatre. The gompa was severely shelled by Red Guard artillery in 1966 and then dismantled by monks. It came to represent the success of Mao's Cultural Revolution in destroying the material fabric of Tibet's nationalism, religion and history. At the beginning of this decade Tibetans began to spend holidays granted from communal labor restoring the Ganden complex, working with laymen's donations of grain and food. The Chinese were to prohibit these spontaneous efforts at restoration which lacked official support or sanction, but shortly thereafter the Chinese themselves began to fund restoration and to hire selected craftsmen. Thus by 1986 sixteen of the apocryphal 108 temples of Ganden had been rebuilt, still mostly by volunteer labour; 200 monks had returned to the gompa; and Ganden had become the mecca of Yellow Hat devotees who had maintained faith with the founder's original principles.

Tsongkapa established Ganden as the centre of the learning and monastic discipline that he found lacking in the Red Hats' tantricism, and although Ganden's abbots were occasionally involved in the political intrigues of the Gelukpas, in general the monastery remained aloof from politics. Its abbots, the Ganden Tripa Rimpoches, were elected from the colleges' most eminent scholars, and after the 16th century they held office for only seven years. The prestige of the position had attached to it the potential Regency of Tibet during a Dalai Lama's absence or minority, and thus the tutorship of the young Dalai Lamas. There were some 2,000 monks in residence in 1959.

Rebuilding at Ganden is proceeding apace. A lhakang containing the Dalai Lama's throne has been constructed to the west of the dormitory houses at the bottom of the site. A red-painted lhakang in the centre is the reconstruction of Ganden's *sanctum sanctorum* containing Tsongkapa's reliquary chorten called the Tongwa Donden, Meaningful to Behold. The master Tsongkapa died in Ganden in 1419. His successor plated the chorten with silver; the Mongol General Gusri Khan's grandson gilded it; the Dzungar general leading the 1717 invasion had a Mongol tent of sandalwood constructed to canopy it. To the right and left of the Tongwa Donden were the reliquary chortens of Kedrub Je and Gyeltseb Je. All this has been destroyed and the present chorten is a copy. The images in front of the chorten are of the *yabsesum*, the Father – Je Tsongkapa – and his two spiritual sons – Kedrub Je and Gyeltseb Je. To the east of this, the lhakang containing the Ganden Sertri, the Golden Throne of Ganden's abbots, is undoubtedly one of Ganden's most vital power-places. Amidst the ruins of the original palace a small, tall building has been constructed for the throne of the Ganden Tripas. The present throne is a copy of the original, a 15th-century product of Nepali workmanship.

Ganden Lingkor

In 1986 the reconstructed buildings at Ganden had not yet gained the sanctity with which use would endow them. However, today as always the Ganden Lingkor amply rewards the pilgrim's energy. This hour-long circumambulatory route around the entire complex is replete with the mystical side-shows in rock that engage and support the pilgrim's faith. Apart from the spiritual therapy inherent in pilgrims' devotions, the devotee is edified by the legends of Tsongkapa related by his guide that are associated with many spots on the *korra*.

The Lingkor begins by climbing to the saddle at the south of the amphitheatre and the following power-spots are located in succession along the route: a self-manifest image of Padampa Sangye; the imprint of Tsongkapa's rosary; images of Tamche

[7] [above] GANDEN: ruins of the monastic town from the south-west (photograph by *Stone Routes*) [below left] GANDEN: giant *tanka* of Sakyamuni Buddha hung during the Monlam festival (photograph by *Stone Routes*) [below right] GANDEN: lama-dance (*cham*) during rite of consecration (photograph by *Stone Routes*)

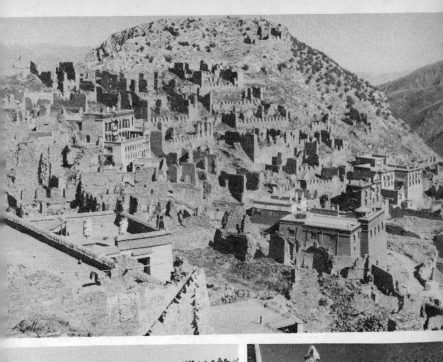

Chogyel, Tsongkapa's Protector, and the Sixteen Arhats; rock paintings of the Protectors of the two colleges, Shartse and Jangtse; the Indian Dundro; the rock where Tsarima Kandroma danced (to be circumambulated thrice on one foot); Tsongkapa's self-manifest hat in rock; the "Dundro of the Indian Wolves"; the *yabsesum* inscribed by Tsongkapa's fingernail, and here pilgrims sidle through a fissured rock to quantify their merit; Tsongkapa's hand-writing in rock and then his "sky-boat"; and finally at the summit, the site of Tsongkapa's prostrations.

On the remainder of the *korra* the following can be seen: the place where Tsongkapa's mother died after the master had shown her the rotten nature of material illusion; a self-manifest Mani-stone; the "Dundro of the Three Bodhisattva Protectors"; the self-manifest Tibetan letter "A" where children repay their parents' kindness with devotion; the calciferous rock through which permeating "milk" gives blessings to the faithful who collect and consume the lime from the rock's underside; the self-manifest depiction of the Rabbit in the Moon; the emission of magical medicinal *chang* from calciferous rock; an image of Senge Dongma, the Lion-headed Dakini; the tongue of Tsongkapa's Protector that assists in recitation of mantra; Chagna Dorje; the chorten Jarungkasor endowed with the same power and name as the Nepali Boudhanath Stupa; and near his hermitage Tsongkapa's handholds in rock.

The climax of the Lingkor is Tsongkapa's hermitage, his *drupuk*, called Woser Puk, Cave of Light, which was the first residence and lhakang on the site. The present hermitage is said to be the original building. The chief images within are five self-manifest images all of which are Talking Buddhas: Gyelwa Dumtompa, Pelden Lhamo, Jowo Atisha, Sakyamuni and Tsepame. There are also several natural prints in the rock.

Only part of the Lingkor sights and legends have been mentioned here. Also of note is the spot where Tsongkapa revealed a conch treasure, the foot-prints of Sakyamuni's disciple Maudgalyayana and the *siddha* Drukpa Kunlek, and the residence of the monkey treasure-protector.

History

Ganden was founded by Je Tsongkapa in 1409, after the Monlam festival of prayer had been celebrated for the first time on the Drok Ri ridge. In 1415 Tsongkapa built the Chicho Kang temple. Jangtse, North Point, and Shartse, East Point, were the two principal original colleges. Jangtse was founded by the first Lama of Ganden, Horton Namka Pelsangpo, and restored by the thirtieth Tripa Rimpoche who renamed it Tosamling. Shartse was founded by another disciple of Tsongkapa Sharpa Rinchen Gyeltsen. Ganden maintained a reputation for intense religious practice and discipline for centuries, but during the 19th and 20th centuries the monks of Ganden joined with Drepung and Sera to form a reactionary political force that hindered attempts at reform, particularly under the thirteenth Dalai Lama.

Lamo Gompa (La mo dgon pa)

The site of Lamo Gompa is to be found south of the highway near the village of Lamo, 49 km north-east of Lhasa. No building remains on the site.

Lamo is renowned as the residence of one of Tibet's principal Dharma-protectors, Tsangpa Karpo, White Brahma, and his Oracle. The wrathful form of Tsangpa Karpo is Setrabchen. Yarlung Trandruk is another of his seats.

History

Lamo is of historical importance because it was here in 1009 that Lume (p.295) built his first monastery after returning from his ordination in Kham. Thus together with Yerpa Neten Lhakang, Sonak Tang, Tsongdu Tsokpa and Dranang, Lamo represents the first product of the second period of propagation of the *dharma* in Central Tibet. The gompa on the site in 1959 seems to have been an 18th-century establishment.

Gyama Trikang (rGya ma khri khang)

The jeep-road that ascends the Gyama[7] Valley on the left bank of the Gyamashing Chu turns south from the highway (at km 1510) some 58 km from Lhasa and 10 km before reaching Medro Kongkar. This valley was an important adjunct to Penyul during the Kadampa period. Three Kadampa monasteries were located here: Gyama Trikang, Gyama Rinchen Gang and Dumbu Ri. We were unable to visit this valley and lack any contemporary information.

Close to the highway is the large walled enclosure that belonged to the noble and highly influential Horkang family in which Gyama Trikang is situated. In 1959 the complex consisted of a *dzong*, some cottages and two lhakangs. In one of the lhakangs was the reliquary chorten of Sangye Wonton, the founder of Trikang and second abbot of Rinchen Gang.

Gyelpo Kang (rGyal po khang): Emperor Songtsen Gampo's Birthplace

On the hillside to the east of Trikang is a small, rebuilt lhakang containing an image of the Emperor Songtsen Gampo who was born in a small house nearby.

Gyama Rinchen Gang (rGya ma Rin chen sgang)

A short distance up the Gyamashing valley from Trikang, also on the left bank of the Gyamashing Chu, is the site of the monastery of Rinchen Gang.[8]

History

Rinchen Gang was built by a disciple of Neuzurpa, the Geshe Gyar[9] Gomchempo Shonnu Drakpa (1090-1171), and some 300 monks gathered here. It was rebuilt in 1181 by the founder's nephew Sangye Wonton (1138-1210), the second abbot, also known as Wonton Rimpoche, who also had a strong reputation as a scholar during his lifetime. Kache Panchen Sakya Sri twice visited Rinchen Gang at Wonton Rimpoche's request. Rinchen Gang was one of the Kadampa gompas that under Sakya control retained a strong tradition for centuries. Lama Dampa Sonam Gyeltsen (p. 136) belonged to the Rinchen Gang school.

Dumbu Ri (Dum bu ri)

At the foot of a spur on the right bank of the Gyamashing Chu, opposite Rinchen Gang, is the site of the Kadampa gompa Nongyi Gyama Dumburi.[10] It was founded by the Bodhisattva Dumburipa Dawa Gyeltsen (c. 12th century) who was a disciple of Jayulpa and also Neuzurpa.

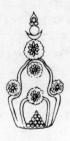

5

THE DRIGUNG MANDALA

The Drigung District still presents the geographical, cultural, political and religious unity that has characterized it for 800 years. The major religious institutions of the Drigung Valley and adjacent tributary valleys belong to the Drigung branch of the Kagyu school founded in the 12th century by Rinchen Pel, an extraordinary, charismatic disciple of Drogon Pakmodrupa, in the lineage of Milarepa. The Drigungpas form one of the four major Kagyu sub-schools with their principal gompa at Drigung Til. In the centuries after their founder's remarkable lifetime, the Drigung Kagyupas were a powerful force in Tibet's religious life. Even in the 1980s the emphasis that this school places on solitary retreat and yoga derived from the original ethos of Milarepa's practice is evident at Drigung Til and Terdrom, where hermitages have blossomed over the hillsides at the expense of monastic reconstruction.

However, in their founder's lifetime the Drigungpas also enjoyed a period of secular ascendancy when they formed a bulwark of Kagyu power against the Sakya hegemony. In this period the school became entrenched in the Kailash and Labchi areas in western Tibet, at Tsari, and also in Eastern Tibet. Then and later other gompas were built in the Drigung area – at Tsel up the Lungsho Valley, at *Yude in a valley running east of Drigung Dzong, and at Drigung Dzong itself. This period generated the wealth for which Drigung Til became famous. It was said that the pilgrim should visit Drigung Til at the end of his pilgrimage through Central Tibet, otherwise the splendours of that gompa would blind him to the inferior glories of less well-endowed monasteries.

The Drigungpas's kinship with the older Nyingma school is demonstrated at several sites in the district, particularly at Terdrom with its caves associated with Guru Rimpoche, Yeshe Tsogyel and the treasure-finders of both schools who have meditated there down the centuries. That the most auspicious and efficacious pilgrimage in the Drigung area circumambulates these caves attests to their power. Further evidence of the importance of the district during the period of empire may be gathered at Shai Lhakang where a pillar records the life of Nyang Tingedzin, the Emperor Trisong Detsen's minister and first Tibetan abbot of Samye, whose birthplace this was. Further, at what may be considered the entrance to the Drigungpa preserve, north-east of Medro Kongkar, are the remains of Katse Gompa, one of the Emperor Songtsen Gampo's four original temples erected to bring the power of Buddhism to Bonpo Central Tibet in the 7th century (p.287).

Access
Three hours by bus, 68 km north-east of Lhasa in the Kyichu Valley lies Medro Kongkar,[1] the centre of the new district in which the Drigung valley system is located. The main highway from Lhasa to the East turns south-east up the Medro Kongkar valley, while the jeep-road to Drigung continues for 35 km to the north-east up the Kyichu Valley to Drigung Qu, the administrative sub-centre of Drigung. Here the Kyichu, running down the Lungsho Valley, makes a 100-degree turn to the south-west. The Drigung Chu, known also as Shorong Chu, is the Kyichu's principal tributary in the north-east, running for 60 km through the broad, fertile valley of Drigung. Before the Lhasa-Chamdo highway was built to the south of Drigung over the Gya La, the Drigung Valley provided an alternative route from the Kyichu Valley to Kongpo and the East. The journey from Medro Kongkar to Drigung Til Gompa takes three hours by jeep or two days by foot.

The Name "Drigung" ('Bri gung)
Three etymologies of the word Drigung[3] have been offered.

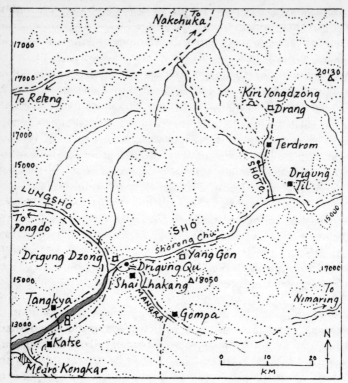

Map 7 The Drigung Area

Firstly, the Drigung district is said to have been the fiefdom of the Emperor Trisong Detsen's minister Dre, while the second syllable may have been derived from the archaic Tibetan *sgar* or *sgang* meaning "camp": thus Dre's Camp. Secondly, the first syllable, Dri, can mean "she-yak": thus Camp of the She-yak. Thirdly, a false etymology provided after the foundation of Til interprets the word as "the hump of the she-yak", indicating the shape of the ridge above Til, which does indeed have that shape.

Katse (sKa tshal): A Songtsen Gampo Temple

Although Katse is located at the bottom of the Kyichu Valley's eastern scarp, it is close to the confluence of the Kyichu and Medro Valleys and on the far side of the Medro River from Medro Kongkar. Thus it is sometimes referred to as Medro Katse.

The original lhakang of Katse was built by the Emperor Songtsen as the north-eastern temple of the inner mandala of four temples binding the Tibetan Demoness. Katse binds her right shoulder (p.287). Another lhakang was founded here after Guru Rimpoche subdued the *lu* serpent that had subjected Bonpo devotees. These two lhakangs formed the nucleus of the small Katse gompa until it was partially destroyed during the Cultural Revolution. Katse would have been a Nyingma foundation that was adopted by the Drigungpas in the 13th century, and acquired by the Gelukpas in the 17th. Today the Drigungpas are once again in possession. The old gompa still lies in ruins, the monks' original quarters inhabited by the Katse commune, but the lhakang built by the Emperor Songtsen Gampo, the Tukdam Tsuklakang, has been restored on the old pattern.

The original temple struck Hugh Richardson as the most ancient in Tibet, untouched by later restoration. The *konyer* assured us that the present small, country-built building is identical in design to that which Richardson would have visited. It has a small portico leading into the small pillared dukang with the inner lhakang surrounded by a *korsa* passage. Above the lhakang on the roof is another small shrine-room. Notable in the dukang are murals of the Drigung lineage, a new image of the Drigung Protectress Apchi in her form of Yudronma, and old *tankas* of Pelden Lhamo, Guru Rimpoche, Santaraksita and the Emperor Trisong Detsen. Images of the Buddhas of the Past, Present and Future are the principal objects of worship in the lhakang. At the back of the dukang is the *lukang*, the residence of the serpent that Guru Rimpoche subdued. Few relics of former times remain in Katse.

Tangkya Lhakang (Thang skya lha khang)

A few kilometres upstream from Katse is an old bridge that crosses the Kyichu to Tangkya Qu. In the middle of this modern administrative complex the Tangkya[4] Lhakang still stands in fair condition, but in 1986 it was locked and barred. It appears that this temple, like Dranang Gompa, is victim to the local Party, which prohibits restoration. The original lhakang built by the Emperor Songtsen Gampo, which stood on the mountainside to the north of the present lhakang, was destroyed long ago, but three of its ancient clay statues were preserved in the later temple. There seems never to have been any Drigung Kagyupa connection here.

History

The first Tangkya lhakang is believed, like Katse, to have been built by the Emperor Songtsen Gampo in the 7th century, perhaps as a temple to subdue the Tibetan Demoness. It was restored by the master Lume in the early 11th century after the period of suppression. In the 12th century a lhakang was built to enshrine the remains of Lama Shikpo Rimpoche (1149-99). Tangkya was the gompa in which Taklung Tangpa took refuge after running away from home in the 12th century, and this connection was sustained by some of his Taklungpa disciples. Later, Tangkya belonged to the Jonangpas until the Gelukpas appropriated all Jonang gompas in the 17th century. Thereafter it became attached to the Namgyel Dratsang in the Potala.

Drigung Dzongsar ('Bri gung rdzong gsar): The Drigung Fort

The original Drigung Dzong was located on the left bank of the Kyichu where the river cuts through a low ridge into the area of its confluence with the Mangra Chu and Shorong Chu. From its height above the rivers it commanded the entrances to both the Lungsho and Sho Valleys. The fortress destroyed during the Cultural Revolution probably dated from the 16th century. The large Drigungpa lhakang within its walls was an important place of pilgrimage. A small lhakang has recently been built on the site. On the opposite side of the Kyichu is the empty site of *Yuna gompa.

Shai Lhakang (Zhwa'i lha khang): Nyang Tingedzin's Residence

The Shai Lhakang[5] is located in the south-west corner of a village on the left bank of the Mangra Chu, 1.5 km to the east of Drigung Qu. The Nyang Clan of Tibetan antiquity gave its name to the valley that descends from the south-east by Shai Lhakang. The Nyang Clan's most famous son was Nyang Tingedzin Sangpo, who was a strong supporter of the Emperor Trisong Detsen in his efforts to promote Buddhism in Tibet, and who became the first Tibetan abbot of the Samye monastery. Nyang Tingedzin founded Shai Lhakang at the end of the 8th or the beginning of the 9th century.

During the Cultural Revolution the principal lhakang, together with the Guru Tsengye Lhakang and the Rignga Chorten, were totally destroyed. Only the ancient building used as monks' quarters that stands to the north of the site was preserved. Of the two *doring*s that stood one on each side of the lhakang's portico, the one on the left side of the door still stands on its base carved with a swastika in the empire style, while only remnants remain of the pillar that stood on the right side. Recent and continuing rebuilding has only restored a single small lhakang to the right of the portico. This lhakang contains images of the three Dzokchen Protectors – Ekajati, Rahula and Dorje Lekpa – and of the omniscient Longchempa.

History

Shai Lhakang's great importance to historians lies in the two inscribed *doring* pillars that stood one each side of the Lhakang's portico. Both *doring*s record exceptional grants of land and privilege to Nyang Tingedzin and his heirs by the Emperor Senalek in the early 9th century. It appears that having made himself indispensable to Trisong Detsen and having become Senalek's guardian, when in the year 800 a dispute arose over the Emperor Murub's successor, Nyang Tingedzin assisted Senalek who eventually gained the throne in 804. The ample rewards that this monk obtained for his service to his royal Buddhist masters are attested to by the inscription on the pillar.

Shai Lhakang's early and abiding religious importance was derived from its founder's status as the principal recipient of the essential Dzokchen Precept Class (*man ngag sde*) instruction of the Indian master and *pandita* Vimalamitra. As the Emperor's preceptor Nyang Tingedzin induced Trisong Detsen to invite Vimalamitra to Tibet. After Tingedzin had founded the Shai Lhakang in the early part of the 9th century, under the protection of the Guardian Deity Dorje Lekpa, it was here that he hid the Vimala Nyingtik texts as treasures for discovery in a later period. These texts were recovered from Shai Lhakang by Dangma Lhungyel, who was born in nearby Sho in the 11th century. In the 14th century the Shai Lhakang was restored by Longchempa, the synthesizer of the various Dzokchen lineages. Later the Lhakang came under the authority of the Gelukpas, and in the 18th century it was restored by the seventh Dalai Lama.

A fold high on the side of the mountain to the south of Shai Lhakang hides the site of a hermitage of Nyang Tingedzin.

Yangri Gon (Yang ri dgon)

The site of Yangri Gon[6] is located 10 km up the Sho Valley at the base of the scarp on the left bank of the river. The Shorong Chu runs in a gorge up to 75 m below the valley floor for this part of its course. The entire gompa was razed to form the site of a military base in the 1960s. It is revealing, however, that although the military would have liked to destroy every last trace of Yangri Gon, until 1985 a single stretch of wall remained standing within the military compound. This wall was a special residence of the Guardian Goddess Apchi. Apchi is said to have been a Kandroma who during the empire period married an ancestor of the Drigung Kyapgon, an exorcist. Apchi, or Drigung Apchi, became the Protectress of the Drigungpas and most of the many *sungkangs* found throughout Drigung belong to her. As the Protector of Yangri Gon, legend had it that anyone tampering with the goddess' residence would die soon thereafter. A series of deaths amongst those engaged in the destruction left the wall standing for twenty years. Tibetans finally demolished it in 1985. This story may indicate that the destruction of the gompas during the Cultural Revolution was done by the Red Guards out of fear of the power within them, rather than with the clean conscience of scientific rationalists. The Red Guards were undoubtedly burning with a fanaticism that can only be derived from zeal of a religious nature, but millennia of obeisance to the gods was not eradicated by a change of political leadership.

To the east of Yangri Gon, on the northern slope of a side-valley, is a pleasant grove hiding the site of an old hermitage that was attached to the gompa. A new lhakang has been built here and several monks maintain the tradition of Yangri Gon.

History

A large appendage of the Drigung Til gompa, Yangri Gon was founded by Trinle Sangpo, the eighth incarnation of the Drigung Kyapgon. As many as 500 monks were in residence before 1959. Its enormous wealth, particularly demonstrated by the gilt chortens enshrining Drigung Lamas, attested to the continuity of Drigung prosperity.

Drigung Til ('Bri gung mthil): Seat of the Drigung Kagyupas

Drigung Til,[7] or simply Til, the greatest of the Drigungpas' gompas, is located some 40 km from Drigung Dzong up the Sho Valley. On the right bank of the fast flowing river, 300 m above the broad valley, the monastery is built on the brow of a long ridge. The slope under the ridge was so steep that ladders were used to connect the lhakangs and residences that had been built after excavation of the mountainside. To the east and north-east passes give access to the valleys of Kongpo and the plains of Nakchuka.

The Drigungpas are one of the three surviving Kagyu schools derived from Drogon Pakmodrupa's disciples, and Drigung Til is the Drigungpa seat. Their tradition is rooted in the ascetic practices of Milarepa, but they have absorbed many Nyingma characteristics, so that some would say that there is little distinction between the Drigungpas and Nyingmapas.

The rebuilding of this important institution in Tibet's spiritual and political history began in 1983. The greatest achievement is the reconstructed assembly hall and chief lhakang built upon a

high platform with foundations 30 m below. On the same lowest level of construction to the east, close to the site of Drigung Kyapgon Rinchen Pel's original place of retreat, where the hermitage of the present meditation master Pachung Rimpoche is situated, is the gomkang, which is the Guardian Goddess Apchi's principal residence. To the west of the assembly hall is a ruined building enshrining Drigung Kyapgon's broken reliquary chorten. Further to the west the large impressive ruins are of a *labrang* residence, and then higher up the remains of the Yangri Gon Dratsang and Dukang. On this level is the new residence of the present Drigung Rimpoches. Spread over the ridge are innumerable rustic hermitages belonging to the ninety monks, nuns, yogins and laymen now committed to three years of retreat.

The principal relics enshrined in the Assembly Hall include Drigung Kyapgon's footprint, and his personal conch and trumpet (*gyaling*). The founder's image takes pride of place on the altar, and on the right side are images of Apchi as Pelden Lhamo and as Dorje Chodron, her wrathful form. Signs of Drigung's original wealth of sculpture can be seen in the many large and small bronzes that have been unearthed during the reconstruction.

History

The history of Til began in the year 1167, when a yogin disciple of Drogon Pakmodrupa called Minyak Gomring founded a small hermitage on the ridge. Twelve years later, in 1179, another disciple of Pakmodrupa fulfilled a prophecy by accepting the land that Minyakpa offered him and by establishing a major Kagyu lineage. This Lama's name was Rinchen Pel (1143-1217), a Khampa of the Drukgyel Kyura clan, with a background in the Nyingma school, who had left his homeland a decade before to sit at the feet of Drogon Pakmodrupa at Densatil. He was to become known as Drigung Kyapgon, Saviour of the Drigungpas, and Drigung Choje, Master of the Drigung Dharma, and Jigten Sumgon, Lord of the Three Realms, and Kyupa Lama.

The 13th century was Drigung's period of greatest vitality and expansion. Aligned with the Kagyu opposition to the Mongol-

[8.] [above] TERDROM: the Ani Gompa, hermitages and hot-springs (photograph by K. Dowman) [below] DRIGUNG: the Kagyu gompa of Drigung Til, founded 1147 (photograph by *Stone Routes*)

supported Sakya power, Drigung Til became a target for the invading Mongol general Dorta in 1240, when its abbot's power saved it from destruction. Legend has it that the Guardian Goddess Apchi was responsible for the Mongols' defeat by imprisoning many of them in her lhakang in the valley below the gompa and incinerating them. However, in 1290 Drigung was destroyed by another Mongol army, this time commanded by a Sakya general. But the Drigungpas were already established in gompas and hermitages throughout Tibet and their future was assured.

Drigung Dundro ('Bri gung dur khrod): Til's Sky-burial Site
The Drigung *dundro* to which bodies were, and still are, brought from as far away as Kongpo and Nakchuka, is as it ever was. This power-place for disposal of the dead is famous throughout Tibet. It is considered identical to the most famous of the Eight Indian Charnel Grounds, Siwaitsel (Sitavana) near Bodh Gaya. Legend has it that a rainbow connects Sitavana with this place and that the Guardian Deity *Yibkyi Chang presides over both. A vulture's footprint in stone still to be seen here is said to belong to Siwaitsel's Protector. The site is located at the western extremity of the ridge on which Til is built, and the path of circumambulation that passes outside the entire Til complex encompasses it.

Within a perimeter of chortens, lhakangs and prayer flags, a circle of boulders 12 m in diameter represents the mandala of Demchok (Cakrasamvara). A larger standing stone at the top and a flat stone near the centre are those employed by the *rogyapa* butchers. Another standing stone painted red is a self-manifest mani-stone. Behind the stone circle is a shrine-room with new paintings of the Wrathful and Peaceful Deities on its walls. To the right of it is a small room filled with hair shaven from the dead, and further to the right is a chorten that marks the place of Drigung Kyapgon's throne, also marked by his footprint in rock.

Shoto Terdrom (gZho stod gter sgrom): "Box of Treasures"

Terdrom[8] is undoubtedly the pearl in the Drigung oyster. Its spectacular mountain ranges of limestone and schist, its medicinal hot springs, its meditation caves, its historical associations, and the sense of power emanating from the yogins and yoginis who continue the Drigung tradition of solitary retreat in its hermitages, combine to give the pilgrim an initiation into the meaning and purpose of such power-places. Terdrom is located at the head of a side-valley that enters the Sho Valley 2 km west of Til. A rough jeep-road climbs slowly for 16 km to the north-east through the meadows of the narrow Shoto Valley with its sides covered by dwarf rhododendrons and other flowering shrubs. There are several medicinal hot springs by the river.

There are two focal points in the Terdrom area: the lower one is at the confluence of two rivers where the principal hot springs emerge and where the Ani Gompa is situated, and the upper one is at the Guru Rimpoche cave several hours' walk to the north. These two power-places are linked by the Nangkor, the inner circumambulatory path, that may be compared to the outer circumambulation of Kailash in terms of duration, difficulty and sensory and supersensory impact.

Terdrom Nangkor (gTer sgrom nang 'khor): The Inner Circumambulation

The starting point of the Terdrom Nangkor is the rest house by the hot springs. The two 50 cm deep pools of hot mineral water arise from sacred springs where once only the Drigung Kyapgon could bathe. Residences of the Guardian Goddess Apchi attend both pools. Just below the springs is a ridge of limestone running across the valley through which the river runs in a tunnel 15 m long. Legend has it that a poisonous lake was once contained behind this ridge, its waters so noxious that birds flying over it would succumb to its fumes, and in the lake lived malignant water spirits and other elementals. On Guru Rimpoche's first visit to Terdrom he stayed in a cave at the bottom of the scarp behind the triangular plateau bounded by the rivers that now converge at the springs. Throwing his *dorje* at the ridge the tunnel was formed that drained the lake. The shape of his *dorje* can be seen protruding from the rock within the cavern-like opening of the tunnel. Subjecting the elemental spirits of the lake he bound them to serve the *dharma* and its practitioners, and as a residence he gave them the red-coloured rock that now stands on the right bank of the river just north of the tunnel (more recently a Drigung Lama poked a hole in this rock with his stick). As a further gift to the yogins and yoginis who would later meditate at Terdrom, he caused the hot springs to emerge, promising that their waters would cure every ailment of the body.

From the hot springs the Nangkor path leads to the Ani Gompa close by to the north. Crudely rebuilt on the old pattern, half of the square compound is courtyard and half dukang and lhakang combined. On the altar built of rock and clay, the central image is of Guru Rimpoche. Terdrom's renowned Drigungpa nunnery is the only monastic establishment in Terdrom and it serves now both men and women, monks and nuns, yogins and yoginis. The Drigung Kagyupas place little emphasis on celibacy, and their married *ngakpa* yogins wear the red and white sash of the Nyingmapas and wear their hair tied up on top of their heads. Their hermitages have been rebuilt around the gompa, along the river valleys and on the low plateau above the gompa. The site of the Ani Gompa is associated with Guru Rimpoche and a rock nearby is called Guru Shuktri, Guru Rimpoche's Throne.

Crossing the bridge to the north of the gompa, the path climbs the ridge to the west, passing a chorten on its crest. From this vantage point the shape of the plateau above the Ani Gompa and the mountain behind it can be seen as the form of the elephant's head and trunk that gives it its name. Further on is a spring said to flow from Guru Rimpoche's cave, and beyond the spring is the ruined gompa of *Tinkye. The path then ascends steeply to the Norbu(?) La, Jewel Pass, and then negotiates a sharp ridge and steep scarp around a large cirque. In the rock-face close to the chorten that marks the point of descent down an ice-covered scree slope into a valley to the north, is a hole in which Guru Rimpoche hid a treasure. Some way down the valley on the north side is an important cave and a ruined circular hermitage called *Bugung Sumdo. Further down, the path ascends the south side of the valley to a place where the bodies of Terdrom anchorites are disposed of through exposure to jackals. A yogin's nest underneath an overhanging boulder close to this power-place is used by practitioners of *chod*, invoking the demons and spirits of the place to feed on their bodies. The path continues along and up the valley-side over scree slopes, until a pass crosses the ridge. From this point until Kandro Tsokchen Kiri Yongdzong is reached, the path vanishes on a limestone rock face which is traversed following natural hand and foot holds. The cave is located at about 5,400 m in one of the tall limestone pinnacles that form this massif.

The size of the vast cavern at the base of a limestone tower gives this power-place the name Kandro Tsokchen Kiri Yongdzong, The Assembly Hall of the Dakinis. Within this 50 m high cavern are two hermitages of nuns in retreat there and the ruins of a former lhakang. A ladder leads to an ascending passage 8 m above in the side of the cavern roof, and this passage reaches a cell enclosed high in the limestone tower. Ice fills the chimney into which the ceiling vanishes. A small shrine indicates that this is the cell called the Tsogyel Sangpuk, Tsogyel's Secret Cave, in which both Guru Rimpoche and his Tibetan consort, Yeshe Tsogyel, spent periods of retreat.

In the 8th century, after Guru Rimpoche had answered the Emperor Trisong Detsen's invitation to visit Tibet, during an interim of pro-Bonpo sentiment the Guru and his consort were banished from the kingdom. But escaping from their retreat at Yamalung they found refuge in the Kiri Yongdzong cave in Terdrom until the political climate at Samye had improved. Tsogyel received her three Kandro Nyingtik initiations and precepts here, and during the Guru's absence she visited Nepal, returning with her consort, Atsara Sale, to spend seven months in retreat in the Tsogyel Sangpuk. Again, returning from Samye after the initiation of the Twenty-four Disciples, Tsogyel practised her Guru-yoga in Terdrom and afterwards spent three years on the snowline performing austerities as The White-cotton-clad Yogini. Towards the end of her life, after Guru Rimpoche had left Tibet, she performed her final Dzokchen retreat here, and after her ultimate accomplishment she remained to teach in whatever way was required of her. Tsogyel hid part of the Kandro Nyingtik in Terdrom.

To complete the circumambulation, returning across the limestone rock-face, the way of descent is 500 m down one of the steep scree slopes that flank the ridge. In the valley the path leads to the ruins of the *Drang gompa, located on the left bank of the river where a side-valley converges. In the centre of the gompa's ruins is a small hut containing a sleeping-box and altar. This was the hermitage of Rinchen Puntsok, a Drigungpa *terton* who discovered some of Guru Rimpoche's treasures in Kiri Yongdzong. The rebuilding of the lhakang has begun at this gompa, and a rough track leads down the gorge that descends to the hot springs and the Ani Gompa.

At the end of this circumambulation the path skirts the "elephant trunk" plateau and gives access to the meditation caves at the base of the scarp. The principal cave, associated with both Guru Rimpoche and Yeshe Tsogyel, is only a meditation cave in name, but the hermitage rebuilt in front of it is the residence of the Drigung Kandroma, presently a young yogini considered to be an incarnation of Kandro Yeshe Tsogyel. In her final testament, Tsogyel promised to project an emanation who would always live at Terdrom. Below the cave are the ruins of hermitages, many of which are in process of rebuilding.

Chikor

A longer circumambulation, the *chikor*, encompasses the entire Terdrom area and Drigung Til itself. This can take as long as a week to perform. Further, in the limestone folds of the area there are many other meditation caves, some of them associated with Guru Rimpoche.

History

Two important Dzokchempas are associated with Terdrom. In the 11th century Dzeng Dharmabodhi, a disciple of Padampa and Bagom, meditated here and received a vision of the Deity Dutsi Kyilwa in a cave of rock crystal. Dzeng was a vital link in the Dzokchen Space Precept (*klong sde*) lineage. The second of the two Dzokchempas who meditated in Terdrom was the Second Royal Terton Dorje Lingpa (1346-1405). He discovered a variety of treasure-texts here. Many of the Drigung Rimpoches were Dzokchen initiates.[9]

*   *   *

A footnote to the Drigung Mandala: just before the only right-angle bend halfway up the Shoto Valley, below Terdrom, on the north side of the road, are to be found a number of saucer-sized concavities in the rock-face. It was explained by a local informant that these hollows were formed by laymen who would rub the top of their heads in the hollows in prayerful appeal to the Drigung treasure-finders to reveal Guru Rimpoche's teaching, to provide instruction for these difficult times, and to replace the losses of the Cultural Revolution.

6

TOLUNG: THE KARMAPA'S DOMAIN

Upper Tolung is the stronghold of the Karma Kagyu school. The principal gompa of the Karmapas, the Black-Crown Karma Kagyu Lamas, is at Tsurpu. To the north of Tsurpu is Yangpachen, the seat of the later Shamarpas, the Red-Crown Karma Kagyu Lamas. Below Tsurpu is Nenang Gompa, the seat of the Pawo Rimpoches, belonging to the Shamar school. From the time of the foundation of the Karma Kagyu school in the 12th century until the final suppression of their political power in the 17th century, this school played a notable part in the history of Central Tibet, particularly as Lamas of the Mongol Emperors of China and in opposition to the rise of the Gelukpas. Further, the Karma Kagyupas are the principal holders of the spiritual tradition of Milarepa. Masters of the lineage have immeasurably enriched the spiritual life of Tibet, and also, since the diaspora of the 1970s, of many western countries.

Access
The *Tobing Chu, the chief river of the Tolung valley system, joins the Kyichu 12 km to the west of Lhasa. Before the Donkar Bridge the highway forks, the right-hand road turning north, ascending the Tolung valley on the left bank of the river. Some 30 km up this wide, fertile valley (at km 1897) a jeep-road crosses the Lungpa Sampa bridge and ascends Dowo Lung to Tsurpu. The principal Tolung valley continues to the north, providing a corridor to Yangpachen where the highway divides. The eastern route leads to Damsung, Namtso and Golmud. This

is the main route from Lhasa to Qinghai Province and northern China. The highway to the west of Yangpachen forms the so-called northern route to Shigatse from Lhasa.

Nenang Gompa (gNas nang dgon pa): Residence of the Pawo Rimpoches

Nenang is located thirty minutes' walk over the ridge to the north of the village of *Kado, which is on the north side of the river some 10 km up the Dowo Valley. The gompa was completely destroyed during the Cultural Revolution, but restoration has begun. The chief buildings were the Jampa Lhakang and the Lhakang Chempo, both of which will be rebuilt. The relics remaining to the gompa consist of a number of bronze portraits of Lamas of the Shamar lineage. In 1959 110 *gelongs* studied here; at present eight *trapas* are attached to the monastery.

The practices of the yogins of this Shamar (Red-Crown) Kagyu gompa, like those of the Shanak (Black-Crown) gompa of Tsurpu, are derived from the teaching of Milarepa, which stresses control of the breath and energies of the subtle body, with the final goal of the Buddha's enlightenment and the relative powers of the *siddha*.

History

Nenang was founded in 1333 by the first Shamarpa, Tokden Drakpa Senge (1283-1349), whose relics were preserved here. With the foundation of Nenang the Karma Kagyu school split into two complementary but often rival parts, the Shanak (Black-Crown) and Shamar (Red-Crown). The hierarchs of each school acted as Regents and tutors to the other during the minorities of their respective incarnations. The Shamarpas became engaged in the anti-Geluk movement of the 16th and early 17th centuries. From 1499 to 1523 the fourth Shamarpa, Chokyi Drakpa, was the Supreme Ruler of Tibet, and Yangpachen (see below) was built under his auspices. This was the period in which the Karmapas usurped the authority of Sera and Drepung and built

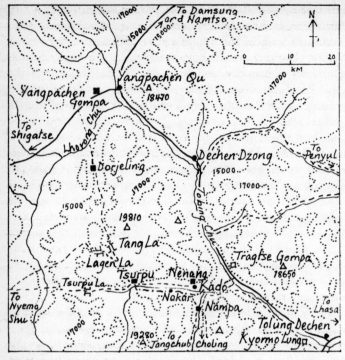

Map 8 The Tolung Area

Red Hat gompas in Lhasa to support the Shamarpa's power. After Yangpachen became the chief seat of the Shamarpa, Nenang was guided by the Pawo Rimpoches. The first incarnation was the *siddha* Pawo Chowang Lhundrub (1440-1503). The second Pawo Rimpoche, the historian Pawo Tsuklak Trengwa (1504-66), is probably the best known incarnation in the Pawo lineage.

Tolung Tsurpu (sTod lung mTshur phu): Seat of the Karmapas

The Tolung Tsurpu gompa[1] is located some 28 km up the Dowo Lung Valley. It is built on the north side of the river and climbs up the valley side. In 1985 the first impression was of a ruined biblical city preserved for millennia by a desert climate, a city that Ozymandias, king of kings, would have been proud to rule. The truncated walls of the 300 m square complex are as much as 4 m thick, bastions standing at the corners. The ruined walls and chimneys of masonry, indicating the former strength of the principal buildings, dwarf the maze of monks' residences on the eastern side. To realize that the destruction of this extraordinary gompa occurred less than a generation ago is to be stunned by the historical forces and human emotions that were engaged. It may be supposed that a gompa with such strong historical connections with China would have been in part preserved; but it is said that the Karmapa's prescience in leaving Tibet with the bulk of Tsurpu's treasure in advance of the Communist invasion, and the later use of the gompa as a haven by Tibetan freedom-fighters, angered the authorities, who vented their wrath on the gompa itself. The sixteenth Karmapa, Rangjung Rikpai Dorje (1924-81), re-established his monastery and his lineage at Rumtek in Sikkim, where many of the portable treasures of Tsurpu are stored. But the late Karmapa's disciple Drupon Dechen Rimpoche is now in residence at Tsurpu, overseeing the work of reconstruction and teaching more than seventy monks.

Restoration of Tsurpu was not far advanced in 1986. In the north-west corner a *labrang*, now called Dratsang, had been rebuilt. The lhakang on the ground floor is the repository of Tsurpu's surviving relics. The upper storey comprises a gomkang with fine new murals, and the lamas' quarters. Below and to the east of Dratsang are the red-painted ruins of the Lhakang Chempo which contained the most revered relic of Tsurpu, the Dzamling Gyen, the Ornament of the World, an image of Sakyamuni created by the second Karmapa, Karma Pakshi, in which relics of Sakyamuni were enshrined. This was the largest cast bronze statue in Tibet. During the Cultural Revolution it was packed with dynamite and blown to smithereens, and fragments of its metal are to be found throughout the ruins. Below and to the east of the Lhakang Chempo the immense Tsokang that was the Karmapas' residence was being reconstructed in 1986. East of the Tsokang are the ruins of another monastic college, called *Suri Dratsang. The fine workmanship of these great buildings is evidence of the wealth and eminence of the early Karmapas.

On the higher ground at the top of the compound are the ruined walls of the vast 17th-century, five-storey residence and college of the Gyeltseb Rimpoches called Chogar Gong. Gyeltseb means "regent", and the Regents of Tsurpu governed their own independent monastic establishment contiguous to that of the Karmapas after the tenth Karmapa had given the college to the sixth Gyeltseb. The first Gyeltseb, Goshi Peljor Dodrub (c. 1427-89), installed the seventh Karmapa.

Outside the walls of Tsurpu are several important remnants of the past. About 150 m above the gompa, perched on a spur, is a reconstructed *drubkang*, a retreat building, and behind this is the *drupuk* where Karma Pakshi and also the third Karmapa, Rangjung Dorje, performed their retreat. It is called Pema Kyungdzong, the Lotus Eagle Citadel. A footprint of Karma Pakshi is found in the lhakang. This reminds the pilgrim that, despite the evidence of his eyes, of all Tibetan schools the Karma Kagyupa were concerned with emulation of the arch-ascetic Milarepa, and particularly with control of the subtle energies within the body. Perched on crags to the west of Pema Kyungdzong are the ruins of several other *tsamkangs* – two for *anis* and one for monks – in which only one of the four rooms in each building had windows. On the south bank of the river are steeply inclined steps upon which gigantic *tankas* were exhibited on festival days.

The *korra* of the entire site can be entered upon by way of the southern gate of the monastery. The path leads west to the confluence of two valleys dominated by Jampa Ri, and here is the site of a garden where the Gyelwa Karmapas had a wooden summer residence. A short distance to the north, at the *dundro* site, the path climbs the mountainside to connect several places of importance as it weaves its way back to the Pema Kyungdzong. On the spur to the east of this retreat is the rebuilt *sungkang* residence of Pelden Lhamo, and above it are the ruins of the lhakang of the Protector Tamdrin. Then descending, by the road is a painted engraving of the principal Karma Kagyu Protector Bernakchen. This *korra* takes about three hours to complete.

[9.] [above] TSURPU: the ruins of the Karmapas' gompa, founded 1185 (photograph by K. Dowman) [below] TSURPU: the Pema Kyungdzong "eagle's nest" hermitage of Karmapa Rangjung Dorje (photograph by *Stone Routes*)

History

The founder of the Karma Kagyu school and Tolung Tsurpu was Dusum Kyempa (1110-93), who, like Drigung Rimpoche and Pakmodrupa Dorje Gyelpo, was born in Kham. His principal Lama was Je Gampopa, but he received instruction also from Milarepa's disciple Rechungpa and various Kadampa sages. He was considered to be an incarnation of the Indian *siddha* Saraha. He was known as the Black-Crown Lama (Shanakpa) after he had been presented with the crown of Indrabodhi, a hat made of the hairs of Dakinis. After travelling widely throughout Tibet, meditating at many power-places, towards the end of his life, in 1187, he settled at Tsurpu. The institution of a series of incarnate lamas or *tulkus* attached to a particular gompa and office was established by Dusum Kyempa when he prophesied his immediate rebirth as the second Karmapa, Karma Pakshi (1202?-83). Karma Pakshi spent most of his life propagating the Kagyu *dharma* while travelling in Tibet and at the Mongol court of Kublai Khan in China. Particularly, his feats of magic, for which he is renowned, impressed the Mongol Emperor – they were remarked upon by Marco Polo. The enormous wealth he received as gifts in China allowed him to rebuild Tsurpu which had been destroyed earlier. The Lhakang Chempo (1287) and the Tsokang date from this period. The political power of the Karma Kagyupas *vis-à-vis* the Sakya school was rooted in this wealth. The third Karmapa was Rangjung Dorje (1284-1339), who repeated his predecessor's visit to the Chinese court. He installed the Emperor Toghon Temur (r. 1333-68) in office during his first visit (1332-4). He died in the third year of his second visit (1339). This third Karmapa, like the first two, spent much of his life meditating in caves, notably at Samye Chimpu and in Pema Kyungdzong. He was an initiate of the Dzokchen Nyingtik of Vimalamitra. Both the fourth and fifth Karmapas also visited China, the fourth at the end of the Yuan dynasty, and the fifth at the beginning of the Ming.

During the decline of the Pakmodrupa hegemony in Central Tibet, the Karmapas were associated with the Princes of Rinpung in eastern Tsang in their stance against the Gelukpas. In the 17th century when the King of Tsang made a strong stand against the unifying policies of the Great Fifth Dalai Lama and the rising

Geluk power, as the King's Lama the tenth Karmapa was aligned with the anti-Geluk forces. After the Gelukpas' Mongol general Gusri Khan had subjected eastern and central Tibet he marched on Shigatse, and in the subsequent battle defeated the King of Tsang and captured and executed him. Gusri Khan then marched on Tsurpu and the Karmapa fled to Bhutan. With the sacking of Tsurpu by the Mongols in 1642 the political influence of the Karmapas ended.

Dorjeling (rDo rje gling)

This Kagyu Ani Gompa is located two days' walk to the north of Tsurpu. Taking the path up the north-western branch of the valley just beyond Tsurpu, after half a day's walk the village of Lagen is reached. Above this village the valley divides and the northern branch crosses *Tang La (approx. 5,300 m) and descends into the valley of an affluent of the Lhorong Chu. Beyond the pass the landscape is more reminiscent of the Changtang than of Central Tibet, with the high Nyenchen Tanglha range forming a backdrop to the north. Dorjeling is also accessible from Yangpachen in a day's walk. Magnificently situated at the bottom of the eastern side of a long ridge, the lhakang and domestic quarters of Dorjeling Ani Gompa have been rebuilt and some thirty *anis* are in residence. In 1986 the lhakang had yet to be decorated.

Tubten Yangpachen (Thub bstan yangs pa can): Seat of the Shamarpas

The Shamarpa's Kagyu gompa of Yangpachen[2] is located on the northern side of the Lhorong Chu valley just above the Lhasa-Shigatse highway. It is accessible from Dorjeling Ani Gompa after a half-day trek. The road from Lhasa follows the *Tobing Chu for some 75 km to Yangpachen Qu passing through Dechen Dzong. To the west of Yangpachen Qu are the hot springs that were once a place of pilgrimage but which now are engulfed by a geothermal plant that irrigates the hot-houses that provide vegetables for Lhasa. 10 km further west is the village of *Shungtse. The gompa is located above it.

Tubten Yangpachen was totally destroyed, but it is now in process of rebuilding. The principal lhakang contains some new images; the Pelkor Gomkang contains an original image of Chakdrukpa (Mahakala) that resisted attempts to destroy it; but the image of Chakdrukpa in the Sinon Gomkang has vanished, along with the glory of Yangpachen.

History

Yangpachen Gompa was founded by Murab Jampa Tujepel in 1490 under the auspices of the fourth Shamarpa and financed by the Prince of Rinpung. It was the residence of the Shamarpas for only 300 years. The Shamarpas' ties with Nepal were their downfall. When the Gorkhalis under Pritvi Narayan Shah, king of the newly unified Kingdom of Nepal, invaded Tibet in 1792 to be defeated by a Chinese army, the tenth Shamarpa was accused of traitorous support of the Nepalis. Yangpachen was confiscated by the Gelukpas, the Shamarpa's hat was buried and recognition of future incarnations was prohibited. In Nepal the present thirteenth Shamarpa has resumed his full status amongst the Karma Kagyupas.

West of Tolung

Just beyond Tsurpu the Dowo Lung Valley divides. Ascending the north-western branch for half a day, just beyond the village of Lagen the valley again divides. Here the western branch ascends to the Tsurpu Lagan La and passes into the upper reaches of the Lhorong Chu. Another pass takes the pilgrim into upper Nyemo Lung, called Nyemo Shu. This valley descends to the larger Nyemo Valley and thence to the Tsangpo to the east of Rinpung and west of Chushul (see map p.266). A power-place of Guru Rimpoche is located in Nyemo Shu, and Nyemo Gyeje is the

Nyemo Jeke that was the birthplace of Bairotsana. Kyungpo Neljorpa (990-1138?) was born in Nyemo Ramang; this was the Bonpo yogin and Dzokchempa, and disciple of Niguma (Naropa's wife) at Nalanda, who founded the Shangpa Kagyu school at Shang Shong.

North of the Lhorong Chu Valley

To the north of Yangpachen is the Nyenchen Tanglha range. Its highest peak at 7,088 m is "a peak resembling a chorten of pure crystal". This is the residence of the very important Mountain God of the West, Nyenchen Tanglha. This Protector was an ancient Bonpo deity, and by the Buddhists he is considered to be the god-king of all the oath-bound Protectors and as such he is one of the most powerful Guardians of the Buddha-*dharma*. His retinue consists of the mountain gods of the 360 lesser peaks of the range. Nyenchen Tanglha, or simply Tanglha, is also a Protector of the Potala's Marpo Ri.

Beyond this range of mountains to the northwest is the holy lake called Namtso, better known to Europeans by its Mongolian name, Tengri Nor, Heaven Lake. Access to this lake is gained via Damsung over the *Large La.

7

THE HIGHWAY FROM LHASA TO CHAKSAM BRIDGE

The 65 km highway from Lhasa to Chaksam down the right bank of the Kyichu passes several monastery sites hallowed by time, but with two notable exceptions these places have little interest for anybody but the historian and the truly inveterate pilgrim. The exceptions are the Drolma Lhakang at Netang and Namkading on Chuwo Ri. Virtually unspoiled the Drolma Lhakang is the one remaining temple of the Netang Gompa. This is the gompa which Jowo Atisha made his chief residence during his 11th-century sojourn in Central Tibet. Namkading is the Guru Rimpoche hermitage on top of Chuwo Ri, a place of extraordinary geomantic power. Both of these places are easily accessible.

Gadong (dGa' gdong)

Gadong[1] was located on a spur behind the present industrial enclave to the west of Drepung and 1 km before the road junction at the bottom of the Tolung valley. The gompa, the cavern in which a school of logic was founded, and the *drupuk* where Je Tsongkapa talked with Jamyang (Manjughosa), have all disappeared.

History
Gadong was the residence of Gya Dulwa Dzinpa (1047-1131) an

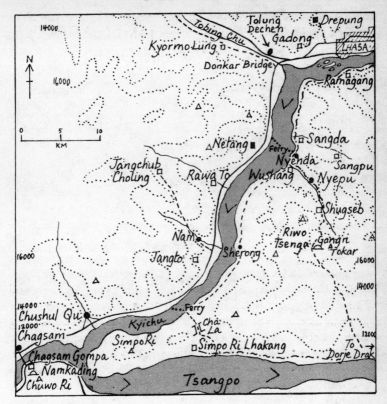

Map 9 The Kyichu Valley Below Lhasa

early exponent of monastic discipline (*dulwa*) in Tibet. Later,
Gadong was the seat of a famous oracle.

Kyormo Lung (sKyor mo lung)

The site of Kyormo Lung[2] is located in lower Tolung on the west
bank of the Tobing Chu some 6 km upstream from the highway
at the Donkar Bridge. In Kadampa days it was a famous school of
logic and metaphysics and remained so at Tsongkapa's time. But
by the 19th century it was much decayed and only a few Geluk

monks remained there. It was dilapidated in 1959 and has now entirely vanished.

History

Kyormo Lung was founded in 1169 by the Arhat Balti Wangchuk Tsultrim (1129-1215) of Yarlung, who was a master of monastic discipline. Tsongkapa studied discipline here under Loselwa. An abbot who was a disciple of Tsongkapa converted it to the Geluk persuasion.

Shongwa Lhachu (Zhong ba Iha chu)

At Lhachu is a spring brought forth by Guru Rimpoche. In 1959 a small building enclosing two pools of fish was to be found there. The lhakang contained a blessing-bestowing Jowo facing Lhasa that was built by Balti Rimpoche (see Kyormo Lung), and the most sacred relic was Guru Rimpoche's staff. Lhachu is located near Kyormo Lung but we have no knowledge of its exact location or its present condition.

Drolma Lhakang (sGrol ma Iha khang): Jowo Atisha's Residence

The Drolma Lhakang is located at Netang (km 17). This Lhakang, also known as Nyetang Wor, with its garden surrounded by a high wall, gives the appearance of a nobleman's villa. The Lhakang was saved from the Red Guards by order of Chou En-Lai. Several Geluk monks are the present stewards of the Lhakang, which is now a museum-gompa.

The Lhakang, surrounded by a circumambulatory passage, consists of a single building divided into three chambers built at the rear of a courtyard. Fine new murals of the triad of Atisha and his favorite disciples Dromton and Naktso Lotsawa, and the triad of Sakyamuni with the Bodhisattvas Jampa (Maitreya) and Jamyang (Manjughosa) decorate the wall of the lhakang's porch, and newly painted clay statues of the Guardian Kings dating from a very early period stand by the doors. In the first chamber, the Namgyel Lhakang, are two bronze chortens, one containing Atisha's robe and the other some relics of Milarepa's Lama,

Marpa. The statue of Atisha, regarded as his own likeness, is found in this room and there is also a remarkable image of Sangdu Yabyum. The central lhakang, which gives the building its name, has tiers of old gilt bronzes of the Twenty-one Drolmas, forms of Tara, the Goddess of Devotion and Service, adorning its walls on three sides, surrounding a statue of Jowo Sakyamuni. In the centre of the room is a glass-faced box containing several small statues. Jowo Atisha's personal deity, Drolma, a talking image, was once amongst them, but today the most sacred relic is an initiatory vase (*bumpa*) containing pieces of Atisha's bones. In front of the relic case is an image of Atisha's chief disciple, Dromton. Except for the loss of Atisha's Drolma, nothing seems to have been moved in this room during the past twenty-five years. The third chamber, the Tsepame Lhakang, contains the Buddhas of the Three Times surrounded by the Eight Bodhisattvas. In the centre of this room is the stone throne from which Jowo Atisha taught his disciples. The reliquary chorten facing one upon leaving this lhakang is said to contain relics of Atisha. Another chorten in the courtyard contains Dromton's sheepskin robe.

History

A building must have stood on this site when Jowo Atisha arrived in Central Tibet. But it was the Drolma Lhakang that was built during Atisha's period (1045-54) – it may have been Dromton who had it constructed – and it is this building alone that has been preserved at Netang. Atisha Dipankara, the Bengali savant known to the Tibetans as Jowo Je, Lord and Master, was abbot of the famous tantric academy of Vikramasila. He was invited to Tibet in 1042 at the age of sixty-one by the King of Guge, to establish a pure monastic base to Tibetan Buddhism after a century of decay. He came to Central Tibet in 1045 at Dromton's urging, although the three years' leave his superiors had allowed him had elapsed. He visited the monasteries of the Tsangpo Valley, particularly Samye and Chimpu, and then came to Netang. He also stayed at Yerpa and other monasteries in the Kyichu Valley. Netang was his principal seat for the remaining years of his life and he died there in 1054. His relics were divided; Reteng also has a claim to them. Atisha taught the *mahayana sutras*, inveighing against practice of the *tantras* without a firm base, and he was responsible for an entire school of translation. He was the Root Guru of the Kadampa School.

Three hundred years later one of the most renowned Tibetan *panditas* was associated with Netang. The Sakya Lama Dampa Sonam Gyeltsen (1312-75) taught the founder of the Geluk school, Je Tsongkapa, in Netang when this prodigy was a mere boy. Later, Netang was converted to the Yellow Hat sect. The gompa that grew up around the Drolma Lhakang was called Dewachen. It was destroyed after 1959 along with Lama Dampa Sonam Gyeltsen's reliquary chorten.

Druk Sewa Jangchub Choling ('Brug se ba Byang chub chos gling)

Between Netang and Chaksam are the sites of several old gompas, but only one of importance – the Jangchub Choling gompa at the head of the Nam valley. Nam village is about 12 km south of Netang. The gompa was founded in 1189 by Tsangpa Gyare, the root guru of the Drukpa Kagyu school. It is said that Drukpa Sewa Jangchub Choling gave the Drukpa school its name. Druk means "thunder" and "dragon". The present condition of this gompa is unknown. Below Netang is RAWATO gompa, which was the mother gompa of Dungpu Chokor (p. 156). More recently it was controlled by the Yellow Hats. Below Nam is JANGTO gompa, an important site in the history of the Gelukpas. To the east of the road at km 40 is a small lhakang called SAKYA LING, now a farmstead.

Chaksam (lCags zam): Ironbridge, Tangton Gyelpo's Residence

At the Tsangpo, some 65 km from Lhasa, a modern bridge has now replaced the 600-year-old suspension bridge built by Drubtob Tangton Gyelpo (1385-1464) that stood a hundred metres to the east of the new structure. Tangton Gyelpo's bridge was of the usual ancient design: "two thick chains are tied to heavy wooden beams underneath the pillars, from the top of which they are suspended; 12' (4 m) ropes hang from the chains and support wooden boards a yard (1 m) long and a foot (30 cm) broad, allowing passage for one man. The bridge is a hundred paces long." In the rainy season the river extended beyond the old bridge's northern end. In 1948 the old bridge was unused and in need of repair and the crossing was made by ferry. It was destroyed when the new bridge was opened.

Tangton Gyelpo, who belonged to the Nyingma school, was a treasure-finder and yogin of considerable renown. But it was as Tibet's master bridge-builder that he gained universal fame. He is said to have built 108 iron suspension bridges throughout Tibet, of which the Tsangpo bridge at Chaksam was one of his greatest. Particularly, the invention of heavy iron chains to support the bridges is attributed to him. At the south side of the Tsangpo bridge was the site of Tangton Gyelpo's chief gompa, known as Chaksam Chuwo Ri. The Chaksam Labrang, the assembly hall and chief building of the complex, was his residence. The large chorten known as Tangton's Kumbum, which stood at the southern end of the bridge, contained his relics, and a chapel inside the top of the kumbum contained his image. The 100 monks of this gompa were supported by the bridge toll. All evidence of its existence has now vanished.

Chuwo Ri (Chu bo ri): Mountain of 108 Springs and Hermitages

The mountain that towers behind the Tsangpo bridge is known as Chuwo Ri, and it is magically related to Tibet's prosperity. 108 springs are said to rise on its flanks, 108 hermitages were built here, and 108 yogins have achieved the Buddha's enlightenment here since Guru Rimpoche's visit. The original hermitage on Chuwo Ri, the location of which is uncertain, was founded by the Emperor Trisong Detsen and it was from here at the beginning of Langdarma's persecution that three monks fled to Kham with the lineage of ordination that Lume eventually brought back to Central Tibet. Taton Joye (c. 12th century), the favorite disciple of Shikpo Rimpoche, had his hermitage on

Chuwo Ri; the first Karmapa and Tsangpa Gyare stayed here; and Rigdzin Lekden Dorje (b.1290) lived in a cave above Chaksam Chuwo Ri.

Namkading (Nam mkha' lding): Guru Rimpoche's Cave
On the summit of the mountain above Chaksam Chuwo Ri is a cave residence of Guru Rimpoche. It is considered by some sources as one of the eight principal caves of the Great Guru. Prayer flags festoon this small hermitage, which has been restored, although it was uninhabited in 1986.

Tsechu Kopa Labrang (Tshe chu bkod pa bla brang)
On the east of Chuwo Ri overlooking Gongkar is the site of Tsechu Kopa Gompa, also known as Tsechu Ling. The gompa has vanished. Nearby is a long-life spring and also Tsechu Puk, Long-life Cave.

Pema Wangchuk Gompa (Padma dbang phyug dgon pa)
Above the road that passes around the west side of Chuwo Ri, north of the western-most spur, 30 m above the road in a protected fold in the hill, is the site of the Pema Wangchuk Gompa.

8

BELOW LHASA TO SIMPO RI

The places of pilgrimage on the left bank of the Kyichu, below Lhasa, from the Lhasa Bridge to the confluence of the Kyichu and Tsangpo rivers at Simpo Ri, are historically rich and various. The unique Kadampa monastic academy at Sangpu Neutok was called "the source of all learning" in Tibet and Ushangdo was the site of the Emperor Repachen's nine-storey pagoda. Unfortunately nothing remains at these sites today. However, Shugseb, the seat of the most recent of Lhasa's female Gurus, is again a flourishing nunnery; and Gangri Tokar, which provided the solitude where Longchempa composed his marvelous works of mystical commentary, is again a thriving centre of religious practice. On the slopes of Riwo Tsenga, Jamyang's (Manjusri's) mountain home in Central Tibet, is a Guru Rimpoche cave. There is no highway on this side of the Kyichu, but a rough jeep-road connects Lhasa to Shugseb. Access to places beyond Shugseb involves some hard trekking.

Karchung (sKar chung): The Emperor Senalek's Temple

On the south side of the Lhasa Bridge the highway divides: to the east is Dechen Dzong while the jeep-road to Shugseb turns to the west. Some 10 km down river, to the south of the road, is a village called Ramagang. Here the Buddhist Emperor Senalek (r.804-14) built the important temple of Karchung Dorying and erected a *doring*, a stone pillar. The site was all but forgotten when Tucci visited it in 1948. Four chortens marked the corners of the temple's foundations and the *doring* stood in its north-east corner. The village has been built on the site of the temple and the whereabouts of the *doring* is now unknown. Guru Rimpoche is said to have consecrated the Dorying temple and taught the Nyingma *tantras* to the Emperor Trisong Detsen's sons within it. The *doring*'s inscription recorded an oath taken by the Emperor Senalek, his ministers and officials, to protect the Buddha-*dharma*, and it enjoined people of succeeding generations to do the same.

On a spur between Ramagang and Sangda are the ruins of the palace of Neudzong from which the ancient Lang family ruled for their relatives, the Tai Situs of Neudong, during the Pakmodrupa ascendancy.

Sangda (gSang mda')

Some 15 km down river from Ramagang is Sangda village, where the affluent of the Sangpu valley meets the Kyichu. This place was known only for its small lhakang in which stood the reliquary chorten of Ngok Lotsawa Loden Sherab (1059-1109), the nephew and successor of the founder of Sangpu Neutok. The lhakang has been destroyed and the nearby chortens are in ruins.

Sangpu Neutok (gSang phu Ne'u thog): "The Source of Learning"

A straight road runs for some 10 km to the south-east of Sangda to Sangpu, and the ruins of the old monastery lie above the village. The significance of Sangpu Neutok to Tibetan culture cannot be underestimated. Jowo Atisha taught the need and set the seeds of an academy of Buddhist learning in Tibet on the model of the Indian monastic academies. As Tibet's only non-sectarian university it gained the epithet "source of all learning". The names of the Kadampa and Sakya abbots and scholars of

Sangpu are mostly obscure, but amongst the students who studied there during its heyday are some of Tibet's most renowned yogins: the first Karmapa Dusum Kyempa, Lama Shang, the third Karmapa Rangjung Dorje, the first Shamarpa Drakpa Senge and his disciple Yakde Panchen founder of EWAM Gompa, Longchempa, Rendawa and Rongtonpa. Sustaining a high tradition of logic, *madhyamika* philosophy and debate, Sangpu provided a base of learning to future accomplished mystics.

The Protector of Sangpu is Setrabchen, Wearer of the Leather Cuirass, the wrathful form of Tsangpa Karpo (p. 103), whose gomkang has now vanished.

Neutok began as a school "in a mountain cave". In its centuries of unique glory (12th-15th centuries) it was an academy of thousands of students. In the 19th century it had become a village of laymen. The places of pilgrimage that remained – a lhakang, the cells of various famous monks, Chapa's reliquary chorten, the gomkang – were all destroyed after 1959. A small lhakang was in process of reconstruction in 1985.

History

The most renowned scion of the Ngok clan, Ngok Lekpai Sherab, founded Neutok Chode at Sangpu in 1073, twelve years after the death of Jowo Atisha who had prophesied its foundation. Born in Yamdrok, Ngok had come to Central Tibet in 1045 and attached himself to Jowo Atisha, becoming one of his closest disciples. After Atisha's death he became a pupil of the "First Kadampa", Dromton. Ngok's nephew, Loden Sherab (1059-1109), succeeded him as abbot. Loden Sherab studied in Kashmir and participated in the Tabo Council that brought together the human strands of resurgent Tibetan Buddhism in 1076. He was a noted translator of the Indian scriptures and he also established his New Logic at Sangpu. Less than a 100 years after its foundation Sangpu was controlled by the Sakya school, and the Sakya scholar Chapa Chokyi Senge (1109-69) became abbot in 1152. Originally Neutok Chode was divided into two Kadampa colleges, Lingto and Lingme. In its Sakya heyday there were fourteen colleges in Sangpu Neutok, and these colleges of *gelongs* were seasonally ambulatory, visiting various gompas for debate and study. With the waning of Red Hat dominance some of these colleges founded their own gompas (see pp.153 & 160). In recent times seven Sakya and four Geluk colleges, such as Ganden Shartse, would visit Sangpu for the summer retreat, but only caretakers were resident there.

Wushang ('U shangs): Repachen's Pagoda Temple

About 5 km south of Sangda is the village of Wushang.[1] Nyenda, close to Wushang, is accessible by ferry across the Kyichu just north of Netang. Wushang was the site of the 9th-century nine-storey pagoda temple with "a Chinese-style dome of blue turquoise"[2] built by the Emperor Repachen (r.815-38) and called Wushangdo. A royal palace, probably built by the Emperor Senalek, stood in the same vicinity. Repachen was the last Buddhist Emperor of Tibet. He was assassinated by supporters of his brother Langdarma, who was responsible for the Bonpo suppression after 838. The period of the ancient temple's destruction is unknown. When Kyentse Rimpoche visited Wushangdo in the 19th century he found a recently constructed temple with a remarkable Jowo inside. In 1948 Tucci found a temple built "according to the ancient pattern consisting of porch, the cell and the circumambulation corridor".[3] In 1985 only ruins were to be found there.

Shugseb (Shug gseb): Jetsun Lochen's Residence

At Wushang the jeep-road turns south-east to ascend the Nyepu valley through Nyepu and *Raden villages to the Shugseb Ani Gompa. Shugseb gompa was totally destroyed after 1959, but the energy of the Nyingma *tulku* whose seat it is, and the nuns themselves, have given the nunnery a new lhakang, several hermitages and an apartment for the reincarnation of the Shugseb Jetsunma, a young man who is presently working in an office in Lhasa. A new image of Machik Labdron is at the centre of the lhakang's altar.

The Shugseb nunnery arose out of obscurity early this century due to a most remarkable woman called Jetsun Lochen Rimpoche. This incarnation of Machik Labdron (p.248) was renowned throughout Central Tibet as a yogini and a healer, having gained a reputation in Lhasa as an itinerant, enlightened beggar. As abbess she presided over 300 nuns until she passed on at a great age in 1951. Today the forty resident *anis*, including twenty-five who remember the old regime, continue the tradition of the Longchen Nyingtik, taking their inspiration from Longchempa's retreat at Gangri Tokar.

History

Nyepu Shugseb was founded in 1181 by Gyergom Tsultrim Senge (1144-1204), a disciple of Drogon Pakmodrupa and a holder of the *shije* lineage of So Chungwa. This Nyepu Gyergom Chempo is considered to be the founder of the Shugseb Kagyu school. Longchempa once taught the Nyingtik to his disciples at Nyepu Shugseb. Later, after the gompa fell into disrepair, it was adopted by the Yellow Hats and remained a Geluk establishment until 1959. At present it is a Nyingma Ani Gompa devoted to the Dzokchen Nyingtik.

Gangri Tokar (Gangs ri Thod dkar): "White Skull Mountain"

The path behind Shugseb connects the ruins of the *anis'* retreat huts, and then, in an hour's walk, climbs steeply through the scrub and sparse juniper growth amongst rocks to the ridge of Gangri Tokar. Gangri Tokar is also accessible in a two day walk over yak pastures from the Dorje Drak valley in the south. There is a path linking it to the Riwo Tsenga *korra*.

Gangri Tokar lies at the heart of a naturally-manifest image of Dorje Pakmo, the Vajra Sow, formed by the shape of the Gangri Tokar ridge. Two springs generating milky water are her breasts; Shugseb is on her left knee; and her *yoni* is the source of the major stream feeding the north side of the ridge. Thus the site is replete with natural sacred symbols independent of the artefacts human beings have endowed with sanctity.

The principal power-place at Gangri Tokar is the cave called Orgyen Dzong Wosel Tinkyi Kyemotsel, "The Citadel Of Orgyen, the Clear-light Cloud Grove". The cave is small and low-roofed, formed by a large overhanging slab of rock walled up at its sides for support. The lhakang that was built in front of the cave was destroyed but is now restored. Quarters for the guardian-keepers of the power-place are to be rebuilt. A new small statue of Longchempa himself has taken pride of place on the cave's altar. This meditation cave had a magnificent prospect to the south, although the restoration work has obscured it. The Riwo Tsenga is visible at the end of the ridge to the west. In the chief cave at Gangri Tokar Longchempa (Longchen Rabjampa) wrote many of his most famous works, amongst them the *Dzodun*, The Sevenfold Treasury, commentary upon the Dzokchen Nyingtik tradition.

To the left of the cave (looking out) is the stump of the juniper tree in which resided the guardian deities who assisted Longchempa with his writing. Close by is the prayer-flag bedecked boulder-residence of the female protectress Dorje Yudronma, who invited Longchempa to this spot. Down the slope to the right is the large rock-slab on which Kandromas and Guardians ground the material for ink.

Four other "sleeping caves" associated with Longchempa are located along the same ridge to the east: the Samten (Meditation), Melong (Mirror), Dewa (Bliss), and Shar (East) Simpuks. The Shar Simpuk, a considerable distance across the scarp to the east, is renowned as an excellent retreat spot for Dzokchen *togel* practice. These caves are now occasionally in use by Shugseb *anis* or visiting yogins, and in 1986 these were the sole inhabitants of Gangri Tokar. Previously, Mindroling (p.165) provided keepers for Tokar.

History

The one great scholar and yogin associated with this place is the peerless Kunkyen Longchen Rabjampa (1308-63). Longchempa was born at *Derong in Dranang (p.169). He was educated at Samye, Neudong and Chimpu, and Rigdzin Kumaraja was his Dzokchen preceptor. He meditated and taught at Chimpu where Guru Rimpoche himself initiated him into the Kandro Nyingtik tradition and gave him instruction. Then, receiving an invitation from the Gangri Tokar Protectress Dorje Yudronma, he came to this cave and began a highly productive period of meditation and writing. Vimalamitra gave him his Nyingtik teaching in a vision, inspiring him to write his commentary on the Kandro Nyingtik. He also wrote the *Lama Yangtik* at Gangri Tokar. At Tokar he attained the Dzokchen level of Optimal Knowledge through *togel* practice.

Riwo Tsenga (Ri bo rtse Inga): The Five-peaked Mountain

Riwo Tsenga is the five-peaked mountain in Central Tibet sacred to Jamyang, Manjusri, the Bodhisattva of Intelligence. It is one of the five sacred mountains of Central Tibet. Situated to the east of the Kyichu, south of Wushang and south-west of Shugseb, its *korra* path is accessible from Wushang or Gangri Tokar. Riwo Tsenga is a spur of the ridge that forms the divide between the Tsangpo and Kyichu Valleys. It is called the "Central Tibetan" Riwo Tsenga to distinguish it from Manjusri's five-peaked mountain abode called Wutaishan in western Shan-hsi in China. Manjusri is particularly honoured in China since he is the source and patron of the mystic arts of astrology, divination and geomancy.

On the Riwo Tsenga *korra* are two important cave power-places. The first is called Lharing Longchen Drak, Vast Space Rock of the Long-life Protectresses. It appears to be a coincidence that the word "Longchen" forms a part of this name, although Longchempa's hermitage is nearby at Gangri Tokar. The second cave is called Drakmar Sangyak Namka Dzong, the Red-Rock Infinite-Sky Fort, or simply Sangyak Drak. This is a meditation cave of Guru Rimpoche where he hid various treasures. He prophesied that the treasure-finder Guru Jotse would recover these treasures. Guru Jotse, an incarnation of the Emperor Senalek, appeared in the 13th century and discovered texts and *purbas* here. These caves are said to be located on opposite sides of the mountain, but since we have no firsthand experience of the Riwo Tsenga *korra* the location of the caves is in doubt.

Simpo Ri (Srin po ri)

At the confluence of the Kyichu and Tsangpo is the hill called Simpo Ri[4] or Yarto Drak, a narrow neck of land that separates the two valleys. The village and gompa of Simpo Ri is located on the Tsangpo side opposite Gongkar Dzong. It is accessible from Chushul[5] by ferry; about 30 km from Wushang by the difficult path along the Kyichu Valley and over the Cha La; and from Dorje Drak in the east by the path along the barren north bank of the Tsangpo. The gompa in the village, small but renowned, is located at the bottom of the path that crosses the mountain from the Chushul ferry station over the Cha La and down to Simpo Ri village. We have no knowledge of the fate of the gompa since 1959.

History

Simpo Ri, or Drangsong Simpo Ri, is mentioned frequently in the early Lamas' biographies. There appears to have been a gompa here before Kache Panchen visited in the early 13th century. The principal power-place at Simpo Ri Gompa was the Demchok Lhakang built by the Bengali *pandita* Vibhuticandra (probably a refugee from Bengal after the ravages of the Muslim Turks in the late 12th century) in expiation for the sin of calling the Drigungpas liars. Kache Panchen Sakyasri, who was then visiting Simpo Ri, imposed this penance. Thus this lhakang dated from the early 13th century. The talking image of Demchok in this temple was a bestower of potent blessings. The gompa was a Sakya establishment, but by the 19th century it had become a village of laymen.

Morchen (rMor chen)

Kyentse Rimpoche mentions the Morchen gompa which he locates inside a valley to the east of Cha La. This was probably the residence of Morchen Kunga Jungne (c.16th) of the Tsarpa branch of the Sakya school. We have no information regarding the location of this gompa or its condition.

9

THE SOUTH BANK OF THE TSANGPO: FROM GONGKAR TO TSETANG

The old district of Gongkar had its western limit at Chuwo Ri, near Chaksam, Iron Bridge, where the Lhasa road crosses the Tsangpo. Today a metalled road runs from Chaksam to the Gongkar Airport, and a good unmetalled road continues from Gongkar Xian through Dranang Xian to Tsetang, 158 km east of Chaksam. Thus the five major and several minor valleys to the south of the Tsangpo are easily accessible. Most of the older gompas in these valleys are situated in the fertile plains close to the Tsangpo, and thus they, also, can be visited with ease.

There is a unity amongst seven of the gompas found between Gongkar and Tsetang: they are all gompas belonging to the Sakya school and the principal buildings of all of them have survived the Cultural Revolution. Gongkar Dorjeden and Dakpo Dratsang in Namrab, Tubten Rawame in Rame, Dungpu Chokor in Chitesho, Dranang Gompa and Gyeling Tsokpa in Dranang, and Tsongdu Tsokpa in Drachi, are not of germinal historical importance, but each has some claim to fame. An indefensible site indicates in most cases the happy period when Tibet still had not known foreign invasion. Gongkar Dorjeden is of special significance to the art historian as it gave birth to the Central Tibetan style of painting known as the Kyenri style. The auspicious device by which these seven Sakya gompas were preserved was their transformation into granaries and Party offices by their local communes. Since grain must be kept dry, the only damage to the murals of many of these gompas has been the superimposition of a layer of whitewash that can easily be removed by a professional restorer. Some of the gompas have been restored while others are in the process of restoration.

Between Gongkar and Tsetang, besides the seven Sakya gompas, the pilgrim can visit two Drukpa Kagyupa establishments, one of the largest chortens in Tibet, the important Guru Rimpoche treasure-cave of Wokar Drak in Jing, and at Jasa the site of one of the oldest lhakangs in Tibet.

The two valleys that contain power-places in their upper reaches are Dranang and Drachi. Since they are not easily accessible from the main road and belong to the Nyingma school, a separate section has been devoted to them (p.164).

Gongkar (Gong dkar)

The Lord (*dzongpon*) of Gongkar[1] ruled the entire stretch of rich farmland on the south bank of the Tsangpo from Chuwo Ri to Rawame. His seat was Gongkar Dzong, the ruins of which may be seen on the ridge to the west side of the main Gongkar valley opposite Gongkar Dorjeden. During the Sakya ascendancy Gongkar Dzong was an important pillar of Sakya power in the Tsangpo Valley. Tai Situ Pakmodrupa consolidated his power in the 15th century by defeating the Gongkar Ponchen.

Gongkar Dorjeden (Gong dkar rdo rje gdan): The Origin of Kyenri Art

Gongkar Dorjeden[2] lies just south of the main road (km 75)[3]. The large three-storey building containing the dukang, lhakangs, the Rimpoche's quarters and the kitchen has survived in good condition. The Drepung Dratsang building behind to its right and the lhakang known as the Keutsang to its left are in poor condition. All these buildings date from the 15th century. Kyentse Rimpoche remarks that the Gongkar Chodra "has a perfect arrangement of hermitages and colleges". All but the three buildings mentioned above have vanished, and the large

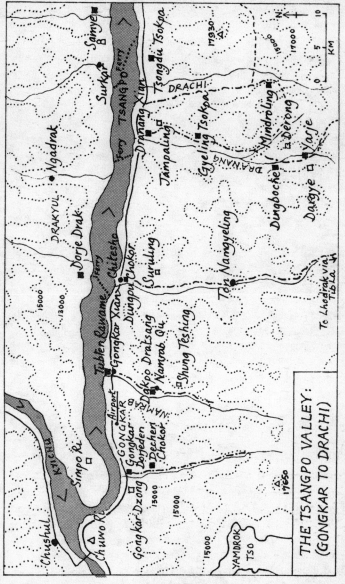

Map 10 The Tsangpo Valley: Gongkar to Drachi

walled compound is bare. Restoration of the main building is almost complete and an abbot is in charge of the education of more than twenty young *trapas*.

The gompa's dukang is a large and highly impressive space. The inner lhakang surrounded by a *korsa*, has been gutted and was not restored in 1986, the gompa's relics and images standing on a makeshift altar in front of its doors. Images of the gompa's founder, Dorjedenpa, and the Sakya savant Sakya Pandita, took pride of place on the altar. Dorjeden's most sacred relic, a skullcup engraved with Sakyamuni's image, belonging to the 11th-century Indian *pandita* Gayadhara (p.278), is missing. Original murals still decorate the dukang's walls. Particularly, on the front wall of the lhakang are paintings of the six Sakya lamas most important in Dorjeden's lineage: (from left to right) Lama Dampa Sonam Gyeltsen, Sakya Pandita, Pakpa, Jetsun Drakpa Gyeltsen, Kunga Nyingpo and Lopon Sonam Tsemo. The murals of the Buddha's life in the lhakang's *korsa* are said to be the original 16th-century work of artists painting in the Kyenri style, but the coat of whitewash permitted no judgement upon the date or style.

The lhakang on the left side of the dukang is the gomkang, the residence of Dorjeden's Protectors. The mural in the outer chamber of Nakpo Chempo (Mahakala) done in gold on black is particularly fine.

In the second storey of the gompa two remarkable rooms have retained murals in excellent condition. The room above the dukang's portico contains four oval panels of early work in a good state of preservation. One of these shows Gongkar Dorjeden in its former glory. These panels are reputed to have been painted by the originator of the Kyenri style, Jamyang Kyentse, in the 16th century. The other notable room in the second storey is a lhakang whose murals depict the *yidam*, or principal deities, of the Dorjedenpa lineage. These include (from the left) Namse, Yangdak Tuk, Dorje Purba, Sangdu, Dukor, Kye Dorje, Demchok, Tsokdak, Demchok Kandro. These deities belong to the highest, non-dual level of tantric practice.

[10.] [above] GONGKAR: Dorjeden, a well-preserved 15th century Sakya gompa (photograph by K. Dowman)
[below] DAKPO DRATSANG: the fully-restored Sakya gompa at Namrab Qu (photograph by K. Dowman)

In the third storey at the front of the building are the Dorjedenpa Rimpoche's quarters, meditation room and shrine, in process of restoration.

History

Gongkar Dorjeden was founded in 1464 by Tonmi Kunga Namgyel (1432-96), known as Gongkar Dorjedenpa. Dorjedenpa, a highly renowned saint and scholar, was a disciple of the renowned Sakya master Lama Dampa Sonam Gyeltsen (p.136) and he also studied with Panchen Jampa Lingpa of Dranang (p.159). In the tradition of Sakya tantric practice Dorjedenpa was known as a meticulous purveyor of tantric ritual on all its four levels. He established the Gongkarpa lineage renowned for its ritual practice of forty-five mandalas belonging to the four tantric classes and also a famous school of *cham* (Lama dance).

Little is known of the 16th-century Jamyang Kyentse (b.1524), otherwise known as Tulku Jamyang, who painted in the style later to be called Kyenri, except that he lived in Gongkar and painted murals in Dorjeden gompa. Although highly stylized his work possessed a fluid vitality not to be found in later centuries of development of the Central Tibetan Menri style.

In the 16th century the Pakmodrupa *dzongpon* of Gonkar was one of the first and most reliable allies of the Yellow Hat reformation. An abiding effect of this alliance was the right of Gongkar monks to perform certain of the rituals perfected by Dorjedenpa at the Potala, a tradition that ended in 1959.

Dechen Chokor (bDe chen chos 'khor)

Dechen Chokor is located 4 km up the jeep-road behind Gongkar Dorjeden and 150 m up the eastern side of the valley. This large complex was completely destroyed, but a new dukang and lhakang have been built for the twenty monks now in residence. In the tradition of meditation retreat of the Drukpa Kagyu school to which the gompa belongs, new hermitages have been constructed for the married monks amongst the grove of trees on the south side.

History

The history of Dechen Chokor is obscure. A hermitage was probably founded here by Lama Yongdzin in the 13th century. Later it became one of the chief centres of the Drukpa Kagyu school in Central Tibet. The Rimpoches of Dechen Chokor were the Lamas of the kings of Ladakh.

Namrab Valley

Dakpo Dratsang (Dwags po Grwa tshang)

The Namrab[4] Valley, in which Dakpo Dratsang is situated, is a broad fertile valley to the east of Gongkar airport. Just west of Rame village (Gongkar Xian), at km 35, a jeep-road turns south off the highway, and Dakpo Dratsang, the second of the Sakya gompas, is found in the village of Namrab Qu, 5 km up the valley. Another "granary gompa" Dakpo Dratsang is in good state of preservation. It is built in the old *vihara* style with the temple on the west side of a large quadrangle surrounded by monks' quarters. The central building has been restored and an abbot is installed as head of fifteen monks and many young students.

The small dukang has been well-restored and repainted. In the lhakang some good murals from the 15th century have been preserved. The portraits of Marpa and Milarepa above the door are of exceptional quality. The central image on the altar is of Sakya Pandita; to his right is the gompa's founder, Tashi Namgyel; and to his left is the 15th-century Sakya scholar Gorampa Sonam Senge. The long chamber on the left side of the dukang is the gomkang, which still retains some original murals.

Amongst the Protectors of the gompa is the *sungma* *Pangboche whose image is found in the box to the right of the lhakang door and also on the back wall of the dukang. In the courtyard close to the walnut tree, which is a *lashing*, and next to the *sangkang* is his principal, red-painted residence.

A plaque erected in 1984 on the kitchen building wall makes obeisance to the Sakya hierarchs — Kunga Nyingpo, Jetsun

Drakpa Gyeltsen, Lopon Sonam Tsemo, Sakya Pandita and Pakpa
– and to Tashi Namgyel.

History
This Dakpo Dratsang which is a Sakya establishment should not
be confused with the Geluk gompa called Dakpo Shedrubling but
more commonly known as Dakpo Dratsang, located at Gyatsa
Xian (p.262). Sakya Dakpo Dratsang was founded by Dakton
Tashi Namgyel (1398-1459). He was head of one of the fourteen
gelong colleges of Sangpu that wandered from monastery to
monastery for part of the year, and it was at Dakpo Dratsang that
his college found a permanent base. Tashi Namgyel, renowned as
both scholar and yogin, belonged to the Kadampa tradition but
favoured the Sakya school. He was Rongtonpa's favorite disciple
and his Lama's successor as abbot at Nalendra in 1449. He was a
teacher of Sonam Gyatso (p.159).

Shung Teshing (gZhung sPre zhing)

A few kilometres south of Namrab Qu and 150 m up the eastern
side of the Namrab Valley lie the ruins of the great Kagyu gompa
of Shung Teshing. The most important objects of worship here
were Marpa Lotsawa's relics and a talking image of Lhamo
Dusolma, a form of the Protectress Pelden Lhamo. We have no
information on the fate of the relics of Teshing.

History
Ngokton Chokyi Dorje (1036-1102) was a disciple of Marpa
Lotsawa (1012-97) who was also Milarepa's Lama. Ngokton's
residence was at Teshing and a famous meeting between Ngokton
and Milarepa occurred here. Ngokton achieved his *parinirvana* at
Teshing. However, it was Ngokton's grandson, Ngok Kunga
Dorje (1157-1234) who founded the Teshing gompa. It was
enlarged by his son, who built a *vihara* and a residence and who
also transported Marpa's relics to Teshing and enshrined them in
a chorten. This reliquary became the principal object of
veneration at Teshing. Descendants of Ngokton maintained his
lineage of Marpa's teaching intact and for 400 years the influence
of the masters of Teshing spread through Central Tibet.

Tubten Rawame (Thub bstan Ra ba smad)

The offices and garrison of Gongkar Xian are located in the old village of Rame[5] (km 36). The small Sakya gompa of Tubten Rawame at the north end of the village has been utilized as Party offices but it is now in process of restoration. A transmission aerial is prominent on the gompa roof.

At the front of the dukang on the throne Sakya Trichen's image takes pride of place. Although Tucci[6] dates the dukang's murals as 17th century, at least part must have been repainted in the years prior to 1959, as the thirteenth Dalai Lama's portrait is still to be seen on the left-hand side wall. Opposite is a painting of Won Rimpoche (1138-1210) associated with the gompa's foundation. In the lhakang are cases of new images of the gompa's lineage lamas and small new bronzes, but the ancient statues that Tucci mentioned have vanished.

Chitesho

The large village of Chitesho[7] (km 52) is situated at the crossing of the east-west Tsangpo highway and the old caravan route from Lhasa to Lhodrak via Dorje Drak. The ferry station to Dorje Drak gompa is at km 48. The ruins of the Chitesho Dzong can be seen high above the village on the east side. Chitesho was renowned for its woolen cloth, particularly its aprons (*pandens*) striped red, green, orange and blue, dyed with colour from Bhutan. Its weaving industry is still operational. Its chief gompa, Dungpu Chokor, has been preserved.

To the south, up the Tib Chu valley, is the site of the large Geluk gompa of Suruling. Higher up the valley, about 12 km to the south of Chitesho, is *Ton Namgyeling Dzong, an attractive, wealthy village where the Gongkar *dzongpon* once lived. At the head of the valley, 25 km south of Chitesho, is the Tib La, which crosses into south-west Lhoka.

Dungpu Chokor (gDung phud chos 'khor)

Behind Chitesho is the Sakya gompa of Dungpu Chokor,[8] which was a "granary gompa" and thus preserved from the Red Guards. The large three-storey building faces a wide courtyard surrounded by monks' quarters. Wooden stairs lead up to the portico of the dukang and lhakang.

In 1948 Tucci reported that the Dungpu Chokor gompa had been completely restored. Only a Chinese inscription on a lhakang door and a pillar's plinth with carved arabesques remained from an ancient period.[9] However, the murals of the dukang and lhakangs of Dungpu Chokor are of considerable interest. The principal relic on the altar is an original statue of Drolma Sungjonma, Talking Drolma. The chief image in the lhakang on the right side of the dukang is Nampar Nangdze (Vairocana), and he is surrounded by Drolmas. To the left of the dukang door are paintings of the gompa's Protectors, Bramze and Gompo Gur.

A room at the top of the gompa has been restored to memorialize the stay of the fourteenth Dalai Lama, Tendzin Gyatso, on his flight to India in March 1959. From the Norbu Lingka, Yishinorbu crossed the Kyichu and rode by way of *Che La to the Tsangpo, and after crossing the river by coracle to Chitesho he stayed in this room at Dungpu Chokor. He then continued south over the Tib La into Lhodrak, east to Jayul, and across the Assam border. Amongst several remarkable small bronzes treasured in this room is a notable image of Guru Rimpoche.

History

Dungpu Chokor was founded by a disciple of Rongtonpa (p.85) called Shedrong Panchen Lodro Chokyi Gyelpo in the 15th century. It was a branch of the Kyisho Rawa To gompa.

Suruling (gSung rab gling)

About 4 km on the jeep-road beyond Chitesho and 2 km up the

eastern valley side lies the Geluk gompa of Suruling.[10] This large gompa of 500 monks was completely destroyed but it is now in process of restoration. A rebuilt chorten stands at the base of the site. There was a nunnery nearby at *Peru.

South of Tib La

Beyond the Tib La the path of the ancient caravan route to Bhutan and India descends to the shores of the eastern arm of the Yamdrok Tso in Lhodrak (see also p.204).

Lower Dranang

The ancient importance of the Dranang Valley, the Valley of Thirteen Buddha-Lamas, has been sustained with the location of the centre of Dranang district at Dranang Xian. The 2 km jeep-road to Dranang Xian leaves the highway at km 76. The plethora of monastic establishments in the Dranang Valley is indicative of the wealth of this valley. The Sakya Dranang Gompa is situated in the centre of Dranang Xian. A short distance further up the jeep-road the amazing ruins of Jampaling and its enormous chorten become visible. At 5 km beyond Dranang Xian are the ruins of *Roi Namgyel Gompa on a spur above the road. The village of Gyeling is reached 3 km further up, and here the Sakya Gyeling Tsokpa gompa and its ancillary hermitage Gasa Puk are located. At the head of this long valley are the Dingboche and Dargye gompas, and the hermitage of Orgyen Lingpa and birthplace of Longchempa: these are described in the section on Upper Dranang and Upper Drachi (pp.164-70).

Dranang Gompa (Grwa nang dgon pa): Drapa Ngonshe's Residence

Dranang[11] Gompa in Dranang Xian is one of the two of our seven Sakya gompas that in 1986 had not been restored from their state as granaries and Party offices. The original temple is in good condition but its ancillary buildings have been destroyed. It has suffered from its position in the middle of an important administrative centre. It was founded at the beginning of the 11th century.

Permission to enter the dukang and lhakang was being denied pilgrims in 1986, but it appears that the murals which excited Tucci[12] in 1948 are still extant, covered only by a coat of whitewash. Tucci also mentioned the Jowo and the Eight Bodhisattvas in the lhakang, which in his opinion had never been restored, and also the statues of Dorje Jigche, Gurgon, Pelden Lhamo, and *Putraminsin in the Chinese style, in the gomkang, images which affected him considerably. Particularly, he considered the murals influenced by the Central Asian Hellenistic school and admired them greatly. However, although the structure, statues and murals of this temple were modelled on the original Samye Utse and were of that same period, their condition was endangered by disrepair in 1948. Their condition today remains to be discovered.

History

A gompa at Dranang, known as Dratang gompa, was one of the four chief temples built during the lifetime of Lume at the beginning of the second period of propagation of the *dharma* in Tibet. However, later in the 11th century, Dranang was the residence of the important treasure-finder Drapa Ngonshe (1012-90) and to him is ascribed the foundation of Dranang Gompa in 1081.

Drapa Ngonshe is renowned for his revelation of the Four Medical *tantras* (Gyushi) which became the canon of Tibetan medicine and which every doctor memorizes. One of the most significant figures of the 11th-century restoration of the *dharma* in Tibet, he was a disciple of Padampa Sangye (p. 281) and Machik Labdron's Lama.

At its inception Dranang was a Nyingma establishment, but it must have been usurped by the Sakya school early in the Sakya ascendancy. Sonam Gyatso (1423-82) had Dranang gompa repaired. The most renowned Sakya scholar associated with Dranang is Tendzin Puntsok, a commentator upon the entire Sakya *dharma*.

Jampaling (Byams pa gling): The Great Kumbum

On a spur to the eastern side of the valley, 1 km south of Dranang Xian, are the fantastic ruins of the Yellow Hat gompa of Jampaling.[13] Innumerable chimneys of masonry packed together over several acres, dwarfed by the vast ruin of what is said to have been the largest chorten or kumbum in Tibet, attest to thorough work of destruction by explosives. The area of ruined buildings covers only a part of the extensive site still surrounded by fortified walls. The colossal pile of the Kumbum ruins stand guarding the site 150 m above the plain. It is called the Kumbum Tongdrol Chemo, the Great Chorten of a Hundred Thousand Images that Grants Liberation by Sight of It. Like the Gyangtse Kumbum, but somewhat later in construction, it was a chorten of many doors to many lhakangs (Gomang Chorten), a decreasing number on each of its nine levels. The outer wall of the lower level is approximately 25 m square, and the giant image of the Bodhisattva Jampa in the central lhakang is said to have been 50 m high. The only work of restoration begun at Jampaling is work on the Kumbum.

The Kumbum was dedicated to Jampa, Maitreya, by its builders, the Panchen Jampalingpa Sonam Namgyel (1401-75), who was the brother of the founder of the Jampaling Gompa, and Lochen Sonam Gyatso. The Jampaling Gompa was founded in 1472 by Tumi Lhundrub Tashi, a descendant of Tonmi Sambhota.

Gyeling Tsokpa (rGyal gling tshogs pa)

The Sakya gompa of Gyeling Tsokpa[14] is located in Gyeling village, 8 km up the jeep-road from Dranang Xian. The principal building is in good condition, for like Dranang Gompa it is still used as a granary, and the towering, unadorned walls demonstrate the superb quality of Tibetan stone-dressing. Although the building's function as Party offices has lapsed, in 1986 a picture of Mao still took pride of place in the original abbot's quarters on the first floor. Whitewash coats the murals on this floor, while in the granary, the original dukang, some murals still appear to be in good condition.

A kilometre behind the gompa, built against the valley wall by a spring that watered a willow grove and monastic gardens, is the hermitage associated with Gyeling Tsokpa called *Gasa Puk. This small rebuilt lhakang contains the sacred relics of Gyeling Tsokpa, and several gelongs maintain the gompa's traditions.

History

The origins of Gyeling Tsokpa are unclear. While it is claimed that Sakyasri, the Kashmiri pandita, founded a lineage here between 1204 and 1214, and that Gyeling is one of the Tsokpa Shi gompas (see p.176), one of the travelling Sangpu colleges is also supposed to have settled here and founded the gompa (p.142). Further, as the tankas and images of Gasa Puk demonstrate and as the affiliation of some of the gelongs now resident imply, there is a strong Nyingma influence in the gompa's lineage.

Lower Drachi

The Drachi[15] Valley (km 78-83) is broad and long, but infertile in its flood plain. The turning at km 79 leads to Drachi's chief monastery, Mindroling, 15 km up the valley: this is described in the section on Upper Drachi (p.165). On the eastern side of the valley (km 83) is the village in which the Sakya Tsongdu Tsokpa gompa is situated. The ferry station for Samye is located on the main road 5 km further east (km 88).

Tsongdu Tsokpa (Tshong 'dus tshogs pa)

The last of the seven Sakya gompas between Gongkar and
Tsetang is the Tsongdu Tsokpa[16] of the lower Drachi Valley. It,
also, has been used as Party offices, and although in 1986 it had
not yet been restored it stood empty awaiting restoration. Like
the Dungpu Chokor gompa it has three storeys with wooden
stairs leading to the portico, and it stands facing a courtyard
surrounded by monks' quarters. To the west of the gompa is the
gutted Jampa Lhakang, surrounding a small courtyard, still
utilized as farm buildings.

History

The history of Tsongdu Tsokpa begins during the early period of
the renaissance of the *dharma* in Central Tibet after the century of
persecution. Lume, one of the Central Tibetans who at the end of
the 10th century travelled to Kham to obtain ordination, built
Tsongdu Ne upon his return. Drachi was the home of the
Lotsawa Kyok Sherab Jungne, a disciple of Drumer whose Lama
was Lume. Kyungpo Neljorpa (990-1138?), the Bonpo who
founded the Shangpa Kagyu school (p.131), was associated with
this gompa in the 11th century. His relics remained here until
1959.

In 1204 the Kashmiri Pandita Sakyasri(bhadra) (1145-1243)
visited Tibet to teach and translate, and during his ten year visit
he founded four particular lineages that became known as the
Tsokpa Shi. One of these lineages was established at Tsongdu.
The Sakya school ascribes the foundation of the gompa to Sakyasri
and one of the gompa's most sacred relics was a statue of Sakyasri.

In the 15th century the Tsongdu Potang was the residence of
Go Lotsawa Shonnu Pel, the compiler of the *Blue Annals*, from
whom much of our knowledge of Tibetan religious history is
derived.

Jing Wokar Drak

From the highway, where it crosses the barren flood plain of the
Jing Valley towards the giant sand dunes on its eastern side, a

rough track turns south (km 105). The village of Jing[17] is reached after an hour's walk, and another one and a half hours takes the pilgrim to the top of a valley to the south-west of the village where Wokar Drak is located. This is a meditation cave of Guru Rimpoche, an important site of hidden treasure, and a power-place where many Nyingma yogins have meditated. The hermitages of Wokar Drak have been destroyed, the site deserted, and only prayer-flags and a spring mark the place. But the virtues of its location are still evident and it is planned to rebuild a lhakang here. The hermitage of Guru Rimpoche was built into a high shallow overhang – there is no natural cave at the site.

Wokar Drak[18] may have been the place mentioned in the Guru's biographies from where he and his consort were transported by the Twelve Goddesses to Shoto Tidro after their exile from Samye. The Dzokchempa Dzeng Dharmabodhi (1052-1169) meditated here and another lineal holder of Dzokchen *semde* and *longde*, the Third Sovereign Treasure-Finder, Dorje Lingpa (1346-1405), discovered a horde of treasures at Wokar Drak. Minling Terchen Gyurme Dorje (p.167) also discovered treasure here. This may be the Yarlung Wokar Drak where Tsongkapa studied the *Samvara* and *Kalacakra-tantras*.

Jasa Lhakang (Bya sa lha khang)

The site of Jasa Lhakang[19] is located at km 119/120 on the south side of the highway and to the west of the village of Jasa, which is close to Tsetang (see map p.172). The Jasa Lhakang was one of the oldest foundations in Tibet, dating from the end of the 9th century. It was renowned for its statue of Nampar Nangdze (Vairocana) whose cult was dominant in Tsang at the beginning of the period of the second propagation of the *dharma* in Tibet. Tucci[20] found the lhakangs in a good state of preservation, and considered that the statues were made during the period of the temple's foundation. The site now consists of small heaps of rubble marked by a *tarchen* pole.

History

The Jasa Lhakang was built by Chogyel Pel Kortsen, the grandson of Emperor Langdarma whose reign saw the destruction of Buddhism by the resurgent Bonpos. Pel Kortsen, the son of Wosung, ruled eastern Tsang at the end of the 9th century after the political fragmentation of Tibet. Jasa was the birthplace of the Dzokchempa Upa Shikpo (1126-95). The Ja Clan produced several notable Lamas in the early period. Kadampa *gelongs* were the temple's custodians before being superceded by the Sakyapas, who retained control until 1959.

10

THE UPPER DRANANG AND
DRACHI VALLEYS

The lower parts of the Drachi and Dranang Valleys and their Sakya Gompas have been described in the itinerary "From Gongkar to Tsetang". The upper reaches of these two valleys (see map p.149) contain power-places of great importance to the Nyingma school. In Dranang are the birthplaces of Longchen Rabjampa, Orgyen Lingpa and Minling Terchen. Longchempa was the most important yogin-scholar of the Nyingma school; Orgyen Lingpa was one of its greatest treasure-finders; and Minling Terchen Gyurme Dorje founded its most important gompa in Central Tibet, Mindroling in Drachi. In the 17th century Old Mindroling, Dargye Choling in Dranang, was superceded as the principal centre of mainstream Nyingma study and meditation by the new establishment in Drachi. Mindroling is being restored as a showpiece monastery

Upper Drachi

The jeep-road to the upper part of the Drachi Valley and to Mindroling leaves the Tsangpo Valley highway at km 79. The Mindroling village and gompa are located 16 km up the valley. Upper Dranang is accessible over a pass to the west and the Chongye Valley over a difficult route to the east.

Mindroling (sMin grol gling): Minling Terchen's Residence

The village of Mindroling is situated in Upper Drachi in the upper part of a rich and fertile side valley. Above the village a paved walkway approaches the original gate of the Mindroling gompa, and here the dressed stonework, forming a patchwork quilt on the walls of ancillary gompa buildings, demonstrates the splendour of old Mindroling. In the stairway inside the gateway are some good murals.

On the west side of the courtyard is a fine three-storey building that was the Minling Terchens' *labrang*. The fabric of this *labrang* was spared destruction, although the building was gutted, and after restoration it now contains the monastery's lhakang and dukang. The principal relic in Mindroling was a statue of Minling Terchen Gyurme Dorje containing his relics; this statue was destroyed, but a new representation of the treasure-finder in his bearded likeness takes pride of place in the lhakang by the altar. A new statue of Sakyamuni is the large central altar-piece. On the left side of the dukang is the gomkang. A locked room on the second storey contains a collection of small statues derived from every century and in varying states of preservation. The printing shop can be seen in operation on the same floor. On the top of the gompa is the room containing the best murals in Mindroling.

The Tsokchen, the great Assembly Hall, has been used by the local commune as a granary for the last twenty years, but it has now been returned to the monastery and is in process of restoration. The murals in the portico reflect a vision of Minling Terchen, and are said to be the only paintings extant as old as the gompa. The interior of the Tsokchen with its murals is in good condition. Behind the Tsokchen is another courtyard where restoration work is proceeding. The buildings on the north side still retain fine murals of the Five Dhyani Buddhas, and although the roof is in a state of decay, in 1985 two hermits were living in constant prayer beneath it.

New monks' quarters on the east side of the main courtyard house thirty-three students ordained during Kyentse Rimpoche's visit in 1985. Unfortunately, as in most "teaching-gompas" in

Tibet today, there are insufficient teachers from the pre-1959 generation to instruct them.

These few buildings are all that remain of the small monastery town that was Mindroling twenty-five years ago. The ruins high above the gompa are those of the retreat centre of the Mindroling monks. A rebuilt chorten at the end of the ridge to the south is a residence of the Protectors of Mindroling. On the face of that ridge the giant legend "Long Live Mao Tse Tung" is depicted in white stones.

History

This most important centre of the Nyingma school in Central Tibet was founded by Minling Terchen ("The Great Treasure-finder of Mindroling"), Pema Garwang Gyurme Dorje (1646-1714), also known as Terdak Lingpa. This prolific discoverer of treasure-texts initiated the lineage of abbots, succeeding each other in patrilineal descent, who ruled Mindroling until 1959.

Minling Terchen Gyurme Dorje was one of the greatest minds to ornament the Nyingma lineages. He was born the son of the incarnate lama of Dargye, and evidently a prodigy at an early age he was ordained by the Great Fifth Dalai Lama. He received comprehensive instruction in *sutra* and *tantra* from his father and other savants of his day. His most important meditation retreat was done at Chimpu. In 1676 he built Mindroling, providing images, scriptures and officials. As a Treasure finder he discovered the Rigdzin Tuktik cycle, Dzokchen treatises, and *sadhanas* of the Wrathful and Peaceful Deities, at Wokar Drak, Shawuk and Yamalung. His treasures formed the basis of the teaching methods of *lhoter*, the Southern Treasure, in contradistinction to *jangter* – Northern Treasure – of Dorje Drak (p.206). But perhaps Minling Terchen's greatest contribution to the Nyingma *dharma* was the compilation of the Nyingma Kama, thirteen volumes of Guru Rimpoche's teaching on the methods of attaining Buddhahood.

In 1718 the monastery was sacked by the Dzungar Mongols. The murals that remain today date from the period of restoration, after this early 18th-century catastrophe.

[11.] [above] MINDROLING: the 17th century *labrang* of Minling Terchen (photograph by *Stone Routes*)
[below] CHOLUNG: formal portrait of the Geluk abbot, four *gelongs* and two *trapas* (photograph by *Stone Routes*)

Upper Dranang

The upper part of the Dranang Valley, the Valley of the Thirteen Buddha-Lamas, is accessible by a jeep-road which leaves the Tsangpo highway at km 76. Dingboche is 14 km, and Yarje Lhakang 18 km, from Dranang Xian. Upper Dranang is also accessible from Drachi and Mindroling over the ridge that divides the two valleys.

Dingboche (sDings po che)

Dingboche gompa was built on a flat-topped spur falling precipitously 300 m to the valley below. That this Drukpa Kagyupa establishment was founded in the 16th century, when Central Tibet was ravaged by civil war and foreign incursion, explains the defensive site and martial aura of a gompa belonging to a school devoted to meditation retreat. At the top of the path that winds up from the village to the southern side of the hill is a reconstructed Namgyel Chorten. Then within the fortified walls are the ruins of a vast Tsokang and other monastic buildings. In 1986 reconstruction had begun and the twenty-five monks in attendance had been provided with *tsamkangs*. Above the gompa on the ridge is a *dzong*, also with extensive walls and fortification.

Dingboche was founded at the end of the 16th century by Rinchen Pelsang, who was a disciple of one of Tibet's great polymaths and the Drukpa Kagyupa's most famous scholar and treasure-finder, Pema Karpo (1526-92), who lived in Bhutan.

Dra Yugang Drak (Grwa gYu sgang brag): A Guru Rimpoche Cave

Yugang Drak, a cave in which Guru Rimpoche meditated, is located in the cliff face behind and above Dingboche. A single monk is in residence. The hermitages that surrounded it have been destroyed. Orgyen Lingpa discovered several treasures here.

Derong Ani Gompa (sTod rong): Longchempa's Birthplace

Derong,[1] the birthplace of Kunkyen Longchen Rabjampa, is located in the broad side-valley to the south-east of Dingboche. It is situated 150 m up the northern side of the valley in a gully where a spring emerges to water a grove of trees. The original Derong Ani Gompa has been destroyed, but in 1986 it was in the process of reconstruction. A house occupied by the Party marks the site.

The Derong Ani Gompa memorializes the birthplace of the Omniscient Longchempa, Kunkyen Longchen Rabjampa, a Second Buddha and pre-eminent scholar of the Nyingma school, who was to systematize the Dzokchen Nyingtik precepts. He was born in his father's family house in 1308. His father belonged to the Rok Clan and was a respected tantric yogin. He taught his son reading and writing, ritual practice of the Peaceful and Wrathful Aspects of the Lama (Lama Shidrak), medicine and astrology. Longchempa left Derong in 1320 for Samye where he took ordination. Thereafter he studied at Sangpu and the principal power-places associated with him are at Samye Chimpu and Gangri Tokar.

Yarje Lhakang (Yar rje lha khang): Orgyen Lingpa's Hermitage

Some 4 km along the jeep-road above Dingboche is the village of Yarje and Yarje Lhakang. The birthplace and residence of Orgyen Lingpa is situated by the river. The original building of this small lhakang has been preserved, and the interior has been restored to its original condition. It is now the residence of a Nyingma *ngakpa*. The design of the building is that of a prosperous villager, although the ground floor is utilized as a lhakang and the upper storey, half exposed to the sky, contains a chamber for retreat and a living-room. It is said to be the place of Orgyen Lingpa's birth. An image of Guru Rimpoche stands at the centre of the altar of the ground floor lhakang and the newly painted murals show a portrait of Orgyen Lingpa. The upper-storey shrine contains a large image of Chenresik Senge Drak,

Chenresik with the Lion's Roar, sitting upon a snow-lion.

Orgyen Lingpa (1323-c.1360) was one of the great treasure-finders (*tertons*) of the 14th century. He discovered texts, images, ritual objects and jewels, chiefly at Shetak, Yugang Drak, and Drachi Drakpoche. Of the 100 texts that were revealed by him, the *Katang Denga* are the most important to have survived. These five volumes chronicling the period of the Emperor Trisong Detsen include the *Pema Katang*, the most authoritative legendary biography of Guru Rimpoche. Orgyen Lingpa was born at Yarje in 1323. His father was a tantric yogin. Although Orgyen Lingpa was also a *tantrika*, to all outward appearances he was a monk – he neither married nor drank alcohol. He was a contemporary of Longchempa, who was born in the same valley, and also of Tai Situ Jangchub Gyeltsen who ruled Tibet from Tsetang, and who persecuted him for his supposed Drigungpa loyalties.

Dargye Choling (Dar rgyas chos gling)

Dargye Choling[2] was built in a spectacular defensive position high on a spur to the west of Yarje Lhakang. Its walls enclose an acre of high density ruins. No reconstruction had begun in 1986 and the site was deserted, not even a lhakang sanctifying the place.

Dargye Choling is also known as Old Mindroling. It was founded in the middle of the 16th century by Tulku Natsok Rangdrol and until Minling Terchen Gyurme Dorje founded Mindroling in Drachi in 1676 it was the most important centre of practice of Dzokchen Nyingtik in Central Tibet. Natsok Rangdrol was an incarnation of Ratna Lingpa, and became learned in all schools but especially in the tradition of Longchempa. He cultivated his Dzokchen view at Chimpu and Shetak in meditation retreat. His successors at Dargye, all of whom transmitted Longchempa's tradition, were Tulku Tendzin Drakpa (1536-97), who was an incarnation of Pema Lingpa; Tulku Dongak Tendzin (1576-1628), the incarnation of Natsok Rangdrol; and Rigdzin Sangdak Trinle Lhundrub, whose son and disciple was Minling Terchen Gyurme Dorje.

11

YARLUNG: THE HEART OF TIBET

The Yarlung Valley was the cradle of Central Tibetan civilization. In this valley the monkey and demoness copulated to produce the first human inhabitants of Tibet. Here in Yarlung the first king of Tibet descended from the sky to land on the top of a sacred hill and establish Tibet's first dynasty. Here in Yarlung Central Tibet first heard news of the Buddha-*dharma*. Here the armies of the great emperors set out to conquer Central Asia, and in nearby Chongye the emperors were buried. A small valley indeed to have formed the nucleus of an immense empire, but the fertility of the land that provided the basis of Yarlung's wealth is still evident, and the few western travellers who reached this obscure corner of the earth in the past have commented on the prosperity and contentment of its people.

Guru Rimpoche meditated in the mountain cave of Shetak and left hordes of treasure there. The translator Bairotsana, Tibet's first Buddhist master, and Milarepa's rebellious disciple Rechungpa, both watched the nature of their minds in Yarlung caves. Great monasteries belonging to all four schools of Tibetan Buddhism were established in Yarlung. In the 14th century under Tai Situ Pakmodrupa, Tibet was again ruled from Yarlung. In the 20th century Tsetang has become the principal city of the Tsangpo Valley.

Access

The Yarlung Valley is one of the many fertile valleys that run into the Tsangpo artery from the south. It is 158 km from

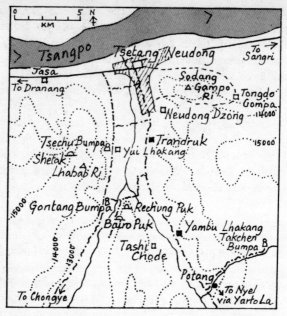

Map 11 The Yarlung Valley

Chaksam, where the Kyichu joins the Tsangpo. The Tsangpo Valley highway, that runs along the river's southern bank, now links Yarlung to Lhasa and Shigatse and also to the provinces of Dakpo, Kongpo and Kham to the east. The ancient, direct route from the Kyichu Valley takes the pilgrim from Dechen Dzong over the Gokar La to Samye and then crossing the Tsangpo down river to Tsetang. The route continues up the Yarlung Valley, over the Yarto La and south to the Indian border.

Tsetang Xian, at the neck of the Yarlung Valley just south of the Tsangpo, is not only Yarlung's principal town it is also the capital of Lhoka Province (the province between the Tsangpo and the Bhutan border) and the largest centre of population in the Tsangpo Valley. It is a garrison, administrative and commercial town and has a considerable Chinese presence. Previously Tsetang guarded the valley entrance and the village of Neudong was a separate entity two to three kilometres up the valley. Now Tsetang/Neudong forms a small conurbation. At Neudong the valley has opened out into a broad plain about 2 km wide, stretching 10 km to the confluence of the Yarlung Chu and the Chongye Chu. The Yarlung Chu is the vital source of most of the valley's water. It is said that in ancient times Yarlung was the most prosperous valley in Tibet, even more fertile than it is today, but an extraordinary monsoon brought a disastrous flood down from Yarlha Shampo mountain, destroying the villages and drowning the people. When the lake so formed subsided the valley floor was covered with infertile detritus.

"Three Sanctuaries, Three Chortens" (gNas gsum rten gsum)

The circular Yarlung pilgrimage includes six chief destinations — three sanctuaries (nesum) and three chortens (tensum). Kyentse Rimpoche's three sanctuaries are the Shetak cave, Trandruk gompa, and either Rechung Puk cave or Yambu Lhakang palace — he admits controversy over the third site. The three chortens are the Takchen, Gontang and Tsechu Bumpas. Lama Tsenpo[1] lists the same three chortens, and then Trandruk, Yambu Lhakang and the Tsentang Yui Lhakang — Shetak is added in a separate cave category. Chandra Das[2] gives an idiosyncratic list of the nesum tensum: Shetak, Trandruk, Takchen Bumpa, Rechung Puk, Sangri Karmar (p.246), and the Tsentang Yui Lhakang. Apart from Rechung Puk and the Takchen Bumpa, the precise ages of which are unknown, all the power-places mentioned in these lists belong to the first period of propagation of the dharma in Tibet (7th-9th century) and they are all of renown.

The Yarlung nekor is traditionally performed clockwise from Tsetang. To begin, the circumambulation of Sodang Gangpo Ri takes a full day. The route then passes through Trandruk and Yambu Lhakang to the Takchen Bumpa, all on the east side of the valley. From Rechung Puk, at the confluence of the two rivers, to Gontang Bumpa in the mouth of the Chongye Valley, it then passes to Tsechu Bumpa and Shetak on the west side of the Yarlung Valley. From Rechung Puk the pilgrim can travel south-west up the Chongye Valley to the tombs of the kings near Chongye Qu and to other Chongye shrines. On foot this entire circuit can take as much as two weeks.

Tsetang (rTse thang)

Nothing remains of the four gompas that constituted the larger part of Tsetang in 1959. The Yellow Hat gompas of Ganden Chokorling and Ngacho, and the Sakya gompas of Samten Ling and Drebuling, have all vanished beneath the modern town. However, facing north-west between two major spurs of Sodang Gangpo Ri, is a small, reconstructed Geluk Ani Gompa lying in the field of ruins that was Samten Ling.

History

The foundation of Tsetang is attributed to Pakmodrupa Tai Situ Jangchub Gyeltsen in 1351, when he built the Tsetang Gompa that became an academy with an eclectic base. Sustaining a strong link with Densatil, but attracting scholars of different schools, Tsetang became an important centre of learning. The growth of Tsetang and the importance of this gompa were a function of the Pakmodrupas' temporal power at Neudong Dzong.

The Sakya gompa of Samten Ling was founded in the vicinity before Tai Situ's Tsetang Gompa. Lama Dampa Sonam Gyeltsen (1312-75) (p.136), a teacher of Tsongkapa, was associated with it contemporaneously with Tai Situ Pakmodrupa. As a holder of the Tsarpa lineage of the Sakyapas, Senge Gyeltsen, a disciple of Sonam Gyeltsen, brought renown to Samten Ling.

Sodang Gangpo Ri (Zo dang gangs po ri): Yarlung's Mountain Protector

This mountain, situated to the east of Tsetang, is one of the four sacred mountains of Central Tibet. Its spurs protect the town from the elements and create a defensible nexus at the valley's mouth. It rises some 800 m above the town. Sodang Gangpo Ri is the residence of Yarlha Shampo, the powerful mountain god who is one of the most ancient divinities of the country, at once the apotheosis and nemesis of Yarlung. However, the principal residence of Yarlha Shampo is on the peak of that name at the head of the Yarlung Valley where the Yarlung Chu rises.

The Sodang Gangpo Ri *korra*, starting in Tsetang, crosses the northern spurs of the mountain and passes the ruined *Tongdo Gompa before climbing up to a low pass at its eastern extremity. On the southern side the path passes by Chenresik's Cave, and the cavern called Tubpa Serlingma.

Cave of the Monkey Bodhisattva
According to legend, the most ancient site in Tibet, the place where the race originated, is the cave where Chenresik, incarnate as a red monkey, copulated with a *sinmo*, a white ogress, and conceived the first men of the Tibetan race. The six sons produced by this union were the ancestors of the six original clans to populate Tibet. Telgom Jangchub Sempa, Meditating Bodhisattva Monkey, was the name of Chenresik's simian *tulku* emanation. Monkeys, unknown on the Tibetan plateau, are seen as only one step below man on the evolutionary scale of karma. The *sinmo*, ogress or cannibal-demoness, can be conceived as either corporeal or incorporeal – here she is evidently the former. She is nasty, brutish, malicious, jealous and hubristic. Thus, in the cave on Sodang Gangpo Ri we have the Bodhisattva of Compassion, the Protector of Tibet, self-sacrificially dedicated to the enlightenment of Tibet, incarnate as a monkey and mating – out of compassion – with a savage but powerful female.

Tubpa Serlingma (Thub pa gser gling ma)
The cave of Tubpa Serlingma served as the Assembly Hall for the monks of the Tsetang Ngacho gompa.

Neudong Dzong (sNe'u gdong rdzong): The Pakmodrupa Citadel

To the south-west of Sodang Gangpo Ri is the site of the Pakmodrupa palace. Tai Situ Pakmodrupa ruled Central Tibet and Tsang from this palace during the 14th and 15th centuries. The site of Neudong Dzong has been empty for more than 150 years.

History

Known also as Kunsang Tse, Neudong Dzong is associated primarily with Tai Situ Pakmodrupa Jangchub Gyeltsen (1302-73). This outstanding figure on the stage of Tibetan history belonged to the family of Drogon Pakmodrupa Dorje Gyelpo (1110-70), the disciple of Gampopa and the founder of Densatil and its Pakmodrupa Kagyu school. As local myriarch (ruling the district established by the Mongols) Jangchub Gyeltsen was the man to appear in the hour of Sakya weakness in the early 14th century and from a humble position re-establish kingship in Central Tibet. From his base at Neudong, in two decades he defeated the Sakya forces based at Gongkar and then later at their headquarters in Tsang. Pakmodrupa power lasted until the 15th century when Neudong Dzong was captured by the Prince of Tsang, patron of the Karma Kagyupas. Although one of Tibet's greatest yogins was a Pakmodrupa and part of the family was strictly Kagyupa, the kings at Neudong appear to have been first Kadampa and later Gelukpa, so that finally they were to suffer at the hands of the Kagyupas of Tsang. The succession of abbots at Tsetang Gompa and of kings at Neudong was determined on the principle of uncle to nephew descent.

Neudong Tse Tsokpa (sNe'u gdong rTse tshogs pa)

This Sakya gompa was situated at the foot of the hill of Neudong Dzong, and close to the Yarlung river. No trace remains of it. Sakyasri, the Great Pandita from Kashmir (1145-1243), founded Tse Tsokpa and the other three of his Four Communities (Tsongdu Tsokpa in Drachi, Gyeling Tsokpa in Dranang and

Cholung Tsokpa in Tsang north of Gyangtse) during his visit to Central Tibet from 1204 to 1213. The principal relic in this gompa was a clay statue called the Talking Kache Panchen.

Namgyel Lhakang (rNam rgyal lha khang)
This small lhakang is reputed to be the place where Tsongkapa received his final ordination. It was attached to Tse Tsokpa, and stood to the south of it near Trandruk. We were unable to locate it and assume its destruction.

Trandruk (Khra' 'brug): The Emperor Songtsen Gampo's Gompa

The temple complex of Trandruk lies on the eastern side of Trandruk village 5 km south of Tsetang. A temple was built at Trandruk by the Emperor Songtsen Gampo in the 7th century to enshrine a self-manifest statue of Drolma, which vanished long ago. In the 8th century it was one of the Emperor Trisong Detsen's three chief foundations. The wooden buildings that survived the Cultural Revolution represent a style of architecture current in the Kadampa centuries.

Apart from the Dukang the gompa buildings at Trandruk were preserved from destruction during the Cultural Revolution. But use of the remaining parts as Party offices, storehouses and residences, together with rot and subsidence permitted by a pervasive indifference, have left them in such bad state of repair that it is doubtful that the authorities have the knowledge and skill to restore them. The magnificent courtyard within the main gate is surrounded by wooden frame buildings that indicate great age, although it is difficult to date them precisely. The temple's plan of gateway, courtyard and lhakang is similar to that of the Lhasa Jokang, and if the vanished Dukang at the eastern side of the complex replicated the Lhasa Jokang then the belief that Trandruk is a small scale copy of the Jokang is probably true. The small dukang in the south-east wing of the gompa has not been restored. In 1985 the new lhakang in the south-east corner of the monastery complex housed the few images saved from the old temple, together with several important statues from other vanished gompas of the Yarlung Valley. A covered wall to the right of this lhakang protects some interesting slates engraved with Buddhas and *siddhas*. At the end of this wall is a storeroom containing Trandruk's famous Dhyani Buddha statues. In 1986 construction of the new Tsokang was not completed.

Kyentse Rimpoche called the principal lhakang Tashi Jamnyom. He mentions the famous 7th-century statues of the Five Dhyani Buddhas and the precious statue of Drolma who consumed her offerings (Drolma Shesema) as the chief objects of worship at Trandruk. The large stone statues of the Dhyani Buddhas, believed to date from Songtsen Gampo's time, have suffered serious mutilation, but although their heads and most of their limbs are missing they are still suitably venerated. The Drolma Shesema has vanished.

In the new lhakang in the south-east corner of the complex, the central image, behind glass, is Padmapani, depicted in pearls and mother-of-pearl. To Padmapani's right is a remarkable Talking Menlha, the Medicine Buddha. To his left is the Talking Guru Rimpoche known as Ngadrama, affirmed as his own likeness by Guru Rimpoche himself, which was brought from Shetak when that hermitage was destroyed. This powerful and beautiful 60 cm image of the young Pema Jungne with extraordinary piercing eyes, holding a *dorje* at his heart, done in gilt bronze, is capable of answering devotees' questions; it was the chief object of worship at Shetak. On the wall to the right is a small bronze of Pelden Lhamo brought from Sangak Choling Gompa. Also now preserved at Trandruk are a small statue of Drolma drawn by Sakya Pandita, a Sixteen Arhat *tanka* from Milarepa's era, and some small images and chortens sent back from China by the Panchen Lama.

The lhakang that probably marks the site of Songtsen Gampo's first temple at Trandruk is located in a lane to the south of the drive that leads from the road to the gompa gate. This small two-storey structure housed famous images of the Emperor Songtsen Gampo and his queens. Its fine murals are still partially visible. The ground floor lhakang, still containing some important relics, was the sole functioning temple in the entire complex in 1985, and a *gelong* who remembered pre-1959 Trandruk presided there. The upper-storey lhakang was empty in 1985, but it, also, contained remnants of fine murals.

In 1959 the U Ngama (also mGo lnga), a central chorten surrounded by four smaller ones, stood south of the temple compound. The village now covers this area. The U Ngama chortens, like Trandruk gompa itself, were repositories of Guru Rimpoche's treasure.

History

Trandruk was founded by Songtsen Gampo (r.627-50). Tibet's first Buddhist king had it constructed to protect a self-manifest image of Drolma, but it is counted amongst the king's twelve principal temples built to pinion the Demoness who is Tibet (p.287), and to convert the Yarlungpas to the Buddha-*dharma*. In the 8th century Trandruk was one of the Emperor Trisong Detsen's three chief monasteries, together with the Lhasa Jokang and Samye. Guru Rimpoche lived here with Yeshe Tsogyel, and both Guru and consort concealed several major treasures. The gompa must have been destroyed during the period of Bon reaction in the 9th century and rebuilt during the renaissance of Buddhism. The present structure probably dates from the 14th century, but Trandruk was restored by the seventh Dalai Lama in the 18th century, and since that time the temple has been controlled by the Yellow Hats.

Sakya Pandita's Throne (Sa pan kyi zhugs khri)

South of Trandruk, on the road to Yambu Lhakang, Kyentse Rimpoche locates the preaching-throne of the great Sakya hierarch, Sakya Pandita. We could not find it. It may have been a man-made artefact, a self-manifest rock or perhaps a mountain prominence.

Yambu Lhakang ('Om bu lha khang): Tibet's First Palace

Ascending the Yarlung Valley, some 4 km above the confluence of the Yarlung and Chongye rivers, a 100 m high spur juts into the valley from its eastern side. Visible from as far away as the

Tsechu Bumoche, the palace and lhakang of Yambu Lhakang[3] stands in isolated prominence. This is Tibet's oldest building and first palace.

Built in a fine defensive position like a *dzong*, the Yambu Lhakang is essentially a three-storey, 50 m by 30 m rectangular structure, with a stairway and portico at its west end and a four-storey tower at its east end. It is certainly not the palace that the first king of Tibet, Nyatri Tsenpo, built, and it is not the building that stood there in 1959 – it was reduced to a single storey during the Cultural Revolution. The mixture of Indian and Tibetan architectural styles and the ancient stairway and portico that were identifiable before 1959 are no longer evident. Today the Yambu Lhakang is a white-washed stone building un-remarkable but for its tower, now unique in Tibet – during the empire period a network of similar watch-towers is believed to have covered the country.

The ground floor lhakang contains images of the Buddhist kings of Tibet, their queens and ministers: (from left to right) Tonmi Sambhota who devised the Tibetan alphabet; Emperor Trisong Detsen; King Lhatotori who received the *sutra* that fell upon the palace roof in the 3rd century; the Ombu Jowo Norbu Sampel; the first king of Tibet, Nyatri Tsenpo; the first emperor, Songtsen Gampo, and his consorts Bhrikuti and Wencheng; the last Buddhist Emperor, Repachen; Wosung, a Protector; and Songtsen Gampo's minister Lompo Gar. These images were made recently in Lhasa, demonstrating that despite a missing generation of craftsmen the skill has not been lost. In the upper storey, in the main Pakpa Lhakang, the principal image on the altar is of Tsepame (Amitayus), the Buddha of Long-life. On his right is a statue of Jampa that was hidden during the Cultural Revolution and thus preserved. A sandalwood image of Chenresik that had been cut into pieces has now been reassembled and installed here, together with cases of small old bronzes. The newly painted murals are interesting. One wall represents the legendary history of Yarlung: particularly, the coming of the first king, Nyatri Tsenpo, and his installation in the Yambu Lhakang,

[12.] [above right] YARLUNG: The Yambu Lhakang, "Tibet's Oldest Building", a 3rd century palace (photograph by R. Demandre) [main illustration, left] CHONGYE: The emperors' tombs, the Bangso Marpo with lhakang on top (photograph by *Stone Routes*) [below right] CHONGYE: The 8th century royal lion on top of Repachen's tomb (photograph by *Stone Routes*)

and Guru Rimpoche's visit and his meditation at Shetak. Another wall shows the Eight Forms of Guru Rimpoche, and in these depictions it becomes clear that in the Tibetans' minds Guru Rimpoche is a composite, transcendental Guru, as well as an historical figure. Another series of murals depicts Sakyamuni and his forms of manifestation. On either side of the main door are Yarlung's Protectors, Pelden Lhamo and Yarlha Shampo. Kyentse Rimpoche mentions the Ombu Protector Nyenpo Sangwa, whose name was unknown to the monks in residence in 1985.

The tower has three small rooms, and King Nyatri Tsenpo is reputed to have meditated in one of them. Restoration of the tower was still unfinished in 1986. The rooms on the north side of the building provide accommodation for the five or six Nyingma monks in residence. Encircling the building is a path for circumambulation where Guru Rimpoche hid treasure. On the very end of the spur is an ancient chorten that has been reconstructed.

History
Although legend tells us that Yambu Lhakang was built in prehistoric times for the first king of the first dynasty of kings in Yarlung, documentation first associates the 3rd-century king Lhatotori with this palace. In Lhatotori's reign knowledge of the Buddha-*dharma* first arrived in Tibet, when the *Karandhavyuha-sutra*, a text relating to the mythos of the Bodhisattva of Compassion, Chenresik, fell upon the palace roof together with other Buddhist artefacts. This Sanskrit text was indecipherable at the time, but a prophecy accompanied the treasure predicting that it would be translated after five generations. It was indeed translated by Tonmi Sambhota at the time of Songtsen Gampo. Some Tibetan authorities believe that Lhatotori was the first King to propagate the basic doctrines of Buddhism and to enforce the ten virtues as a legal code, but this would seem unlikely, particularly as histories give the Emperor Songtsen Gampo that honour four hundred years later. The legend of Lhatotori probably indicates that Buddhist missionaries penetrated the Tibetan plateau and the outer darkness of Yarlung with the Buddha's message as early as the third century. If Lhatotori built the Yambu Lhakang it is unlikely that the later kings inhabited

it. It was the Tibetan tradition for each powerful king to build a new palace, since it was considered unlucky to live in a building inhabited by one's forebears. So this palace is more a symbol of Tibet's prehistory and the early dynasties than a habitation of the emperors.

Lhakang Nyenru (Lha khang gnyan ru): Medicine Buddha Temple

We could not locate this two-storey Geluk lhakang dedicated to Menlha, the Medicine Buddha. If the villagers were reluctant for us to visit the shrine it would be the only instance of such an attitude on our entire pilgrimage. Other travellers have asserted that the temple still stands. At Shetak and Yambu Lhakang we were told that the temple was miraculously preserved from the Red Guards. The principal image in Lhakang Nyenru[4] was a revealed treasure. There were eight forms of Menlha in this lhakang.

"Near Lharu is what is traditionally called the first field to be cultivated in Tibet."[5]

Chogyel Potang (Chos rgyal pho brang)

Also known as Potang Dzong, this village lies just beyond the turn to Takchen, about 4 km beyond Yambu Lhakang. It is said to be the oldest village in Tibet, the birthplace of a certain ancient dynasty from which in 1894 the village headman claimed descent.

Takchen Bumpa (rTag spyan bum pa)

The Takchen Bumpa, the first of the three famous chortens of Yarlung, is located on a pass on the old path to Eyul in the east. A jeep-road leaves the Yarlung Valley just south of Potang and follows the course of the river valley for several kilometres to Takchen village. The chorten was damaged during the Cultural Revolution, but it has been fully restored. On a very ancient pattern this chorten has a dome-shaped bumpa and steps in its side leading to a window close to the top of the dome. Within the window a lamp burns for the faithful.

Takchen Bumoche is the name of the small Drukpa Kagyu gompa that stands by the chorten. The chief blessing-bestowing relic is a piece of ossified excrement believed to have been passed by Gotsangpa, the renowned Drukpa Kagyu yogin. Some dozen monks are now in residence at the gompa.

History

"Takchen" is a contraction of Taktu-ngui Chenyon, the Left Eye of the Bodhisattva Sadaprarudita, "Always Weeping", and the chorten enshrines the left eye of the renowned Indian *prajna-paramita* practitioner Sadaprarudita, whose name is well-known to Tibetan monks. Sadaprarudita is said to have taught the Indian *pandita* Asanga, who initiated the Mind-Only school of meta-physics, so Sadaprarudita must have lived in the 2nd or 3rd centuries. Sadaprarudita's tears were shed at the truth and beauty of the *prajnaparamita* teaching. A Kadampa establishment stood near here in the 12th century and Nyak Lotsawa was the abbot. The chorten was built during his period of office by his disciple Geshe Korchen who belonged to the lineage of Neuzurpa.

Yarlha Shampo Gangi Rawa (Yar lha sham po gangs kyi ra ba)

Kyentse Rimpoche includes Yarlha Shampo Gangi Rawa in the Yarlung Valley circuit and locates it above Takchen Bumoche. However, the peak and massif that dominates Yarlung from afar, appearing from the vantage point of Shetak as a snow-walled fortress of the gods, and frequently possessing a cloud-cap that gives it an enigmatic and ethereal look, is the massif to the south of the entire Yarlung Valley. The central peak of this massif, Yarlha Shampo itself (approx. 7,000 m) is one of the mountains that Lama Tsenpo[6] likened to a crystal stupa.

Yarlha Shampo is one of the four chief mountain gods of Tibet. When Guru Rimpoche arrived in Tibet this important Bonpo deity manifested as a white yak to obstruct him and caused snow to fall upon him. Guru Rimpoche subjected him and bound him to serve the Buddha-*dharma* as a Protector.

History
Drokmi Pelgyi Yeshe, one of Guru Rimpoche's Twenty-four Disciples, is said to have performed the *sadhana* of Mamo Botong on Yarlha Shampo in the 8th century. Mamo is the principal deity of the mandala of the wrathful female Protectresses who dominated the hearts and minds of Bon Tibet. They were mountain and pass goddesses, fearsome elemental forces.

Tashi Chode (bKra shis chos sde)

The important Sakya gompa that was situated on the western side of the Yarlung Valley, opposite Yambu Lhakang, and some 3 km from Rechung Puk, is now but acres of ruins. No one had returned by 1985 to reconsecrate this power-place. It was founded by Yolwo Shonnu Lodro, a disciple of the founder of the Tsarpa lineage, in the mid-16th century. Tashi Chode gained renown as an academy of high learning.

Rechung Puk (Ras chung phug): Rechungpa's Cave

The site of the gompa at Rechung Puk is situated between 50 m and 200 m above the confluence of the Yarlung and Chongye rivers. Its prominence on the roman nose of the ridge, and the acute angle at which the valleys converge, give this power-place an extraordinary geomantic setting and provide avenues of vision along three valleys. One path approaches it directly up the ridge while the main path zig-zags up the Yarlung side from the large model commune-village of Rechung that lies in geometrical order below.

Red Guards' dynamite revealed the vast foundations that a large building constructed on a precipitous slope requires. Walls 2 m thick rose 10 m before a level plane was achieved to form a floor for the lhakang and a courtyard for the gompa. Since the ruins run down the ridge it appears that the gompa faced north, but in fact it had the desirable eastern aspect, and it is on the eastern, Yarlung side that rebuilding has begun. The cave of Rechungpa itself, below and to the south of the old dukang, was the first to receive attention. The cave is a mere walled-in rock overhang, forming an L-shaped lhakang where a young Nyingma-Kagyu presides. A larger lhakang is in process of completion a few metres to the south. On the same level a kitchen and several small cells have been built for the *anis* who form the Lama's community. Fifteen metres above the cave is a terrace of five new meditation cells built into the near vertical rock face. Behind and above the ruins of the dukang, where dynamite merely blew out small holes in the vast walls that still stand 10 m high and more, a single new hermitage had appeared in 1985. On the Chongye side, one of the lower structures is a chorten that somehow escaped destruction.

In Rechungpa's cave, on the altar in the recess, is an image of Guru Rimpoche, indication of the resident Lama's school. Five tiers of small bronze images, several of them portraits of Kagyu Lamas, some of them covered with the verdigris of interment, are displayed beneath the Guru's image. An impressive 45 cm high bronze chorten stands on the same altar. Rechungpa's silver reliquary has vanished.

History

If the three valleys radiating from Rechung Puk are conceived as three radial spokes defining a circle of three equal segments, the ridges surrounding the Yarlung and Chongye Valleys being the circumference of this circle, Rechung Puk is at the centre of a mandala. Although this power-place must have been recognized and its power-potential realized long before the 13th century, the *siddha*-yogin whose name finally adhered to it after his prolonged residence there in a cave was Je Rechungpa Dorje Drak (1083-1161). Rechungpa was the most renowned disciple of the yogin-ascetic Milarepa. Rechungpa, the Lightly-clad, sustained his Guru's habit of wearing white cotton cloth, establishing a tradition of Tibetan yogins dressed in cotton, called *repas*.

Born in the village of Kab in Gungtang Rechungpa met his

master in his homeland when he was eleven years old and suffering the persecution of an unsympathetic step-father. At the age of fifteen he contracted leprosy, which he cured through mantra. Thereafter he travelled in Nepal and India, where he studied with the *siddha* Tipuba, receiving one of his major yoga cycles – The Spiritual Dakini – associated with his chief field of practice, the *Demchok-tantra*. Only later did he travel in Central Tibet where Bepo Asu taught him how to beg – one of the many maturing experiences he received under the Nepali master-yogin's tutelage. In Yarlung, where he stayed at this spot, he had the chastening experience of an unfaithful consort, who came of noble birth, and in his disappointment he fled to Shampo Gang. Later, he taught Ratna Lingpa.

The other major figure associated with Rechung Puk is Tsangnyon Heruka (1452-1507). Tsangnyon was born in Nyangto (p.000), and like the treasure-finder Rechungpa he was an inspired writer, most particularly a biographer (his detailed life of Milarepa was commonly believed to have been composed by Rechungpa). His biographies of Marpa and Milarepa are two Tibetan classics, no less impressive in their style and poetry than in their profound insight. Both Rechungpa and Tsangnyon were considered crazy, the latter formally so, Tsangnyon meaning "The Crazy Tsangpa". Rechungpa was introverted, whereas Tsangnyon was excitable and demonstrative – he was expelled from the Sakya gompa where he studied after insulting his royal patron. Both were peripatetic when they were not in contemplative retreat. Tsangnyon travelled to Nepal several times and became well-known there in Kagyu circles. Both were imitators of Milarepa's life-style. Tsangnyon, like Rechungpa, was an initiate of Milarepa's Cakrasamvara lineage. He died at Rechung Puk at the young age of fifty-four. He was a contemporary of Druknyon Kunga Lekpa.

Bairo Puk (Bairo phug): Bairotsana's Cave

Bairotsana's cave is located 1 km up the Chongye Valley on its eastern side. It is situated to the left of a dry waterfall about

50 m up a gully. The prayer-flags surrounding the cave opening are visible from the road from Rechung. Half way up the gully is the rare phenomenon of hundreds of small rock shrines, altars constructed with four rocks – sides, back and roof – built by pilgrims in an acre of open space. The cave itself is 3 m deep and faces a ledge by the waterfall. It contains only a few tsatsa, mani-stones and pilgrims' tokens – and to judge by the evidence of these tokens it is a popular local power-place.

History

Bairotsana (Vairocana) was a Dzokchempa, a Tibetan disciple of the Central Asian Guru Sri Singha who he met in Orgyen, and also of Guru Rimpoche. He attained a status in Tibet superior to any of the other Twenty-four Disciples of the Guru. He was born in Tsang at Nyemo Jeke (p. 130) into the Pagor family. However, according to a local tradition Pagor is located in the Chongye Valley, and because he spent much of his life meditating and teaching in this area the Yarlungpas consider Bairotsana one of themselves. He was chosen by the Emperor Trisong Detsen to learn the art of Sanskrit translation, and after taking ordination under Santaraksita amongst the first seven Tibetan monks he became one of the great translators of the early period. His principal original contribution was of the Mind Section (*semde*) of Dzokchen precepts. He was also a concealer of treasure-texts (*terma*).

Kyentse Rimpoche omits reference to Bairo Puk but mentions Rokpatsa which must be identical to Yarlung Rokpasa where Padampa Sangye meditated and gave instruction in Shije Chod to Machik Labdron and others. Rokpasa may be identified with Bairo Puk.

Gontang Bumpa (dGon thang 'bum pa)

The Gontang (or Guntang) Bumpa is situated at the middle of the entrance to the fertile, flowering Chongye Valley, by the Chongye Chu, at a tangent to Bairo's cave.

The Gontang Bumpa guards the entrance to the Yarlung

Valley. Chortens frequently protect the approaches to a valley or village, keeping demons and hostile forces at bay. About 8 m high with one outer retaining wall remaining, the shape of the original structure of the Bumpa is evident, but the rubble from its dome still gives it the appearance of a large heap of debris. Ditches 1.5 m deep on three sides give the impression that its fallen earth and stone has been recently re-heaped. On its southern and eastern sides fine engraved-slate carvings of *siddhas* and *panditas* are to be found. The village commune has built a People's Temple to the south of the chorten where two lay practitioners live. The lower storey houses a lhakang, while the upper storey is residential.

Sri Chobumpa and Netso (Sri gcod 'bum pa dang Ne tsho 'bum pa)

The sites of these two ruined chortens are located on the west side of the Chongye Valley not far from the Gontang Bumpa. It is possible that a sanctuary once stood in the valley behind them, giving their site more significance. Originally considerably smaller than the Gontang Bumpa they have been destroyed almost to ground level. The Sri Chod Bumpa is also called Kondum. The Netso Bumpa is said to have been founded by King Lhade in a pre-historical period.

Lhabab Ri (Lha bab ri): The First King's Place of Descent

Lhabab Ri[7] is the highest of three hill-tops on a long spur descending from the southern horn of the Shetak amphitheatre into the Yarlung Valley. Paths ascend the hill from both north and south sides. The summit is visible from the road. Lhabab Ri means "God-descending Hill", and it is here that Yarlung's first king, Nyatri Tsenpo, descended from heaven. The Bonpos believed that a "sky-cord" connected heaven and earth, and since this cord was used by the kings to ascend to heaven at the end of their lives it may have been the origin of the notion of an initial descent. Carried down the hill on the shoulders of Tibetans who recognized Nyatri Tsenpo's divine provenance and his purpose, he was called "Neck-enthroned". The Buddhists modified the legend to include the idea of a flight from the ancient state of the Licchavis in present day Bihar, attributing a Sakya ancestry to him, and a claim of descent from Sakyamuni Buddha.

When the Tibetans were ruled by twelve petty demon chieftains, a child with hooded eye-lids and webbed fingers (marks of a Buddha) was born to the Indian king of Vatsa, who out of fear had the child entombed in a lead box and thrown into the Ganga. A peasant rescued him and reared him, until in grief the young prince fled to the Himalayas, and having passed over Lhabab Ri he descended to the Tsentang Goshi where he declared himself a king (tsenpo) and where he was recognized by the Bon priests as a divine gift to them. They built a wooden throne for four men to carry on their shoulders and thus he received the name "Neck-enthroned" (Nyatri).[8] The murals of Yambu Lhakang depict the king's arrival and life in that palace. The Tibetans place these events many centuries before the birth of the Buddha. It is probable that this legend refers to the evolution of the Yarlung kingship out of a primitive system of rule by clan elders sometime in the centuries after the Buddha's birth.

Previously there was a lhakang on Lhabab Ri. This may have been the Tsentang Goshi Lhakang, the Four-doored Temple of the King's Fields.

The Shetak Dundro

The Shetak *dundro* is located on the path to Shetak, some 300 m higher than the deserted village of *Sekang Shika. The chorten on the site is visible from afar.[9] The old custodian of Shetak assured us that he himself had rebuilt this chorten on its original spot. In front of the chorten is a remarkable large stone slab where the corpse-cutters (*rogyapas*) do their work.

The 5 m high chorten is dedicated to Tamdrin, the Horse-necked Deity, who is a personification of the Buddha's Throat-chakra. An ephemeral horse-head effigy protrudes from the chorten's top and another appears in the window in the dome's south side. Tamdrin, an Indian Buddhist deity and the wrathful form of Chenresik, had various elements of the pre-Buddhist horse-cult attached to him, thus preserving them. In the base-wall of the chorten is a window containing devotees' token offerings such as hair and articles of clothing. Knives used for the dismemberment of bodies were scattered around the stone slab in front of the chorten. The entire site is festooned with prayer-flags. However it is apparent that this is not a frequently used site.

Shetak (Shel brag): Guru Rimpoche's Crystal Cave

At the top of the Shetak valley, a hard five hour walk from the Tsechu Bumpa, is an amphitheatre of ridges which is part of Padma Tsek Ri. On the north side is a phallic peak of some 5,500 m and Guru Rimpoche's cave is located at the base of this peak. The path leading to it winds around the contours on the opposite side of the half circle, crossing the streams that run down the precipitous walls of the basin, before climbing steeply up the final 100 m of the rock face to reach it. This is a paradigm of the "eagle's nest" hermitage. It commands the entire Yarlung Valley. The amphitheatre-ridge provides the sense of a mandala while offering protection to a site at a height that normally would receive the full force of the elements. Shetak is one of the five most sacred and efficacious power-places of the Nyingma school, the Power-place of the Guru's Qualities. All the buildings on this site were destroyed during the Cultural Revolution, but an ancient Yarlungpa has taken care of the cave for the last few years, and a Khampa Lama is now in charge of restoration.

The Guru's cave itself is a walled-in overhang about 3 m deep, while the recess containing the altar is 1.5 m high and the same distance in width. The cave-front is some 4 m wide and 2 m high. It faces east. A flight of steps leads down the rock face to what was originally the Upper Temple, the Guru Tsengye Lhakang, the Shrine of the Guru's Eight Forms. This temple fell in on itself so that the ground floor of the two-storey structure is filled in to its ceiling and now forms the floor of a simple lean-to and store-room built by the Khampa Lama in residence. Nearby is a small lhakang about 3 m square built on the site of a hermitage. The Netil Labrang, of which nothing remains, must have been located to the north of the Tsengye Lhakang. A stream issuing from the side of the Shetak peak, reached by descending 50 m, provides the residents of the upper hermitages with water; plentiful water nearby is a potent blessing for these monks. Where the path crosses the streams 100 m below is the site of the original Shetak gompa. The main lhakang was modest in size and the monks' quarters were small hermitages built into the cliff face behind it. About fifty married monks lived there and also many yogins immured in caves to practise yoga in situations of optimal sensory deprivation.

The most precious image at Shetak was the Guru Rimpoche Sungjonma, the Talking Guru, now housed at Trandruk. Today there is a new and unremarkable image of Guru Rimpoche on the altar and another of Drolma. The silver reliquary containing an image of the Guru as a twelve-year-old boy has vanished. As the most sacred artefacts remaining in the sanctuary the custodian produced a crystal ball and a skull cup. Inside and to the right of the door, in the rock of the roof, is a small footprint attributed to Yeshe Tsogyel, the Guru's consort. Kyentse Rimpoche remarks upon an image of Orgyen Rimpoche in the Netil Labrang with "his (own original) monastic robe resplendent like the sun". His staff was also kept there, but with the image and the robe it has vanished. The small new Lhakang near the old Tsengye Lhakang has several new images on its altar.

History

The power-place of Shetak is a site well-endowed with geomantic power, but it is so inaccessible that it is unlikely to have been developed until meditation retreat provided motivation. Probably it is a purely Buddhist site. With Samye Chimpu and Drak Yerpa it gained its great significance during the first period of propagation of the Buddha-*dharma* in Tibet. Guru Rimpoche visited it to exorcise and subject the Bon spirits, gods and demons of the area and to bind their power to Buddhist yogins. Later he returned to conceal hordes of treasure, mostly in Padma Shepuk. His consort, Yeshe Tsogyel, was in retreat here during the late 8th or early 9th centuries and also concealed treasure here. During this same period the Thirty Siddha-magicians (*ngakpas*) of Shetak are mentioned as achieving renown for their magical powers accomplished through mantra. In the Nyingma revival of the 14th century the important treasure-finder Orgyen Lingpa (p.170) was associated with Shetak. In the 17th century Minling Terchen discovered treasures in Padma Shepuk. Shetak has remained a hermitage site of universal renown up to the present time.

Tsogyel Sangpuk (mTsho rgyal gsang phug): Tsogyel's Secret Cave

Shetak was one of Yeshe Tsogyel's favorite places of meditation. Her secret cave was identified to us as an untended rock cave on the wall of the amphitheatre directly across from the Tsengye Lhakang to the south. We did not investigate this spot. There is another "secret cave" 15 m above the bridge by the old gompa.

Padma Shepuk (Padma shel phug): Shetak's Treasure-cave

We received directions to this power-place, called the Crystal Grotto, most vital in the Nyingma tradition, from the Shetak custodian. It is accessible from the path that runs around the Shetak peak and then along and behind the ridge to the north and north-east. It is also accessible by a path that climbs the same ridge from the valley below.

Guru Rimpoche practised the rites of Dudtsi Men, Ambrosia-Panacea, in Shepuk and left a significant horde of treasure-texts there. Orgyen Lingpa discovered some of them in the statue of Rahu that guarded the door to the cave. His most popular revelation was the *Padma Katang*, our chief source of information regarding the Guru's life and the early period of propagation of the *dharma* in Tibet.

Tsechu Bumpa (Tshe chu 'bum pa)

The Tsechu Bumpa is located behind the village of *Kato at the entrance of the valley that leads up to Shetak. It is 5-6 km from the Gontang Bumpa. This is the third of the *tensum* chortens.

The Bumpa's condition is no better nor worse than the other two major chortens of Yarlung, the Gontang and Takchen Bumpas. The area it covers is large, as the original base was about 50 m square, and it is some 12 m high. It is surrounded by many miniature votive stone chortens – three or four stones piled one on the other. A few slate-engravings have been reinstalled in prominent places.

History

Known also as the Chokro Tsechu Bumpa,[10] legend has it that the renowned translator Chokro Lui Gyeltsen gave the Emperor Trisong Detsen an Indian image of rock-crystal that was installed as the heart of the Bumpa. Thus Tsechu Bumpa was built in the 8th century. Kyentse Rimpoche reports that on the day of the full moon, the fifteenth day of the month, water of immortality (*tsechu*) actually flows out of the chorten. Circumambulation of the chorten by local people and by pilgrims from distant places is not curtailed by its ruined condition.

Tsentang Yui Lhakang (bTsan thang g-yu'i lha khang)

Directly east of the Tsechu Bumpa, on the eastern side of the road, in the village of *Kato, is the empty site of the Yui Lhakang, so-called due to its "blue tiles glazed with melted turquoise".

History

The Yui Lhakang was founded by Ngangtsul Jangchub, the mother of the Emperor Trisong Detsen (although Queen Mangmo Je Shiteng of Nanam is the more usual name of Trisong Detsen's mother). She met Guru Rimpoche here at the end of the 8th century. Guru Rimpoche secreted a horde of treasure in this lhakang.

Tsentang Goshi (bTsan thang sgo bzhi)

It is uncertain where the Tsentang Goshi was located. Tsentang means "King's Fields", and thus it may have stood on the spot where the Bonpo priests received Nyatri Tsenpo, on the rolling pastures of Lhabab Ri. However, it is a local belief that the Tsentang Goshi stood immediately to the south of the Tsechu Bumpa on the very tip of the Shetak ridge's spur.

South and South-East of Yarlung

The road that passes through the Yarlung Valley crosses the Yarto La and eventually reaches the old district of Nyel. The Subasiri River drains the valleys of Loro, Jayul, Jarto and Jarme, close to the Assam border. Kyentse Rimpoche did not visit this area. Further east is the major power-mountain of Tsari, previously an important place of pilgrimage for Buddhists and Hindus alike.

12

CHONGYE AND THE ROYAL TOMBS

The Chongye Valley, politically distinct from Yarlung, has its ancient citadel at Chingwa Taktse and its contemporary administrative centre at Chongye Qu, about 27 km from Tsetang. It too has claim to renown in Tibetan history. Foremost, the colossal burial mounds of the emperors are located in Chongye, particularly the Bangso Marpo in which the Emperor Songtsen Gampo was buried in the 7th century. The Great Fifth Dalai Lama was born in the Chingwa Taktse *dzong*. The Yellow Hats are represented in Chongye at the important gompa of Sonak Tang, which is a very early Kadampa foundation, and also at Riwo Dechen, the gompa beneath the *dzong*. Chongye, like upper Drachi and Dranang, took part in the Nyingma flowering of the 16th to 18th centuries, and Peri gompa and Tsering Jong are both of high significance to Nyingma pilgrims.

Pagor Gompa (sPa gor dgon pa)

Both the location and history of Pagor Gompa is obscure. Pagor was the family name of Bairotsana, the first Tibetan Master and a disciple of Guru Rimpoche. Bairotsana was born in Nyemo Jeke (p.130), the seat of the Pagor family. He meditated at Yamalung for three years and his cave retreat is at the mouth of the Chongye Valley. Although no information was forthcoming locally about Pagor Gompa in 1986, a few decades previously this residence of

Bairotsana in Chongye was identified as an Ani Gompa close to the Bairo Cave.

Sonak Tang (Sol nag thang)

The Geluk gompa of Sonak Tang, or Yarlung Tangboche, founded in the early 11th century, is one of the four great gompas built at the beginning of the second period of propagation of the *dharma* in Tibet. It lies on the eastern side of the Chongye Chu, a few kilometres up from the confluence of the Chongye and Yarlung rivers. Tucci considered that the gompa's plan, a row of chortens and surrounding ruins, indicated the

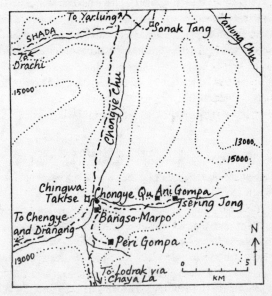

Map 12 The Chongye Valley

gompa's great age, but its walls had been repainted and nothing of note remained. Sonak Tang was totally destroyed after 1959, but a lhakang has been rebuilt and several monks are in residence. Jowo Atisha's cell (*simpuk*), the power-place of the gompa, is situated alone on the north-eastern side of the site. The most precious relic here was a black Prajnaparamita called "Splendid" (Sipachen).

History

Tangboche was founded in 1017 by "Seven and a Half Monks" (Bende Mi Chedangye) under the leadership of Drumer Tsultrim Jungne, who was the disciple of Lume, one of the ten Central Tibetans to travel to Kham for ordination after Langdarma's suppression. In this early period the monastery produced a school of philosophy called Tankor. The famous Kadampa Lama Geshe Kuton Tsondru Yungdrung (1011-75), one of the foremost disciples of Atisha and a teacher of Putowa, was abbot here. In the 12th century Drumer's lineage, renowned for learning in the *prajnaparamita sutras*, came to an end. Je Tsongkapa stayed at Sonak Tang in the 14th century and thereafter it passed into the hands of the Gelukpas.

Further up the valley on its west side is the *Shada Valley where local tradition locates one of the emperors' tombs.

Chingwa Taktse ('Phying pa sTag rtse): The Great Fifth's Birthplace

At 27 km south of Tsetang, the ancient citadel of Chingwa Taktse[1] climbs a ridge from the western bank of the Chongye Chu to the top of Chingwa Ri, commanding the valley of the tombs. All three of the powerful *dzongs* that have graced this ridge, protecting the secular rulers of Chongye, now lie in ruins. Chingwa Taktse means "The Chingwa-Mountain Tiger-Top", and the highest ruins belong to the oldest *dzong*, the chief residence of the early Tibetan kings until the time of Emperor Songtsen Gampo. Beneath the tower at the top of the ridge is said to lie a tomb of an early king.

The *dzong* of the Depas, or Chieftains, of Chongye was built on the back of the ridge below the emperors' fortress. The influential Depas of Chongye traced their lineage back to the royal line of Sahor (Mandi in the Kulu Valley in India). They were patrons of the Nyingmapas until the Great Fifth Dalai Lama was born in Chingwa Taktse in 1617, and thereafter they became firm supporters of the Yellow Hats. The room in which the Great Fifth was born is the principal shrine in the ruined *dzong*.

The last reconstruction of the *dzong* was done on the old pattern by the eighth Dalai Lama in the 18th century. In 1948 the fortifications and most of the *dzong* was in disrepair. The Chongye Depa's large lhakang merely had its roof removed and is to be restored.

Riwo Dechen (Ri bo bde chen)

The Geluk gompa of Riwo Dechen,[2] built on the pattern of Ganden, lies beneath and to the south of Chingwa Taktse. It was wholly destroyed, but the principal lhakang dedicated to Jampa has been rebuilt. The other important lhakangs, indistinguishable from the host of monastic quarters that surrounded them, are the Rinchen Lingme which was the gompa's gomkang, and the Kalsang Lhakang, dedicated to the seventh Dalai Lama.

History
Riwo Dechen was founded by Lowo Pelsang (d.1475), whose Lama was the *prajnaparamita* scholar Kedrub Gelek Pelsang (1385-1438), a disciple and biographer of Tsongkapa and the third Throne-holder of Ganden. The seventh Dalai Lama expanded and restored this gompa in the 18th century.

Bangso Marpo (Bang so dmar po): The Emperor Songtsen Gampo's Tomb

Bangso Marpo, the Red Tomb, is the 7th-century Emperor Songtsen Gampo's tomb. It is the most sacred of twenty-six colossal burial mounds of the early Tibetan kings and emperors that lie in the Chongye area. The Bangso Marpo is located between the jeep-road and the river, 1 km south of the bridge in Chongye Qu. This area is called Chingwa. Rectangular in shape and approximately 100 m long, 70 m wide and 30 m high, the tomb was created from a natural hillock, which is more evident today because the original confining walls, the surmounting *axis mundi* pillar and all trace of artifice, have disappeared. The river has eaten into the mound on its western side, but the traces of walls below the path that Tucci found are no longer visible.

Steps climb the eastern side to a small reconstructed lhakang on the top of the mound. This Nyingma lhakang was originally founded in the 13th century by Nyang Menlungpa Sakya Wo (b.1239), a remarkable pilgrim who travelled throughout India. The three monks who now attend it belong to the Peri Gompa. At the rear of the small chamber are images of the Buddhas of Past, Present and Future, and Guru Rimpoche, flanked by the Protectors Chagna Dorje and Tamdrin. In front of this altar are images of the Bodhisattva-Emperor Songtsen Gampo and the sublime principals of his reign: (from left to right) Tonmi Sambhota who created the Tibetan alphabet; Bhrikuti, the great emperor's Nepali wife; Wencheng Kongjo, his Chinese wife; and Lompo Gar, his roving ambassador. The bas-relief of the Emperor Songtsen Gampo that was seen here last century has vanished, along with the *doring* that stood by the riverside. Although we know the names of the kings buried near the Bangso Marpo in the Chingwa Valley from literary sources, there is no unanimity regarding the identification of their tombs. However, it is probable that the tomb to the north-east of the Bangso Marpo belonged to Senalek (r.804-14), Trisong Detsen's grandson. A *doring* that must have once stood in the centre of this mound is now located to the east of it in a locked enclosure. The inscription describes Senalek's reign, lauding the power of the Emperor and alluding to troubles at the beginning of his reign. The Bonpo terminology of the inscription indicates the continuing prerogatives of the Bonpo priests during the period of the Buddhist kings. A stone lion certainly sculpted in the empire period is to be found on top of the highest tomb situated closest to the eastern valley side. This tomb may belong to Repachen. Some observers have hypothesized that the large holes in the sides of this mound originally held timbers and provide evidence that the mounds were man-made.

At least seven descendants of Songtsen Gampo were buried in this area: his grandson Dusong, Dusong's son Me Agtsom, Me Agtsom's son Trisong Detsen (r.755-97), Trisong Detsen's sons Muni Tsenpo (r.797-8/9) and Murub Tsenpo, his grandson Senalek (r.804-14), and Senalek's son Repachen (r.815-38). The tombs of all these kings are located in the vicinity of the Bangso Marpo or at the foot of the side-valley that runs to the east of Chongye Chu. The tomb of the Emperor Trisong Detsen, which was provided with an identifying inscribed *doring*, now vanished, is located in this latter area.

Originally centred on the top of each tomb, standing on a turtle that symbolizes the foundation of the universe, a *doring* represented the *axis mundi*. It was also the "tree of life" at the centre of the mandala created by the central burial chamber, which contained the mummified body, and its eight surrounding chambers. Certainly in the case of Songtsen Gampo there can have been no Buddhist influence in the burial customs and rites. It is said that the great emperor was mummified and buried in a silver coffin, and that his possessions, wives, servants and horses were buried in the surrounding chambers. Officials impersonating the deceased king, called "the living dead", guarded each tomb, confined to the burial ground prohibited to the people.

The tombs are said to have been desecrated by robbers during the period of persecution in the 9th century, and also in other troubled times, but professional excavation has yet to be undertaken. Archeological excavation will undoubtedly shed further light on these extraordinary funeral monuments.

Literary sources identify the valley of the tombs with the Donkar Valley, although Donkar has also been identified as the valley in which Trisong Detsen's tomb lies. It was on the Donkar plain that the decisive debate between Buddhists and Bonpos was held during the Emperor Trisong Detsen's reign. After the Bonpos' defeat they were killed or exiled, and until this day there is no Bonpo establishment in Central Tibet.

Tsering Jong (Tshe ring ljong): Jigme Lingpa's Residence

From Chongye Qu a jeep-road runs to the east up the side-valley where Trisong Detsen's tomb is located. The sites of several other burial mounds lie in the lower part of this valley. The village of Tsering Jong, Long-life Valley, is located some 10 km from Chongye Qu. Just above the village, by a gully, is the spot that in the 18th century the Dzokchempa Jigme Lingpa chose for the hermitage he called Wosel Tekchok Ling. The small gompa on this site was totally destroyed, but it is in process of reconstruction. In 1959 Tsering Jong was an Ani Gompa and some of the hermitages of the forty *anis* who lived here still remain by the spring in the gully. This spring, "water for meditation" (*drubchu*) bestowing long-life, was discovered by Jigme Lingpa, and the willow trees in the gully are said to have grown from his hair. To the west of the gompa are the five *sungkangs* of the Protectress Tseringma and her Long-life Sisters.

History

Kunkyen Jigme Lingpa (1729-98) revealed the Longchen Nyingtik, the Dzokchen treasures of Longchen Rabjampa, and Jigme Lingpa is considered to be the principal disciple of Longchempa. An incarnation of both the Emperor Trisong Detsen and Vimalamitra, he was born in a village south of Chongye. He gained his realization at Peri Gompa and at Boudha in Nepal, but it was at Samye Chimpu that he received the full transmission of the Longchen Nyingtik in vision (p.228). Thereafter he built Tsering Jong, and his Dzokchen meditation instruction was disseminated throughout Tibet. Another of his accomplishments was the compilation of the Nyingma *tantras* into the collection known as the *Nyingma Gyudbum*. He died at Tsering Jong, but his reliquary chorten has disappeared.

Chongye Peri ('Phyongs rgyas dpal ri)

A few kilometres south of Bangso Marpo the Chongye Valley divides. The south-eastern branch is joined by a side-valley from the east and on its northern side the Peri Gompa is located. Although totally destroyed it has been rebuilt and is now the residence of several Nyingma monks. Peri Gompa was not of great age but it had considerable importance. Previously Samye Chimpu was under its control, and although this governance has now lapsed monks from Peri still maintain the lhakang on top of the Bangso Marpo.

History

Peri Gompa was founded by a lord of the Chingwa Taktse *dzong* in the 16th century, and it became the residence of Trengpo Terchen Sherab Woser (1518-84), a *tulku* of Bairotsana. It became known as the important Nyingma college called Dormin Peri. After Mindroling was established its importance was reduced.

Chengye Lhakang (sPyan g-yas lha khang)

Chengye Lhakang[3] is located to the south-west of Chongye Qu. We have no description of this ancient foundation, no report of damage done in the last twenty years and no news of reconstruction. From Chengye the path continues west to climb over a pass and into Lhodrak.

History

Chengye Lhakang was founded by Geshe Drapa and completed by Geshe Kache, and it was renowned for its school of monastic discipline. Go Lotsawa (p.161) went to school there in the 14th century. Its name was derived from the lhakang's chief relic, the right eye of Sariputra, the beloved disciple of Sakyamuni Buddha.

South and South-East of Chongye

The road that passes through the Chongye Valley crosses the *Chaya La at its head and descends to the west of Drigu Tso into

Lhodrak. Lhodrak is an area of great significance to the pilgrim. Mawo Chok in north-eastern Lhodrak was the birthplace and residence of the First Sovereign Treasure-finder, Nyangral Nyima Woser (b.1135). Neshi gompa is associated with the Second Sovereign Treasure-finder Guru Chowang (1212-73). Senge Dzongsum, one of the vital power-places of Guru Rimpoche, is located over the border in Mon, Eastern Bhutan. In Karchu, the Tibetan border town, is an important Guru Rimpoche cave and the cave where Namkai Nyingpo achieved enlightenment. Nearby is one of the Emperor Songtsen Gampo's principal temples called Lhodrak Lhakang. North-west of Karchu at Dowo Lung was the residence of Marpa Lotsawa, Milarepa's Guru, and the Sekar Gutok, the Nine-story Tower that Milarepa built. To the north of Dowo Lung is Guru Lhakang, which was the residence of Guru Chowang.

13

DORJE DRAK AND THE CAVES
OF DRAKYUL

Drakyul is renowned for one great gompa, a small pond, and two remarkable cave systems. The gompa is called Dorje Drak,[1] one of the two important Nyingma monasteries of Central Tibet; the pond is Kandro Yeshe Tsogyel's life-spirit lake; and the caves are two of Guru Rimpoche's meditation caves – Dzong Kompu and Drak Yongdzong. These caves are not simple holes in the rock. In two separate limestone ridges, behind the large caverns in which Guru Rimpoche meditated, are extensive tunnels, domes, rivers, lakes, cascades, and other phenomena associated with the erosion of limestone. Many of these phenomena have been imbued with the symbolic significance of *tantra* to create a natural iconography.

At the time of the Tibetan Empire, Drak was the independent principality of Karchen and it is well known as the birthplace of Guru Rimpoche's consort, Yeshe Tsogyel. The old district of Drak consisted of several valleys from Samye to the west of Dorje Drak, and north of the Tsangpo to the Kyichu/Tsangpo watershed. Today Drakyul belongs to Dranang Xian. It is a depopulated area due to the ravages of the wind-born Tsangpo Valley sand, to deforestation, and to the district's isolation. Its communications depend on the Tsangpo ferries. In centuries past Drak was renowned for its timber. The forest-covered mountains of Drak were the source of much timber carried on yaks over the Gokar La pass to Dechen, and thence by boat to Lhasa.[2] The last twenty years have seen an acceleration of the process of deforestation.

Access

Two ferries cross the Tsangpo to Drakyul. Approaching by the Tsetang road from Chaksam, before the large village of Chitesho at km 48 is the ferry station for Dorje Drak. In a small village 3 km beyond Dranang, by a new hydro-electric plant (km 73), is the terminus of the Drakda ferry. Drakda is the lower part of the principal valley of Drak.

The pilgrim approaching Drak from Samye or Surkar in the east has a long, hard day's march across sand dunes and the stony flood plains of small rivers and over the low spurs of ridges that protrude into the Tsangpo. The beauty of this walk along the Tsangpo Valley lies in the light over the water and on the hills. The little-known Russian artist, Nicholas Roerich, brother of the Tibetologist and translator of the *Blue Annals*, George Roerich, attempted to catch the ineffable light of the Tsangpo Valley in water colours. Many of his hundreds of canvases can be seen in a gallery at Kulu in Himachal Pradesh, India.

If the pilgrim is approaching Drak on foot from Lhasa by the direct route, he crosses the *Trango La, and descends into the valley above the Dorje Drak Gompa. This path follows the ancient route from Lhasa to Southern Tibet via Chitesho and to the east of the Yamdrok Tso. If the pilgrim approaches by way of Shugseb and Gangri Tokar in the west, he crosses uninhabited high plateau before descending into the valley to the west of Dorje Drak in a two-day walk.

Tubten Dorje Drak (Thub bstan rDo rje brag): The Jangter Gompa

The site of the important Nyingma gompa of Tubten Dorje Drak runs up the hillside behind the ferry terminus and behind a large plantation of willow trees that bind the sand. The gompa is built at the bottom of a ridge shaped like a *dorje*, the form of which can be seen from the road on the opposite side of the Tsangpo and which gives the gompa its name. The centre of the gompa — the red-painted dukang and lhakang together with the monks' quarters — has been rebuilt and restored in the old style. A new image of Guru Rimpoche and a few relics from the past are found on the altar in the lhakang. A large urn of broken bronze images

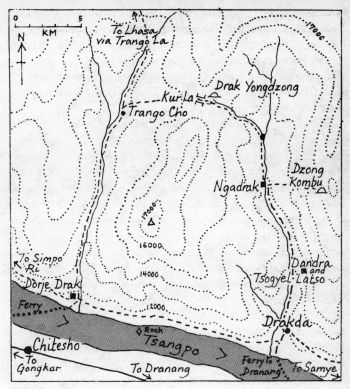

Map 13 The Valleys of Drakyul

and artefacts destroyed during the Cultural Revolution is also found in the lhakang. Above the new building are the ruins of other monastic buildings. In 1959 400 monks studied here. At present a venerable *kempo* trains a bevy of young monks and instructs several *gelongs*. The present incarnation of Rigdzin Pema Trinle is occasionally in residence.

History

The great name at the top of the lineage that founded Dorje Drak, the first of the line of incarnations of Guru Rimpoche who still preside there, is Rigdzin Chempo Ngodrub Gyeltsen (1337-1409), better known as Godemchen, He adorned with the Eagle Feather. Guru Rimpoche wears a similar feather in his Hat of

Victory. Godemchen was one of the greatest of the treasure-finders, the discoverer of the Northern Treasure (*jangter*). Whereas the essential body of instruction given at Dorje Drak is derived from the *jangter*, the rival, sister gompa at Mindroling (p.165) to the south of the Tsangpo is associated with the Southern Treasure (*lhoter*).

Godemchen was born into a family descended from Mongolian royalty in Tsang. He was not associated with Central Tibet during his lifetime. His father, Lopon Dudul, was an adept in the *Purba-tantra* and taught it to his son. At the age of eleven three eagle feathers appeared as a cockade on the boy's head, the three increasing to five when he was twenty-three. At the age of thirty-five he was given a list of treasures concealed at Sangsang Lhadrak, and from this cave he recovered his remarkable and numerous treasure-texts (p.267). His death was a complete dissolution of his body into the space and awareness of the *dharmadhatu*.

It is said that with the propagation of the teaching contained in the *jangter* the whole of Tibet was spiritually revitalized. Certainly the 14th century saw a blossoming of the Nyingma *dharma*. The lineages Godemchen established consisted of lines of *ngakpa* yogins, most of whom achieved bodies of rainbow light as the result of their practice. The method of the *jangter* is known for its simplicity, speed and effectiveness in accomplishing Buddhahood in the form of a rainbow body.

Dorje Drak may have existed in some form before the third incarnation of Godemchen, Tashi Tobgye, moved his establishment to Drak from Godemchen's original gompa in Tsang in the 16th century. But the place received its name of Tubten Dorje Drak at that time and it has become renowned by that name. The fourth incarnation, the greatest of the incarnations of Godemchen was called Rigdzin Shabdrung Pema Trinle (1641-1717), and it was he who did meditation retreat in the Nego Che cave at Drak Yongdzong. This savant and *siddha* is known for his reduction of the *jangter* theory of the Buddhist path to a simple practical method. Like most of the monasteries along this stretch of the Tsangpo Valley, Dorje Drak was sacked by the Dzungars in 1717.

[13.] [above] TUBTEN DORJE DRAK: the *jangter* Nyingma gompa from the Tsangpo (photograph by K. Dowman)
[below] TUBTEN DORJE DRAK: the courtyard with *lashing* and *sangkang* (photograph by K. Dowman)

Drak Yongdzong (sGrags Yongs rdzong): Guru Rimpoche's
  Citadel

The power-places of Drak are best visited as part of a clockwise
korra. From Dorje Drak the pilgrim should ascend the valley for
about 12 km to *Trango Cho, and then climb over the *Kur La
to Drak Yongdzong. This hard day's walk is preferable to the
longer route along the beautiful but barren shore of the Tsangpo
and then up to the head of one of the Drak Valley's side-valleys.

Descending from the *Kur La through meadows and thickets
of flowering shrubs, the pilgrim climbs again to the end of the
ridge that is one of the horns of the amphitheatre in which Drak
Yongdzong is situated. At the end of this ridge is the *dundro* site
of Siwaitsel, Cool Garden, the name of the chief amongst the
Eight Indian Cemeteries. Ruins of hermitages are to be seen
above the site of dismemberment, along with an ancient juniper
tree. A hundred metres from the main cave, on the left-hand side
of the path, is a derelict cave associated with Rigdzin Pema
Trinle, the fourth incarnation of Godemchen, whose residence
was at Tubten Dorje Drak. The name of this cave is Nego Che.[3]
Above the place where the path from the *dundro* joins the path
from the valley is a small opening into a large descending tunnel.
A steep drop marks the point beyond which the pilgrim does not
advance, and here he makes his obeisance and offerings. This cave
is called Nego Sarpa, the New Door to the Power-place.

Drak Yongdzong itself, listed amongst the five principal Guru
Rimpoche caves as the place identical to his Buddha-body, is
located in the side of a sheer, white, limestone cliff. The cliff is
called Shinje Rolpai Potang, "The Citadel of the Dancing Lord of
Death", a name that invokes the powers that transcend mortality.
Climbing the cliff face on bridges of timbers secured with wire,
passing the ruins of more retreat huts, the pilgrim reaches the
entrance to the Guru's cave. Within is a vast space, 30 m high
and as much broad and deep, in which a lhakang was constructed
long ago. This lhakang has been preserved, while other buildings

[14.] [above] DRAK YONGDZONG: Guru Rimpoche and Consorts
on the alter within the cave's lhakang (photograph by K. Dowman)
[below] DRAK YONGDZONG: ladder and tunnel entrance to the
Secret Cave of the Dakini (photograph by K. Dowman) [below
right] DZONG KOMPU: entrance to the vast cavern of Guru
Rimpoche (centre) in limestone peaks (photograph by K. Dowman)

in the cavern, apart from the cells on the left side, have been destroyed. The murals of the Mindroling Gompa and the hierarchy of Minling Terchen Lamas painted on the outer wall of the lhakang are its most notable features. Amongst the new images on the altar is an impressive bronze statue of Guru Rimpoche in semi-wrathful mode flanked by his two consorts, Yeshe Tsogyel and Mandarava. This cave is now the residence of a Khampa Lama and his disciple. In his absence the *konyer* is to be found in Ngadrak (see below).

Outside the cave on the left is a path leading to the upper cave system. A ladder assists the pilgrim to slide up through a difficult narrow tunnel that opens some distance above the floor of a large womb-like cavern. On the far side of the cavern at the same height as the tunnel entrance is a ledge with a small opening at waist height that gives access to the Kandro's Secret Cave, a small circular cave that has a shrine within. This is the heart of Drak Yongdzong. Tiny pearls of crystalline rock may be found amongst the limestone powdered in a hole in the rock: this is the *ringsel* prized by pilgrims for its medicinal and protective qualities. On the same side of the cavern as the entrance tunnel a passage leads back to a gallery overlooking the lhakang in the large, lower cave. At the end of the gallery is the shrine of the Protectors of Drak Yongdzong.

History
After the initiation of Guru Rimpoche's closest disciples in Samye Chimpu, Nubchen Sangye Yeshe, whose birthplace was in Drakda, and Dorje Dunjom, were advised to go to Drak Yongdzong and enter meditation retreat for the purpose of realizing their *yidam*, their tutelary deity, Jampel Shinjeshe (Manjusri Yamantaka). Sangye Yeshe's sign of accomplishment was skill with the *purba*; he gained the power to summon spirits, to liberate them from their existence in samsara, and to pierce rock, all with the movement of his *purba*, the "magical dagger". After the mass ordination of *gelongs* attendant upon the consecration of Samye, one hundred initiates were sent to the meditation school (*drubdra*) at Yongdzong. The result of all the activity at Yongdzong during this period was the legend of the Fifty-five Recluses, yogins or neljorpas, of Yongdzong, who took

their place in the mythology of the Tibetan world as exemplars of meditation retreat achieving extra-sensory power and Buddhahood. In 1959 a *tulku* and eighteen monks lived at Drak Yongdzong.

Yongdzong was a major location of hidden treasure. Guru Rimpoche concealed all the major Dorje Purba texts here, and Yeshe Tsogyel stayed here for over a year, leaving ten major caches of treasure.

An unidentified cave in the area of the upper Drak Valley, called Ngar Puk, belonged to the 13th-century Dzokchen yogin Melong Dorje. This renowned Dzokchempa was born in Drak. He practised the Nyingtik precepts of Dangma Lhungyel and was a disciple of Trulshik Senge Gyelwa. He died in 1303.

Dzong Kompu (?rDzong kham phug?): The Guru's Labyrinth

From Drak Yongdzong the path descends to the Drak Valley, and turning south within three hours the pilgrim arrives at Ngadrak Qu. The Ngadrak Gompa, which is a Karma Kagyupa establishment belonging to the Pawo Rimpoches of Nenang, was preserved as Party offices. It is now is process of refurbishment and two or three monks attend to it. The *konyer* of Drak Yongdzong lives in the village. The *konyer* of Dzong Kompu[4] lives in the part of the village on the east side of the river, and the path to the Guru's Cave ascends the valley behind it. Following the valley up its south-eastern branch, the path climbs steeply through thick vegetation towards the massive opening high in a limestone tower that can be seen even from the south bank of the Tsangpo. The cave can be reached in three hours from Ngadrak.

The cliff in which the Guru's cave is located is called Karchen Drak, Karchen being a name of the Guru's consort, Yeshe Tsogyel. Within the gigantic 30 m opening the cavern is some 50 m wide and deep. The old lhakang that stood in the centre of the cave and the *tsamkangs* that lined the walls have all been destroyed. A new country-built lhakang stands on the site of the old. It contains a new statue of Guru Rimpoche and other modern objects of devotion. A pilgrims' shelter stands adjacent to it. At the left front of the cavern are ancient rock carvings of Guru Rimpoche, the Thirty-three Buddhas and a *siddha* lineage. At the back of the cavern two passageways diverge. The right-hand tunnel culminates after 150 m in a cathedral-like cavern where the object of worship is a stalagmite in the form of a *lingam*, the male principle. The left-hand tunnel of about the same length follows the course of a stream to end by a deep well, symbolizing the *yoni*, the female principle. These two passageways polished by centuries of use are part of a system of tunnels that honeycomb the mountain.

The history of Dzong Kompu is obscure. No legend in Guru Rimpoche's biographies sheds light on it. However, local oral tradition, confirmed by *Kyentse's Guide*, aver that this indeed was a place where the Great Guru meditated with his consort Yeshe Tsogyel.

Tsogyel Latso (mTsho rgyal bla mtsho): Tsogyel's Life-spirit Lake

Rather more than an hour's march below Ngadrak, and an hour from the Tsangpo ferry, is a village called *Dandra, marked by a surrounding grove of tall silver oaks. Within the grove is a deep depression filled with a shallow stretch of water. This pond is what remains of the Tsogyel Latso. On the north side of the lake is a small lhakang belonging to the Nyingma school with two or three *tsamkangs* behind it. The original structure of the lhakang has been preserved and original murals decorate the porch and the walls inside. The old image of Vajra Yogini on the altar is worshipped as Yeshe Tsogyel herself.

The Great Guru Padma Sambhava's Tibetan consort, Yeshe Tsogyel (757?-817?) was the daughter of the King of Karchen. Karchen, comprising all or part of the District of Drak, was one of the seven principalities that the Emperor Songtsen Gampo subjected to form the nucleus of the Tibetan Empire. Seulung is given as the location of the Karchen palace where Tsogyel was born. Local tradition identifies the lake that stood by that palace, the lake that is identical to her life-spirit, her *la* (p.259), as the pond that exists in *Dandra today. The Princess's birth was attended by an increase in the size of the lake and the blooming of red and white speckled flowers around it. This inspired her father the king to call her Tsogyel, Lady of the Lake. The extension of her name to Yeshe Tsogyel, Lady of the Lake of Pure Awareness, emphasizes the nature of the lake as a symbol of the feminine principle. Since in tantric symbolism Yeshe Tsogyel is the ubiquitous, all-inclusive expanse of pure awareness, the Guru's consort and his feminine principle, the lake is identified with Tsogyel herself.

Drakda (sGrags mda'): The Lower Drak Valley

Drakda is the lower part of the Drak Valley (the suffix *da* means "arrow"). This includes the site of the Tsogyel Latso. Kyentse Rimpoche notes that Drakda was also called Drak Drongmoche, and that this was the birthplace of Nubchen Sangye Yeshe. Sangye Yeshe was one of the Twenty-four Disciples who received the transmission from Guru Rimpoche at Chimpu, and he fulfilled his meditation at Drak Yongdzong. He was also a disciple of Bairotsana, and the transmitter of Dzokchen *anuyoga*. The Nub clan was an important force in the courts of the Emperors: Nub Namkai Nyingpo was one of the first seven Tibetan *gelongs*, and a protagonist of the Tibetan *chan* school.

14

SAMYE CHOKOR

Samye Chokor, the Dharmacakra of Samye, will give to many pilgrims the most rewarding experience of their sojourn in Central Tibet. Samye was the first monastery to be built in Tibet, and it was established through the skilful means of Tibet's Great Guru, Padma Sambhava. In the 7th century the Emperor Songtsen Gampo had built many small temples and the Lhasa Tsuklakang, but the construction of Samye by the Emperor Trisong Detsen in the 8th century marked the establishment of monasticism, which has always formed the basis of Buddhist societies. Although Samye has been damaged and restored many times over the centuries, its design and foundations date from its origins. The magnificent plan upon which it was built, copied from an important Indian *vihara*, survived even the Cultural Revolution.

Samye is far more than the oldest monastery in Tibet. To the Tibetan people it symbolizes the root and the glory of their 1200-year-old Buddhist heritage. Today, with the limited religious freedom that the Tibetans have been granted, Samye has resumed the significance that it had lost over the last few centuries. After the blooming of the Geluk reformation and the establishment of political power by the Dalai Lamas and their Regents, the influence of the Red Hat schools diminished and they lost control of many of their gompas. Released from Yellow Hat domination and the corrupting effects of political involvement they are now free to demonstrate the original qualities of their old traditions. The Lhasa Jokang is a focal point of national consciousness for the whole of Tibet; Samye performs functions of the same order in the Tsangpo Valley. During the full moon of the holiday season in June thousands of pilgrims from the surrounding district, from Lhasa and further afield, make their way to Samye.

To yogins of the Nyingma school the Drakmar area in which Samye is located contains other power-places of equal significance to the Samye gompa. Samye Chimpu is the hermitage site originally attached to the Samye gompa, and after Guru Rimpoche himself sanctified it by meditation and by instruction of his Twenty-four Disciples it became associated with many of the great names of the Nyingma lineages. In the mountains north of Samye is the hermitage of Yamalung, a power-place chosen by both Guru Rimpoche and Bairotsana for extended periods of retreat. Close to Samye, at Drakmar Drinsang (Drakmar is an old name for the Samye Valley), is the birthplace of the Emperor Trisong Detsen. Also nearby is Surkar Do, where the Emperor first met his future lama, Guru Rimpoche.

Access
Samye is located at the foot of the valley of the Samye Chu, a northern affluent of the Tsangpo. Thus the valley has no connection with any road system. It is most easily accessible by ferry across the Tsangpo. The ferry station on the south side of the Tsangpo is located to the east of the Drachi Valley (at km 88) and 36 km west of Tsetang. On the north bank the ferry lands at Surkar, 8 km upstream from Samye.

Samye is located on the ancient route linking Lhasa and the Kyichu Valley with Yarlung and the other rich valleys south of the Tsangpo. The path from Dechen Dzong over the famous Gokar La descends close by Yamalung and then continues down to Samye. Another route links Ganden with Samye. Both routes take the pilgrim through valleys rich in flora and fauna up to high yak-pastures, and either route can be traversed in three days.

Samye is also approachable from west or east along the north bank of the Tsangpo. To the east are the Lo, Dolung, Yon and Woka Valleys, and to the west is the district of Drak. Particularly during the spring, the harsh, arid nature of the Tsangpo's north bank with its dunes, wind-blown sand and lack of flora, water and habitation, make for difficult progress. But

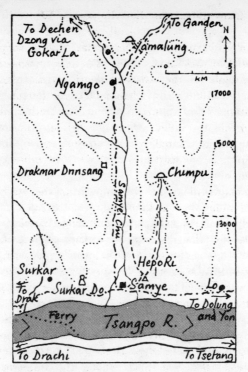

Map 14 The Samye Valley

after rain has fallen, during the months of July and August, when the river is in spate, the ineffable light of the Tsangpo Valley gives the north bank its own attraction.

The pilgrim attached to the notion of *korra* and wishing to avoid the contamination of recent development in Tibet can do so in a two-week trek beginning and ending in Lhasa: Ganden, Yamalung, Samye, Drak, Dorje Drak, Gangri Tokar, Riwo Tsenga, and Sangpu. This route includes five cave-hermitages of Guru Rimpoche (Yamalung, Chimpu, Drak Yongdzong, Drak Kompu and Sangyak Namka Dzong), the cave of Longchen Rabjampa at Gangri Tokar, the gompas of Samye and Dorje Drak, and the life-spirit lake of the Guru's consort, Yeshe Tsogyel. The itinerary that follows describes the route from Samye to the Kyichu.

Surkar Do (Zur mkhar rdo): The Emperor's White Chortens

The village of Surkar lies at the foot of the valley running parallel and to the west of the Samye valley. The ferry station is located on the west side of the valley's mouth, 4 km beyond the chortens. In the 1880s Sarat Chandra Das, a Bengali Brahmin scholar, mentioned the walnut, peach, willow, and poplar groves at the bottom of this valley.[1] After the deforestation of the last decades only newly-planted willow saplings grow there. It is difficult to imagine the hardships of those bitter winters after the trees were cut down.

Surkar is renowned for its chortens. From the south bank of the Tsangpo, more than a kilometre away, they are visible as striking small, white shapes against the brown hillside. They are located on the spur that descends between the Surkar and Samye Valleys. Above the jeep-road, and below a scarp with boulders perched precariously at its top, there are five small, white, dome-shaped chortens carved out of the living rock (p.220). In the holocaust only their long necks were broken, but they have been recently restored. It is believed that they date from Trisong Detsen's reign in the 8th century. Faded, indecipherable inscriptions can be seen in their vicinity.

The chortens mark the place where the Emperor Trisong Detsen met Guru Rimpoche c.765, having come from Samye to greet the Indian Guru according to Sino-Tibetan custom. Legend has it that the Emperor, lacking respect for the Guru, waited for his guest's homage. Not until he became aware of the Guru's resplendent form, and of his entire entourage prostrate upon the ground, did he prostrate himself. Later, perceiving that he had lost face during this encounter, he sought to repair the damage to his merit by building these five chortens. They are known as the Rignga Chortens, the Chortens of the Five Buddha Families, and as such they are worshipped as identical to the Five Buddhas. Orgyen Lingpa (p.170) found two important treasures at Surkar Do.

Another story relating to Surkar concerns Me Agtsom, the Emperor Trisong Detsen's predecessor. His son, Prince Lhawang, was drowned here, and furious at the river gods, the *lu*, the king ordered the river to be whipped. The *lu* came to the king

begging reprieve, promising him that they would show him many good omens. It is said that "the gods' omens at riverbank fort" is the origin of the full name of the place – Surkar Lhatak.

Samye Chokor (bSam yas chos 'khor): Tibet's First Monastery

Approaching Samye over a low ridge from Surkar, the elliptical walled compound of Samye Chokor, with the great Utse temple in the middle, is an impressive sight. It stands at the southern edge of the fertile plain of the Samye Valley. With destruction of tree cover in centuries past, sand from the river has encroached to bury villages and fields between Samye and the Tsangpo. A willow plantation now gives some protection.

The builders' plan of Samye reflected an imperial conception and aspiration. The legend describes Guru Rimpoche provoking the Emperor Trisong Detsen's imagination to conceive a most ambitious design. The result was a symbolic representation of the mandala of the Buddhist cosmos, based on the design of the Indian *vihara* of Odantapuri (S. Bihar). This plan has Mt Meru, or more specifically the Buddha's palace at the centre of the plain at the top of Mt Meru, represented by the Utse Rigsum Tsuklakang in the middle of the mandala. The four continents surrounding Mt Meru are the *lingshi* lhakangs, located in the cardinal directions, and the eight satellite islands are the eight smaller *lingtren* lhakangs, one on each side of each of the *lingshi*. The sun and moon revolving around Mt Meru were represented by the Nyima (Sun) and Dawa (Moon) Temples to the east and west of the Utse. Four chortens in four colours stood at the Utse's corners. Bath-house, dressing-room and residential buildings constructed in later times broke this simple symmetry. The three important lhakangs called the Jomo Lingsum, built by the Emperor Trisong Detsen's queens, lay outside the wall surrounding the mandala of temples. The wall had four impressive gates at the cardinal directions, each with a gomkang for the gates' Guardians, and an inscribed *doring* pillar stood inside each of these gates. 1008 small chortens decorated the top of the wall.

Samye suffered less severely during the Cultural Revolution

[15.] [above] SAMYE: the walled Samye Chokor from Hepo Ri, Utse Rignga at centre (photograph by *Stone Routes*)
[below] SURKAR DO: two of the five 8th-century Rignga Chortens carved from the living rock (photograph by *Stone Routes*)

than many other great gompas of Central Tibet. The Samye
agricultural commune was located within the walls and the entire
complex became a farmyard. The domestic monastic buildings
were destroyed and commune buildings were erected with the old
construction materials. However, most of the *lingshi* and *lingtren*
lhakangs still stand, although in a state of disrepair. The four
storeys of the Utse Rigsum have been reduced to two and the
figures in the fine murals in the cloisters of the *vihara*, for
example, have had their eyes gouged out. The Tamdrin Ling, the
Nyima (Sun) and Dawa (Moon) Lhakangs and the Four Chortens,
and the Jomo Ling Sum lhakangs, have all disappeared. The
encircling wall is still intact but the chortens on the wall, the
gatehouses, the gomkangs and the pillars have all been destroyed.

It is reported that a plan exists to relocate the commune
outside the walls and to restore the original design of the Samye
mandala. By 1985 the lower two storeys of the Utse Rigsum
together with the monks' quarters that surround it had been
refurbished and the Nyima Lhakang was being rebuilt at its
location to the east of the Utse Rigsum. It is to be hoped that the
authorities will restore the entire Samye complex. It was one of
few gompas in the country to be left intact. The satellite temples,
the *lingshi* and *lingtren*, need only internal decoration, as in many
cases their external structure remains in good condition, even
some murals having been preserved. In 1959 some 300 monks
were in residence; but now there are only sixty.

Utse Rigsum

The Utse Vihara stands at the centre of the complex. Outside its
walls on the east side is the Dalai Lama's preaching throne. Stone
elephants guard the doors. On the left side of the door is a *doring*
erected by the Emperor Trisong Detsen, decreeing the everlasting
protection of Samye. Inside the *vihara* original murals decorate
the outer wall of the courtyard, but they have been defaced. On
the eastern side are notable depictions of the cosmos and also of
Samye in its original glory. Monks' quarters surround the
courtyard which is virtually filled by the dukang. Although the
Utse Rigsum has lost the top two of its four storeys together with
its four turrets, the ground floor has been restored and the second
storey is in process of restoration. The characteristic styles of its

three original storeys – Chinese, Indian and Khotanese respectively – are no longer discernible. An inner *korsa* is built into the temple to permit circumambulation of the dukang and lhakangs.

The murals of the assembly hall reflect the mixture of Nyingma, Sakya and Geluk influences at Samye. At the left front of the dukang are images of the protagonists who founded Samye: one of the first monks, Bairotsana; the founding abbot, Santaraksita; an image of Guru Rimpoche as Tsokye Dorje that was discovered as a treasure by Nyangral Nyima Woser; the Emperor Trisong Detsen; and the first Buddhist emperor, Songtsen Gampo. In front of Guru Rimpoche is a stone impressed with the Guru's footprints taken from the Gungtang La, where he departed for the Sangdok Peri Pure-land. At the front of the dukang on the right are images of important Lamas: Dromton, Jowo Atisha, Lekpai Sherab, Longchempa, Gyelwa Ngapa, Sakya Pandita and Tsongkapa.

The central image in the *sanctum sanctorum* is Jangchub Chempo, Mahabodhi, the Samye Jowo, who is Sakyamuni with Bodhisattva ornaments. This stone image (with a new head of clay) is said to be the original 8th-century statue self-manifest on Hepo Ri. It is surrounded by the usual eight standing Bodhisattvas in larger than life size, all new. Two Door Protectors (*go-kyong*) one at each side of the entrance, are said to be the famous King and Kang images, the Protectors of King Me Agtsom. They are Tamdrin (Hayagriva) and Miyowa (Acala).

The gomkang on the northern side of the dukang is certainly the most powerful lhakang at Samye. It contains images rescued from the *lings* and *lingtren* lhakangs: the statue of Pehar that originally stood in the Pehar Lingtren, said to have been made by Guru Rimpoche himself (it was the Guru who first invoked Pehar at Samye) and the Tamdrin that previously stood in the Arya Palo Ling (renamed Tamdrin Ling in honour of this statue). Images of Tseumar and Begtse are also found here. White *katak* offering scarves obscure the features of these Protectors and it is impossible to judge their antiquity. In the gomkang it must be remembered that the anger that the Protectors display is a manifestation of pure transcendental awareness (*yeshe*) and therefore detached and free of all egoism.

On the first storey the walls of the portico are covered with fine murals in the Central Tibetan style. Their age is difficult to assess. Here the lives of Guru Rimpoche are depicted. On the northern side wall is a graphic map of the original Samye Chokor with its temples named. Within the first-storey lhakang is a magnificent image of Guru Rimpoche in his semi-wrathful mode of Kamsum Sinon, Suppressor of the Three Realms through Inner Radiance, in which the Guru affects a ferocious mien, holding his nine-ribbed *dorje* on his knee and his skull-bowl to his heart. Apart from the few images beside the Guru on the altar and the fine murals, this lhakang was empty in 1985.

To the left of the entrance to the assembly hall is an important lhakang housing a repaired image of Chaktong Chentong, the Thousand-armed Thousand-eyed Chenresik. To his left is an image of Bairotsana, the first Tibetan translator and Dzokchempa. Here pilgrims received the blessings of Bairotsana's *chakdar*, his staff, on the day of the full moon. Samye possesses other relics which we did not see.

Lingshi and Lingtren (gLing gzhi gling phran): The Circle of Temples

In 1985 it was impossible to visit the four *lings*, the eight *lingtren* and other small lhakangs. Some were residences, some locked barns and storerooms, and some farmyards. Some examples: the three-storey Jampel Ling (E.) was the commune office, the fabric in good state of repair and now being refurbished; the Tsenmai Ling (E.S.E.) was a residence with murals remaining; the Tamdrin Ling (originally known as Arya Palo Ling)(S.) housing the sacred Tamdrin image, and the most important *ling* shrine, was gutted although murals remain; the Pehar Lhakang (N.), where the Protector Pehar was housed, was locked and barred.

The Nyima lhakang, also known as Yaksha Tawok, located to the east of Utse, enshrined the Protector Tseumar, also known as Yaksha. When Pehar was removed from Samye to take up his chief residence at Nechung, Tseumar became the principal Protector of Samye, and his Oracle became the Samye Oracle, who lived in the Nyima Lhakang. Like the Dawa Lhakang it has been destroyed, but it was in process of rebuilding.

History

Guru Rimpoche, from the Swat Valley, consecrated the ground of Samye in 765(?), subjecting the local deities and forcing the local *lu* to provide timber and stone. The Emperor Trisong Detsen had it built and the Indian Bodhisattva Abbot Santaraksita was its first abbot. Nyang Tingedzin (p.111) was his successor and the first Tibetan abbot. Samye was the Royal Temple and Samye and Chimpu were one of the three pairs of monastic and retreat establishments of the late 8th and early 9th centuries. During Langdarma's repression Samye was boarded up. During the Sakya ascendancy Sakya Pandita had Samye restored and it became the residence of both Nyingma and Sakya monks with a Sakya abbot at its head. Later both Lama Dampa Sonam Gyeltsen and Ngakchang Sakya Sangpo restored Samye. At the time of the Great Fifth Dalai Lama, after it had suffered the depredations of Mongols and Dzungars, Samye was adopted by the Gelukpas and again restored; but the Sakya abbot retained his position. As evidence of continued Gelukpa dominance of Samye, in the 1920s the Reteng Regent was responsible for its most recent major restoration, done with state funds. Today the majority of monks at Samye belong to the Red Hat schools and only a few Gelukpas are present.

Hepo Ri (Has po ri): Bonpo Ridge

The spinal ridge to the east of Samye was a pre-Buddhist, Bonpo site. There was a residence on the top of it associated with the emperors, and during the Emperor Trisong Detsen's reign the embattled Bonpos fought a magical conflict with the Buddhists from this vantage point. The Guru's consort, Yeshe Tsogyel, was instrumental in destroying their power.

Today Hepo Ri is a power-place where offering is made to the protecting deities. *Lhabtse* cairns line the ridge; *lungta* prayer-flags purify the air; and *sangkangs* emit juniper smoke. In the centre, at the top, a lhakang stands in ruins. On the north-east side the Guru Rimpoche cave is now identified as a flat rock. Near this inscribed rock is Guru Rimpoche's *shuktri*, his meditation throne. The Guru hid treasure on Hepo Ri and the Gyege *terne* (p.293) is probably identical to the Guru Puk. A fine view of Samye can be gained from this ridge.

Samye Chimpu (bSam yas mchims phu): Samye's Hermitages

Samye Chimpu gained its enduring power and reputation during the Emperor Trisong Detsen's reign, in the first period of propagation of the *dharma* in Tibet. Guru Rimpoche spent long periods here in meditation, particularly while Samye was under construction, and here he instructed his Twenty-four Disciples, many of whom are associated with Chimpu's various caves. Chimpu is considered to be the Guru's Speech Centre in the mandala of his power-places, and it is counted amongst the Eight Solitary Places of Realization (p.290). Guru Rimpoche, Yeshe Tsogyel, Nyang Tingedzin and others hid treasures here, and during the second period of propagation of the *dharma* treasure-finders (*tertons*) and yogins of the Nyingma school further sanctified its caves.

Chimpu's primacy in the early history of tantric meditation in Tibet alone justifies the detailed description given here. By 1986 it had become once again a vital place of retreat, where upwards of fifty yogins and yoginis, mostly from eastern Tibet, live in caves and hermitages.

Chimpu is at the head of the valley running parallel and to the east of the Samye Valley and some 12 km from Samye Chokor. The ridge of Hepo Ri separates Samye from the Chimpu Valley. It is accessible from Yamalung in the north over a difficult goat path. A direct path from the Dolung Valley enters Chimpu over its eastern ridge.

Chim is the name of the clan that lived in this valley in ancient times, and *pu* denotes the head of the valley. Thus like most *ritro* sites, the Chimpu caves and hermitages are situated high up at the valley head. The chorten marking the entrance to the power-place is located where the valley begins its steep ascent. On the ridge that forms the top of the amphitheatre that is Chimpu its highest cave is located. The gully created by a stream divides this semicircular amphitheatre into two equal parts, and the caves and hermitages scattered over the area are more concentrated closer to this principal source of water. The most significant of the caves — Drakmar Keutsang, Bairo Puk and the caves in and above the

[16.] [above] HEPO RI: laymen burning juniper twigs in *sang* offering to the Protectors (photograph by R. Demandre) [below] SAMYE: the Eight Manifestations of Guru Rimpoche (Guru Tsengye) in Lama-dance (photograph by B. Beresford)

Sangdok Peri Crag – are close to this *drubchu* in the gully. On the far eastern side of the gully is a rockfall in which the wise may see the shape of the sacred Tibetan letter HUNG. The Longchempa reliquary chorten is the hanging vowel of this sacred letter.

All Chimpu's hermitages were destroyed, and the walled caves rendered uninhabitable, during the Cultural Revolution. After the prohibition of religious practice in Tibet was lifted, many of the caves have become occupied, hermitages have been reconstructed, and the gompa rebuilt over the Guru's main cave. The area to the east of the gully where many ruined hermitages were still to be seen in 1985, shows how the entire site appeared in 1980.

Sangdok Peri (Zangs mdog dpal ri): "The Copper-coloured Mountain"

On the western side of the gully and one quarter of the distance up the amphitheatre is a conical crag about 15 m high protruding from the valley side. This is known as Sangdok Peri, the Copper-coloured Mountain Pure Land of Guru Rimpoche. The crag consists of a pile of glacial debris covering a rocky outcrop, and the spaces between the boulders cleared of earth and small rocks form excellent caves, a walled-in overhang, perhaps, forming a detached kitchen. Other hermitages are built into rock overhangs. Sangdok Peri is one of the most remarkable and sacred geomantic features of Chimpu.

Lower and upper *korra* circuits encircle Sangdok Peri. At the bottom of the crag on the lower circuit, and beside a path climbing up the valley, is a small shrine covering a rock with Guru Rimpoche's headprint in it. Above this is a cave called Dronme Puk, Butter Lamp Cave. To the right is Sangchen Metok Puk, Great Mystery Flower Cave, and Nyang Puk Wokma, Nyang's Lower Cave. Metok Puk is the cave in which Jigme Lingpa (p.202) received the three visitations of Longchempa that gave him full understanding of the Longchen Nyingtik and which resulted in his *magnum opus* the *Yonten Dzo*, a commentary upon Longchempa's work. Nyang is Nyang Tingedzin.

Around and up the *korra* path is a shrine marking the spot where Guru Rimpoche expounded the cycle of instruction called the Kandro Gongdu, which is described in an inscription here as "the heart-blood of the Kandroma". Nearby, the upper path branches off behind a 12 m long boulder lying at a 45-degree angle. In this rock is found the 4 m footprint of Guru Rimpoche imprinted after he transformed himself into a giant in order to fly to Yarlung Shetak away to the south-east, where his Tibetan consort Yeshe Tsogyel was in retreat. This rock is also called the Guru's Horse. On the south side of Sangdok Peri, below the upper circuit, is the Nyang Puk Gongma, Nyang's Upper Cave. Nyang Tingedzin was the principal disciple of Vimalamitra and the recipient of the Vimala Nyingtik, which he hid at Chimpu after writing it down in Tibetan. Nyang Tingedzin's Cave was later occupied by Longchempa who employed the Vimala Nyingtik in his synthesis of *kama* and *terma* doctrines to produce his monumental Dzokchen works. Guru Rimpoche's oral Dzokchen doctrines were also hidden here by Nyang. A *terton* called Pema Ledrel Tsel first discovered the *dzokchen mengakde* treasures, but because he lacked the relevant initiation he left them unopened for a later incarnation, Longchempa.

Kyentse Rimpoche mentions only the Upper and Lower Nyang Puks on Sangdok Peri, which he identifies as caves where Trisong Detsen did meditation retreat. There is some doubt about the identification of another important cave, the Tamdrin Puk. Our guides were quite adamant that the cave in which Gyelwa Chokyang, one of Guru Rimpoche's Twenty-four Disciples, performed the major propitiation of his tutelary deity Tamdrin, was the cave inhabited by a young nun on the upper east side of Sangdok Peri on the higher circuit. The *ani* inhabited a small but comfortable cave with a chimney shafting through to the sky, and a short tunnel connecting to her living space in a walled-in overhang. On the south side a flat rock over a precipitous descent gives a magnificent sense of vast space down the closed valley to the open plain of the Tsangpo. But Kyentse Rimpoche locates the Tamdrin Puk below the main Chimpu area, a location confirmed by another local resident who pin-pointed the cave half a kilometre down the valley near a large ruined lhakang on the path by Chimpu's old reservoir. A tree with stones tied to its branches for luck is another feature on the path near the cave. Above Tamdrin Puk is the site of a *dundro*.

Above Sangdok Peri and below the gompa are several caves named after the disciples of Guru Rimpoche who did retreat there. Immediately above Sangdok Peri is the cave of the translator Ma Rinchen Chok, and above that the cave of Shubu Pelseng. Just to the west of the latter is a cave of Yeshe Tsogyel in which the yogini's hand-print is frozen forever in rock. These three caves formed by the juxtaposition of vast boulders are all of a good size and fine caves for meditation.

Drakmar Keutsang (Brag dmar ke'u tshang): The Red-rock Treasury

What Kyentse Rimpoche describes as the mystical centre of Chimpu, Drakmar Keutsang,[2] the Red-rock Cavern, was the chief sanctuary of Guru Rimpoche. About 60 m above Sangdok Peri, just to the west of the gully, a new lhakang has been built over the two most important caves – Drakmar Keutsang and the Bairo Puk – by a Lama from Riwoche in Kham. This building now obscures the rock formation in which the Keutsang is to be found, but it has been described as a fissure about 5 m long, 2 m broad and from between 1 m and 2 m deep.[3] Since the present Drakmar Keutsang is a small cave about 3 m square and 2.5 m high, with an altar across its rear, all its walls solid stone, there is doubt as to the authenticity of this cave. The absence of the self-manifest mandala of the Drupa Kabgye, the Eight Logos Deities, which Kyentse Rimpoche found on the rock roof, strengthens this apprehension. In Drakmar Keutsang the Emperor Trisong Detsen, Yeshe Tsogyel and seven other principal disciples received authorization and empowerment to practise the *sadhanas* of the Drupa Kabgye, and also specific meditation instruction upon them. He also gave them the locations of their places of retreat, where they performed this their most vital meditation practice.

Originally the principal object of worship in the Keutsang was an image of Guru Rimpoche called Jema Atrong, believed to have been made personally by Bairotsana and one Tami Gontson. An image of Yumchen, the Great Mother Prajnaparamitama, who was Trisong Detsen's Heart-Samaya, was another cult-object of great power. An image of the Guru flanked by Mandarava and Yeshe Tsogyel is still found at the centre of the altar, but it is doubtful that this, or the present image of Yumchen, are the original statues.

In front of the cave, in the middle of the floor of the monks' dukang, is the rock on which Princess Pema Tsel, daughter of Trisong Detsen, who had died prematurely, was brought back to life by the Guru. He then gave her instruction in the Kandro Nyingtik, the Kandroma's Heart-drop, which liberated her from the wheel of life. She is supposed also to have been dismembered on this rock before her mortal remains were fed to the vultures, and the imprint of her body can be seen thereupon.

Bairo Puk (Bairo phug): Bairotsana's Cave
The entrance to the cave of Bairotsana, the Bairo Puk, is found in the chamber at the west end of the terrace built above the main sanctuary. It is reached through 4 m of tunnel that opens out into a small chamber barely long enough for a man to stretch out. It has a rough hewn altar but in 1985 no cult-objects, as if it has remained untended since the original structures on the site were destroyed.

The Upper Caves
A half-hour climb above the gompa takes the pilgrim to an important group of three meditation caves. To the left of the gully is a Guru Rimpoche *simpuk*; to the right of the gully is the cave of Atsara Sale, Yeshe Tsogyel's Nepali consort; and below this is the most significant of Yeshe Tsogyel's caves at Chimpu. Here at the top of Chimpu, Kyentse Rimpoche locates the Lompo Gul, the Minister's Cave, or Longchen Gurkar Puk, the Chief Minister's White-tent Cave, which he associates with Guru Rimpoche and Yeshe Tsogyel and others of the Twenty-four Disciples. Here Guru Rimpoche made a three month retreat, and here he concealed alchemical texts. The Lompo Gul may be identical to the Chimpu Dri Gugeu to which the Guru retired after he had instructed Trisong Detsen to build Samye Chokor. Here he subdued the *lu*, the serpentine protectors of the site and guardians of the earth and the construction materials – wood and stone – that the king required. The Guru intimidated the *lu* by transforming himself into an eagle. Also in the Gugeu or Gegung cave Vimalamitra hid his own Vimala Nyingtik treasures. It is possible that both the Lompo Gul and Gugeu are names of the Guru Rimpoche *simpuk*, as we failed to discover any other likely cave in the vicinity.

East of the Gully

On the eastern side of the gully there are many hermitages, most
of them walled-in overhangs, but also a few caves, built over the
uniformly steep hillside. A small lhakang has been restored and is
now functional. The only named power-place we discovered on
the east side belonged to Longchempa. Below the long HUNG of
the rockfall is the Longchen Bumpa which enshrines the relics of
that greatest of the latter-day Nyingma *panditas* and yogins
(p.169). He spent the end of his life at Chimpu. At the age of
fifty-six he died in a *dundro* high on the east side of the Chimpu
amphitheatre, and this, he said, was the closest he could come to
the Bodh Gaya Siwaitsel (Sitavana) charnel ground. The 7 m
high chorten, which has been restored, preserves his relics. A
stele at its side records his life and achievements. Close by is a
low, geomantically unappealing cave that some will identify as a
cave where Longchempa meditated. It is little more than a hole
in the ground. Longchempa gave the Kandro Nyingtik instruction
at Chimpu. It was at this time that Guru Rimpoche appeared to
him and gave him the name Drime Woser. He also taught *trekcho*
and *togel* in Chimpu.

History

The names of the yogins of the Nyingma tradition who have
come to Chimpu to meditate down the centuries include many of
the important treasure-finders of the tradition. Chetsun Senge
Wangchuk (11th-12th centuries) and Shangton Tashi Dorje
(1097-1167) both discovered Vimala Nyingtik precepts in
Chimpu. Sangye Lingpa alias Rinchen Lingpa (1340-96), Dorje
Lingpa the third Royal Treasure-finder (1346-1405), the Great
Engineer Tangton Gyelpo (1385-1510), all discovered treasure
here during the Nyingma renaissance of the 14th and 15th
centuries in which Samye's retreat centre at Chimpu played a
major part. In the 16th century Ngari Panchen Pema Wangyel
(1487-1543) stayed in retreat at Chimpu and was rewarded by
many visions; and Minling Terchen Gyurme Dorje (1646-1714)
also meditated here. After the Sakya school came to dominate
Samye, Chimpu was adopted by Chongye Peri. Today it is again
under Samye.

Drakmar Drinsang (Brag dmar mGrin bzang): Trisong Detsen's
  Birthplace

The site of the ancient lhakang at Drinsang[4] and the Emperor
Trisong Detsen's birthplace is rather more than an hour's walk, or
6 km, up the broad fertile plain of the Drakmar Valley. This
place of pilgrimage is located on the valley-side just to the west
of the jeep-road. The lhakang itself, built on a spur overlooking
the valley, has long since disappeared, but the small house below
the spur which is said to have been the actual place of the
Emperor Trisong Detsen's birth remained in 1959. This house
now lies in ruins, while the red and white sandalwood trees that
once grew large in its courtyard have vanished, along with the
small lhakangs that had been constructed on the site.

The original lhakang at Drinsang was built by the Emperor Me
Agtsom (705-55), Trisong Detsen's predecessor. Built on the
caravan route from Yarlung, the Emperor's winter capital, to
Lhasa, the summer capital, it was a stop in the Emperor's
progress along the route. The Emperor Trisong Detsen was born
here in 742(?).

Yamalung (gYa ma lung): Guru Rimpoche's Cave

Above the village of Ngamgo,[5] where some 18 km from Samye
the valley narrows and rises more sharply, there is a major river
confluence. The western effluent flows from the Gokar La; the
eastern river from the pass on the path to Ganden. The hermitage
of Samye Yamalung[6] is located up the eastern valley. Less than an
hour's walk brings the pilgrim to the base of a high cliff on the
western side of this valley, and another hour takes him to the
hermitage site some 300 m above.

At the bottom of the site is a spring in a grove of trees, which
flows with the Water of Long-life, a gift of Guru Rimpoche, who
also concealed Long-life *sadhanas* here. Slightly higher is the
Orgyen Puk, Guru Rimpoche's cave, which is a large enclosed
overhang in the cliff. Within this cave-lhakang are several self-
manifest phenomena, including the Guru's foot and hand prints.

At the centre of the altar at the back is a new statue of Guru Rimpoche. Higher up the slope is the small *drupuk* of the translator Bairotsana.

History

Yamalung is one of the eight chief hermitages of Guru Rimpoche and a location of the Great Guru's hidden treasure. He instructed his consort Yeshe Tsogyel in the rudiments of the Buddha-*dharma* and she received her first initiation at Yamalung. When the Emperor Trisong Detsen was politically besieged by his Bonpo ministers at Samye he sent letters to his Guru at Yamalung asking for advice and finally with a warning to escape. When the Guru's Twenty-four Disciples were initiated into the Drupa Kabgye mandala at Chimpu, both Bairotsana and Denma Tsemang's initiatory flowers fell upon the *yidam* Mopa Drakngak's section of the mandala, and the Guru sent them to meditate at Yamalung. Bairotsana stayed here in retreat for three years, and his attainment was described as an ability to hold the three realms that constitute the universe in the palm of his hand. The *drupuk* at Yamalung is chiefly associated with this Dzokchempa. In the 17th century his incarnation, Minling Terchen (p.165), discovered the Rigdzin Tuktik at Yamalung.

Yamalung was never developed beyond a centre for mountain retreat, a *ritro*, and during the last few centuries the buildings erected during its more vital period decayed. The hermitages still standing in 1959, occupied by some twenty-five hermits, have all been destroyed. In 1984 a solitary Khampa yogin lived in the Bairo Puk, but after his death, during 1985, Yamalung was deserted. In 1986 Guru Rimpoche's cave, the Orgyen Puk, was walled in and two or three yogins were resident. Another yogin occupyied the Bairo Puk.

From Yamalung to Dechen Dzong Via the Gokar La

Returning from Yamalung to Ngamgo, where the jeep-road from Samye ends, the path to the Gokar La ascends a lush green valley. Traces of the old massive stairway along this route appear in the forest and in the meadowland above it. Below the Gokar La there are *drokpas'* summer camps. The master and translator Bairotsana, who meditated at Yamalung, is reputed to have named the Gokar La, White Eagle Pass. The path descends steeply from the large cairns of the pass by several *drokpa* camps, and through yak pastures inhabited by fearless hares and marmots. After a four-hour walk, and having forded the vicious river, the first village on the north side of the pass is reached. Another five hours' walk through a fertile and prosperous valley on a jeep-road brings the pilgrim to Dechen Xian (p.98), 24 km east of Lhasa.

15

THE VALLEY OF YON

Yonlung, the Valley of Yon,[1] lies on the north bank of the Tsangpo River, east of Tsetang. Away from its barren flood plain and the wind-blown sand of the Tsangpo, the valley is rich and fertile, growing peas and beans besides wheat and barley in its middle reaches, while the meadows and pastures of the upper valley provide excellent grazing. At the head of this beautiful valley is the power-place of Guru Rimpoche called Yonpu Taktsang, at the foot of the valley is the site of the important Geluk academy of Ngari Dratsang, while in its middle reaches is the ancient temple of Keru, and also Choding Gompa and the hermitage of Tashi Doka.

The history of Yon indicates that the people of the valley have much to remember with pride. Tucci noticed relics of the plunder of Central Asian cities by the emperors of the 8th century. The Taktsangpas of Yonpu gave Gurus to the Ming Emperors in the 15th century, and in the 18th century the Gyese of Choding was Regent of Tibet during the Dalai Lama's sojourn on the Chinese border. Today Yon is part of Tsetang District, with its own administrative centre at Yon Qu, but since there is no connection to a road outside the valley, horses and carts are the principal means of transport, and the valley has remained isolated from development dependent upon motor transport.

Also included in this section is the description of Densatil, one of the original Kagyupa gompas, founded in the 12th century by a disciple of Je Gampopa. Although only ruins remain at this site its natural beauty is extraordinary and the historical significance of the place is immense.

Access

The entrance to Yonlung is a two-day walk from Samye in the west, or one day from Sangri in the east. However, it is most easily accessible across the river by way of motor ferry from the ferry station 4 km east of Tsetang on the highway to Sangri. From the north it is accessible from the Medro Valley, east of Chakar Gompa, in a three-day walk over the *Takar La. The

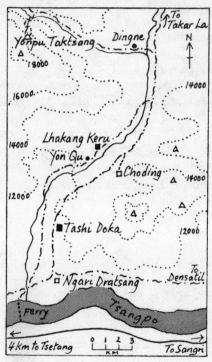

Map 15 The Yon Valley

upper reaches of the Yon Valley leading to Taktse are accessible over a 5,500 m pass from the Lo Valley in the west.

The Yon Valley runs south-west/north-east from the ferry to the *Takar La pass, but where the path begins to rise more steeply during the second day's walk the valley divides, the northern arm continuing to the *Takar La while a western branch turns west and then south-west. This western arm of the valley terminates at Yonpu Taktsang, more than a day's walk from *Dingne.

Ngari Dratsang (mNga' ri Grwa tshang)

The eminence upon which Ngari Dratsang[2] was built dominates the entrance to the Yon Valley. Now only chimneys of masonry indicate the vanished strength of this Geluk fortress-academy. Tucci waxed lyrical to describe it in 1949: "The massive building, as redoubtable and inaccessible as a fortress, dominated the valley from the sharp ridge where it stood planted with a warrior's fine bearing."[3] Tucci found a giant Tang relic container here that he surmised was part of the plunder brought back from Central Asia in the 8th century. It was, undoubtedly, a very wealthy foundation.

History
The Ngari Dratsang was erected for Geluk students from Western Tibet (Ngari) in 1541 under the auspices of the second Dalai Lama, Gendun Gyatso (1475-1542), and financed by a king of Guge. "The Religious King, Lord of the World, Pekarde, and his minister Ngawang Namgyel sent from Ngari many initiates, like a flock of geese, together with an offering of many jewels, to build a college in Gyel, and so even today it is known as Ngari Dratsang."[4]

Below Ngari Dratsang on its north side is the village of *Takkar Sho, and ruins believed to belong to an ancient residence of the Pakmodrupa, who gained their name from the valley below Densatil where Drogon Dorje Gyelpo built his hermitage.

Tashi Doka (bKra shis rdo kha): Tsongkapa's Hermitage

About 8 km up the valley, in a fold low on its eastern side, where a spring emerges to provide a rash of variant greens on the barren hillside, is the hermitage of Tashi Doka. A small gompa lies in the dip surrounded by willow trees, and a tiny lhakang stands above it. Tsongkapa stayed in this ideal spot with its magical spring (*drubchu*) in meditation retreat for two months in 1415. It was here that he met his disciple Gendun Drub, who became the first Dalai Lama. It has been rebuilt since the Cultural Revolution and three monks are now in residence.

Lhakang Keru (Lha khang ke ru): An Ancient Nyingma Temple

Some 15 km up the valley is the new administrative centre of Yon Qu, built on the site of the old Gyekang Dzong. A short distance beyond, set back on the west side of the road behind farm buildings is Lhakang Keru,[5] an unassuming square, two-storey *vihara*. The original Keru temple is attributed to the Emperor Trisong Detsen. The present building, miraculously preserved from the ravages of the Cultural Revolution, in part may date from the 11th century. Very similar in plan to the Muru Nyingba behind the Jokang in Lhasa, it consists of a dukang and lhakang in the centre of a courtyard surrounded on three sides by monks' quarters.

The style of the temple building is of the simplicity associated with very early construction, a few large undecorated beams, without supporting pillars, holding the roof. Original Nyingma murals decorate the dukang: Guru Rimpoche is represented on both side walls; facing the door, the Dzokchen Protectors are found on the right and the Tenma Protectress of the Passes on the left; facing the lhakang, Menlha, the Medicine Buddha, is on the right and Sakyamuni on the left. Within the inner lhakang is a fine 4 m high Buddha in the centre, surrounded by statues of the Eight Bodhisattvas and the two Door Protectors whose faces have been mutilated. The date of the murals and statues is much later than the temple structure.

In the north-west corner of the courtyard is the small room that contained the Chorten Karchung, the Small White Chorten, in the Indian style, that contained some of Jowo Atisha's relics. This chorten has now disappeared. In 1047/8 Jowo Atisha stayed one month at Lhakang Keru, and his portrait on the wall of the room containing the Chorten Karchung was said to have been painted by him. Murals of Jowo Je and his principal disciples, Dromton and Naktso Lotsawa, can still be seen there. Je Rimpoche Tsongkapa also lived in this small room for some time. Next to it is the empty lhakang that was associated with the Geluk tradition.

Previously twenty-eight monks from Dorje Drak were resident here together with a few Geluk monks. In 1986 there was one resident Nyingma monk from Samye Gompa, together with two Gelukpas.

Choding (Chos sdings)

Undoubtedly the gompa that dominated Yonlung economically and politically in recent centuries was the Choding Gompa belonging to the Geluk school. The ruins of this large complex can be seen in a side-valley to the east of Lhakang Keru. Rebuilding had not begun in 1986.

History
Choding was probably founded in the 12th century by four Nyingma yogins, who are mentioned in the *Blue Annals*, but it also has Kadampa antecedents. Later, as a Geluk gompa, Choding was the residence of the Gyese Rimpoches (Jinaputra), incarnations of Shiwailha (Santideva), the Indian *prajnaparamita* commentator, author of perhaps the most renowned work on the *prajnaparamita*, the *Bodhicaryavatara*. The first incarnation's relics were venerated at Choding when Tucci visited in 1948. From 1728-35 the fourteenth incarnation, Jigme Yeshe Drakpa, acted as regent of the seventh Dalai Lama when the latter was exiled to the Chinese frontier.

Yonpu Taktsang ('On phy stag tshang): Guru Rimpoche's Tiger Lair

The most potent power-place of Yonlung is Yonpu Taktsang, the Yonpu Tiger's Lair, another of the Guru Rimpoche caves situated high in the *pu* at the head of a valley. From the Tsangpo two or three days are required to reach it, including more than a day from the village of *Dingne, where the path first veers west, and then south-west and south, up the upper Yon Valley. The cave is located high in the cliff-face. All the construction on the site has been destroyed, but a single small lhakang has been restored. It is a *terne* of Orgyen Lingpa.

The Three Taktsangs

The three "Tiger Lairs" associated with Guru Rimpoche and Yeshe Tsogyel are Paro Taktsang, the cave-hermitage hanging upon a high, precipitous cliff behind Paro in Bhutan (Mon), where Guru Rimpoche became Dorje Trollo and where he hid many Purba treasures; Kham Taktsang, the famous retreat near Katok Gompa in Kham, also associated with Purba; and this Yonpu Taktsang. The Guru identified these three Taktsangs as the external places analogous to his internal focal points of Mind, Speech, and Body, respectively. They may be treated as the principal sites at which *terma*-treasures were hidden, and the Guru's meditation at the place maximized the potential for ultimate maturing experiences beyond what the already powerfully expeditious geomantic environment could provide.

Yeshe Tsogyel and Yonpu Taktsang

Yonpu Taktsang figured significantly in the life of Yeshe Tsogyel, Guru Rimpoche's Tibetan consort. It was here that Tsogyel, the Princess of Karchen, hid from her rival suitors after escaping the prince who had won her in an athletics contest, and here the losing suitor found her and whipped her back to Surkar (p.219). After she had completed her eight austerities, her meditation on the snowline at Shoto Tidro, and her alchemical practices and energy-control yoga at Paro Taktsang, she came here to find Guru Rimpoche awaiting her. He gave her the Dorje Purba initiations at Yonpu Taktsang.

The Taktsang Kagyupa

The significance of Yonpu Taktsang for the Nyingmapas is only surpassed by its importance for the Taktsangpas. The independent Kagyu gompa at Yonpu Taktsang gave its name to a school following the teaching of Milarepa. Established in 1405, its influence spread even as far as the Ming court in China, the Emperor bestowing the title "Defender of the Faith" upon the Taktsang Kyapgon, thus giving this obscure hermitage international recognition.

Densatil

Since Densatil lies several kilometres to the west of Ngari Dratsang, and about the same distance from Sangri in the east, it is in between the geographic and ethnic limits of Yon and Sangri. It is located on a shelf high in the *pu* of a ravine. The ravine opens up at the village of Pakmodru[6] ("Sow's Ferry") on to the Tsangpo flood plain. The path from Yon and Ngari Dratsang begins its ascent 1.5 km beyond the village of *Jang and climbs a spur before following the contours of the ravine-valley to Densatil at about 4,750 m. A road from the Sangri ferry follows the Tsangpo to the west, and a path winds through the ravine to climb very steeply up to the gompa. The path from Sangri Xian crosses the ridge that bounds the Sangri plain on its west side and ascends gradually to cross a ridge into the Densatil valley and thus down to the gompa itself. This last route provides the most impressive approach through luxuriant flora.

Travellers have described the idyllic beauty of the valley immediately above and below Densatil in highly romantic terms. Streams descend its cliffs in cascades; rhododendrons, wild roses and an amazing proliferation of other flowering shrubs cover the slopes below; and under the limestone crags of the broad amphitheatre that forms the backdrop to the gompa is a forest of junipers, which invites comparison with the junipers of Reteng. The remains of meditation caves pocket the cliffs to the west of the gompa at the same level as the emerging springs.

The entire monastic complex of Densatil has been completely

destroyed, the growth of demented vegetation accelerating a process begun by the Red Guards. Within the ruined walls of the Lhakang Chempo, below the dukang pilgrims have placed a canopy of prayer-flags over the spot upon which the gompa's founder, Dorje Gyelpo, constructed his hut. At the foot of the spur on which the Lhakang Chempo is constructed is a restored *sungkang*, the residence of the gompa's Protector. Below it on the east side of the ridge is a walled-in sleeping-cave with its altar intact. Above the path to the west of the gompa, under the cliff that is pitted with meditation caves, is a new lhakang. These were the only signs of human activity at Densatil in 1986.

The Pakmodrupa ascendancy during the 14th and 15th centuries brought vast wealth to Densatil. Pre-1959 travellers noticed the signs of this wealth with some incredulity. Das describes six tablets of gold hanging from the ceiling of the dukang, each six feet long and six inches wide, and he mentions eighteen reliquaries in silver, the repositories of the remains of eighteen successors of Dorje Gyelpo. These chortens were actually copper gilded with silver; Tucci remarks upon the consistency of the quality of the engraving and casting work which covered these reliquaries. Kyentse Rimpoche mentions the statue called the Jisama as the most significant blessing-bestowing image in Densatil, but he does not identify its subject. Perhaps it was the statue of Dorje Gyelpo himself which Lama Tsenpo mentions.

History

The Master Drogon Pakmodrupa Dorje Gyelpo was born in Dokam in the East in 1110, and he came to Central Tibet to study with the great teachers of his day. He was taught *lamdre* by Sakya Pandita; Lama Shang of Tse Gungtang was another of his teachers; but his principal Lama was Je Gampopa (p.261). He met Gampopa late in the Guru's life at Daklha Gampo, and from him he received Mahamudra instruction together with many other precepts originating with Milarepa. After Je Gampopa's death, in 1158 Drogon Dorje Gyelpo founded Densatil where he lived in a small meditation hut constructed of willow sticks. Amongst the 800 monks who gathered at Densatil were Taklung Tangpa Tashi Pel who established the Taklung Kagyu, Drigung Rimpoche Rinchen Pel who established the Drigung Kagyu, and

Ling Repa Pema Dorje who established the Drukpa Kagyu. These became his most renowned disciples. After his death in 1170, conflict between the abbots of Taklung and Drigung resulted in the establishment of Chenga Rimpoche in the Chair of Densatil, and thus Densatil became attached to the Drigungpas. At this time the Great Lhakang was built over the master's hut and the collection of books was gathered for which Densatil became famous.

Immediately after the master yogin and teacher Drogon Pakmodrupa Dorje Gyelpo died, his establishment was involved in political wrangling, and with the rise of his family's political fortunes in the 14th century, when Tai Situ Jangchub Gyeltsen became ruler of Tibet with his capital in Neudong in Yarlung (p.176), Densatil became increasingly politicized. However, the Pakmodrupas of Neudong became detached from their Kagyupa antecedents and allied with the rising Yellow Hats. From the 14th century the succession at Densatil passed from uncle to nephew within the Pakmodru family, the political and abbot's offices often residing in a single person. In the 16th century the Pakmodrupas of Neudong were stripped of their power by their ministers based at Rinpung in Tsang. By the 19th century the reputation of Densatil and the number of monks in residence was much reduced, and the monastery was no longer a fully functioning monastic institution.

16

SANGRI AND THE WOKA VALLEY

Some 40 km to the east of Tsetang the Tsangpo River enters a gorge. Not more than 200 m wide the river that has been more than a kilometre in width for some stretches becomes a raging torrent with angry rocks protruding from its white surface. To avoid this gorge the Tsetang-Chamdo highway turns south-east through Lhagyari to the *Potang La. For the pilgrim the principal route crosses the river to Sangri District and follows the Woka[1] Valley to the north-east.

Sangri Xian dominates a small, rich and fertile plain, and on the eastern side of this oasis on an eminence overlooking the river is Sangri Karmar. This principal power-place of Sangri derives its importance from the 11th-century residence there of one of Tibet's most important yoginis, Machik Labdron.

The Sangri-Woka route was that traditionally followed by the Dalai Lamas en route to Lhamo Latso in Dakpo over the Gyelong La at the head of the Woka Valley, and remnants of the ancient paved way are still visible. But Woka is more than a corridor into Dakpo, for on its eastern side is the mountain Wode Gungyel, one of Tibet's most sacred mountains, worshipped by Bon and Buddhist alike and a favourite resort of hermits. The master Tsongkapa is associated with several hermitages in this area. The Wode Gungyel massif forms part of the area known as Upper Central Tibet, Uto.

At the northern end of the gorge to the west of Wode Gungyel the Woka Valley divides, the eastern fork slowly rising to the Gyelong La while the principal branch continues north to

Dzinchi Qu, the present administrative centre of northern Woka, and the site of Woka's principal gompa. The Lamas of Dzinchi, the Gyeltseb Rimpoches, were incarnations of Gyeltseb Je Dharma Rinchen who was Tsongkapa's disciple. The important role that these Lamas played in the history of Tibet demonstrates the importance of Woka, its wealth and political influence. Woka was once also called Lelung.

Access to Woka can also be gained from the north. The Lhasa-Chamdo road follows the Medro Valley to the south-east up to the Gya La. Near the hot springs of *Rutok Gompa (km 1444) a path turns south up a long valley to Magon La. A further hard day's walk over high yak pastures populated only by *drokpas* brings the pilgrim down to Dzinchi in Woka.

Sangri Karmar (Zangs ri mkhar dmar): Machik Labdron's Hermitage

A vehicle ferry crosses the Tsangpo from the village of *Rong (p.262), and a jeep-road skirts Sangri Xian to pass Samdrub Potang on the eastern side of the Sangri plain. Samdrub Potang is the well-preserved three-storey palace of the Lord of Sangri that dominated the old village. It is now occupied by the proletariat. It lies at the bottom of the "copper mountain" that gives Sangri its name. Sangri Karmar, the Red Citadel, is located on a 50 m prominence at the southern extremity of this mountain over-looking the Tsangpo. The colour of Karmar Drak, Red Citadel Rock, representing the nature of the Dakini who lived there, is derived from the orange lichens that cover its sides.

The entire large complex of Sangri Karmar[2] was destroyed during the Cultural Revolution. Today a single small lhakang has been rebuilt on top of the rock with quarters for three monks beside it. The small square lhakang had not been decorated in 1986 and an old *tanka* depicting Machik Labdron as a Dancing Kandroma was the only original relic remaining. On the cliff-face to the west of the lhakang is Machik Labdron's meditation cave, her *drupuk* restored as a small shrine room. A new statue of Machik with iconography identical to the depiction in the *tanka*

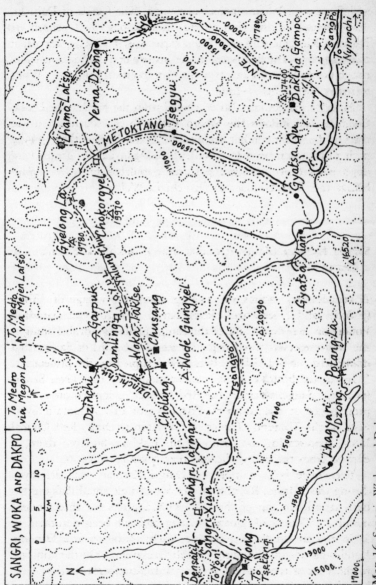

Map 16 Sangri, Woka and Dakpo

in the lhakang – she brandishes a knife above her shoulder in her left hand and holds a bell at her thigh in her right hand – has been erected in the cave. It is a faithful copy of the original Talking Kandroma. At the back of the cave is a hole from which treasures of Guru Rimpoche were recovered.

History

Machik Labchi Dronma (1055-1149) settled at Karmar late in her life. She was ordained by Drapa Ngonshe (p.158) in her youth and became fluent in the *prajnaparamita sutras*. Later she met her root Guru, the Indian yogin Padampa Sangye, at Tingri, and received the entire transmission of the *choyul* tradition, becoming the principal exemplar of this practice. Through exposure to charnel-ground demons in *choyul*, this yoga is particularly efficacious in inducing awareness of the pure nature of all emotion and the empty essence of all kinds of mental obstruction, including disease, which is all reduced to psychosomatic functions. Machik then cohabited with the yogin Topa Bhadra, but scorned as a *samaya* breaker she left Tingri to begin an itinerant existence in eastern Tibet. She gave birth to three boys and two girls. Then she came to Sangri alone, and re-ordained she spent several years in retreat here. The Red Hat establishment of Sangri Karmar was eventually adopted by the Geluk school, becoming a dependency of Ngari Dratsang. The Geluk monks of Karmar were forced to marry during the Cultural Revolution, and this explains the absence of *gelongs* in residence today.

Wode Gungyel ('Od lde gung rgyal): Old Man Mountain

To the east of the Woka Valley is one of Central Tibet's highest and most sacred mountains. Wode Gungyel[3] is the name of a king of the second Tibetan dynasty, the son of King Drigum, who was the first king to be interred rather than ascend the sky-cord to the Bonpo heaven. Wode Gungyel is also a mountain god, a *shidak*, and a Protector of the Dharma. Known as Sipai Lhagen, Old God of the World, and commander of a host of ancestral spirits, he is father of Nyenchen Tanglha (p.131).

A huge dome of rock, it steadily mounted, each ridge topped by the next one, up to its abrupt, toothed, forbidding crests glistening with ice and overhanging the snow-blanketed slopes. The Wode Gungyel was wrapped in an unceasing blizzard. Only in its brief respites did a sudden rend in the clouds and a touch of fugitive sun allow a glimpse of the mountain in all its glory.[4]

A high and difficult circumambulatory path takes the pilgrim around the mountain in three days.

Woka Taktse ('Ol kha stag rtse): The Old Woka Dzong

From Sangri a jeep-road follows the Tsangpo before crossing a spur into the Woka Valley and ascending the long gorge on the western side of Wode Gungyel. Woka Taktse is located on the spur between the two branches of the Woka river. The rich principality of Woka was once ruled from Woka Taktse *dzong*, dominating the confluence of Woka's two valleys. The northern valley, leading to Dzinchi, is fertile and prosperous, while the eastern valley is broad and dry. The wealth of Woka was stolen by the Mongols in their various incursions, and after the last raid in the 18th century the valley never recovered. Taktse was virtually destroyed during that period and nothing of the citadel remains today.

Cholung (Chos lung): Tsongkapa's Hermitage

Cholung lies on the southern side of the valley to the south-east of Taktse. A stream flows by it draining the northern side of Wode Gungyel. It is the most significant of the hermitage sites on the slopes of Wode Gungyel, and it was Je Tsongkapa who sanctified it as a major power-place. A number of hermitages were built here over the centuries in emulation of the 14th-century scholar and yogin who transformed the Kadampas into the Geluk school.

Here were the sleeping quarters of the master Lama, which were constructed according to the *vinaya*, and also the prints of the master's hands, feet and knees, which were made while he was practising ascetic rites. There appear distinctly such things as many letters on the surface of a stone mandala, which were self-originated when Je Rimpoche [Tsongkapa] had visions of the Thirty-five Buddhas of Confession; a *mani* [the Six-syllable Mantra] on the surface of a rock, which was written by the master himself with his finger; and the prints of the master's back and the designs of his girdle and gown.[5]

The restoration of Cholung was begun immediately upon the Chinese policy change that permitted the rebuilding of monasteries. Already, in 1986, with twenty-five monks and young students in residence, the rebuilt dukang and gomkang had resumed an age-old appearance. It is in conformity with the Tibetan schools' general trend of return to their origins that the Gelukpas have restored a hermitage of Tsongkapa to its original vitality.

Chusang (Chu bzangs)

A short distance to the north-east of Cholung is another hermitage site where Tsongkapa stayed. A small lhakang has been rebuilt at Chusang and a solitary monk is in residence. Tsongkapa's foot and handprints can be seen here.

Dzinchi (rDzing phyi): Gyelwa Jampa's Residence

Dzinchi Qu, the old Dzinchi Dzong, is located some 8 km to the north of Woka Taktse up the valley of the Dzinchi Chu. From Dzinchi a path veering west and then north leads to the upper Medro Valley via the Magon La. Two hours' walk directly to the north of Dzinchi is *Mejen Latso, the Life-spirit lake of the Protectress *Mejen, and a path continues north to the Medro

Valley. To the east a path leads to Garpuk and Samling.

The Dzinchi Gompa[6] consisted of three principal buildings: the Tsokang, the Labrang and the Jampa Lhakang. The Tsokang was destroyed only in 1982 to be replaced by a community hall more suited to the new dispensation. The Labrang, which was the residence of the Gyeltseb Choje Rimpoches, has been used as a store-house and undoubtedly will be restored in time. The Jampa Lhakang, which enshrined the Dzinchi Jampa, the most sacred artefact at Dzinchi, had its roof removed during the Cultural Revolution, and the shell of the building was in process of restoration in 1986. The original murals on the walls at the front of the Jampa Lhakang dukang, on both sides of the entrance to the *sanctum sanctorum*, depict Tsongkapa and his disciples. The murals of the Jampa Lhakang are said to have arisen spontaneously according to the Geluk school's founder's vision after intense meditation at Dzinchi. On the back wall of the dukang are original murals of the Dharma Protectors: Chakdrukpa (Six Armed Mahakala), Namse (Vaisravana), and Dorje Lekpa. The original statue of Jampa is lost, replaced by a new image, which, however, retains the feet of the original. A rock impressed with Tsongkapa's fingerprints is one of the few other relics remaining here.

Above and to the north-east of the ruins of an Ani Gompa built into the rock-face behind the village are several caves. At the *Tendi Drupuk are the footprints of Gyelwa Jampa's goat, with palm-prints near the cave's entrance. Further along, near Jampa's life-spirit tree (*lashing*), is one of Jampa's meditation caves, the Jampa Drupuk. A third cave, excavated in the shape of a cube, now filled with *tsatsa*, is another meditation cave in which Jampa is said to have lived. All three of these caves are excellent places for meditation.

History

The original statue of the Dzinchi Jampa is said to have been one of the oldest statues in Tibet. Local oral tradition tells of a revered monk from Dome in Eastern Tibet, who became known as Gyelwa Jampa, the Buddha Maitreya, and who stayed at Dzinchi in the dim and distant past to meditate in one of the caves in the rock-face behind the village. One night the hermit's spontaneously-manifest goat let flow a stream of milk that ran down the hill to the spot where a temple should be constructed. After the Jampa Lhakang was completed Gyelwa Jampa stayed in it one night and then disappeared. The image of Jampa was considered identical to him. From historical sources we know that the statue of the Dzinchi Jampa was the creation of one Garmiton Yonten Yungdrung, who is also credited with founding the Dzinchi temple. Garmiton was a disciple of the Khampa Lama Gongpa Rabsel who was ordained by one of the three monks that escaped from the 9th-century suppression of the *dharma* in Central Tibet. Thus the Jampa Lhakang's origins lie in the 10th century.

The Jampa Lhakang was also renowned for its association with Tsongkapa, a connection that later provoked the Geluk establishment to acquire the monastery from its Red Hat caretakers. Tsongkapa had the temple restored, and in 1393 he had the Jampa image renovated. It is likely that the original image was destroyed by the Dzungars in the early 18th century, as the original image had disappeared by 1948. What indubitably is still in Dzinchi is the notion of the Buddha Jampa, who is destined to incarnate on earth at the end of an unparalleled era of suffering, aggression and destruction.

An important power-source at Dzinchi was the relics of Taranatha enshrined in a silver chorten in the Jampa Lhakang. Taranatha was the founder of the Jonang school and the gompa of that name in the Tsangpo Valley to the north of Lhatse in Tsang. The story has it that his bones were thrown into the river near Jonang only to be rescued from it somewhere east of Sangri Karmar and taken to Dzinchi to be enshrined. The reliquary has now vanished.

Historically, Dzinchi has derived importance from the residence there of the Gyeltseb Rimpoches in the Dzinchi Labrang. The Gyeltseb Rimpoches were incarnations of the foremost disciple of Tsongkapa, Gyeltseb Je Dharma Rinchen, and due to Woka's staunch support of the Yellow Hats before their political success, the Dzinchi Rimpoches were powerful voices in Geluk councils. Further, Dzinchi was the birthplace of the eleventh Dalai Lama. The large, imposing building in which he was born, now converted into a people's residence, stands beyond the communal threshing ground.

Woka Garpuk ('Ol kha mGar phug): Cave of the Dancing Dakini

Guru Rimpoche's cave at Garpuk[7] is located in the grass-covered hills to the east of Dzinchi, and from that village it can be reached by foot in four hours. It lies at the top of a valley draining into the eastern arm of the Woka Valley below Samling (see below), from where Garpuk is also accessible. The cave remains, but all other construction has been destroyed and there was neither caretaker nor yogin resident in 1986.

History
Garpuk is probably the oldest power-place in Woka, as Guru Rimpoche lived in the cave here in the 8th century. While meditating at Garpuk the Great Guru assumed the form of the Dancing Kandroma and was known by that name. He concealed treasure in the cave, particularly a text pertaining to the Kandroma. Later, after Je Gampopa (1079-1153) spent a year giving instruction at Garpuk, a temple of the Dakpo Kagyupas was built there. In the 14th century Tsongkapa meditated there in a *drubkang*, and thereafter the Yellow Hats became entrenched at Garpuk.

Samten Ling (bSam gtan gling)

High above the eastern arm of the Woka Valley, are the ruins of Woka Samten Ling.[8] The place is associated with Je Gampopa and Tsongkapa, who both spent some time in this *ritro* mountain retreat. "An Offering-house was erected here by eight men who could penetrate solid objects with their bodies."[9] Samten Ling was a Geluk gompa at the time of its destruction.

Gyelong La

To the east of Samten Ling the eastern arm of the Woka Valley becomes *Loyul. The path ascends on the south bank of the

*Yulung Chu through a gorge which soon opens out into a broad valley. During a second day's walk from Samling rich vegetation gives way to high yak pastures. At the top of the valley is the Gyelong La (approx. 5,600 m) located above one of the twenty-one lakes of the area sacred to Drolma, and beyond the pass is Dakpo and Chokorgyel.

17

DAKPO AND LHAMO LATSO

In the far east of Central Tibet, close to the border of Kongpo, in the old province of Dakpo, lies Gyatsa District (see map p.247). The old province of Dakpo comprised part of the easternmost "horn" or "wing" (see p.286) of the four administrative districts of the central part of Songtsen Gampo's empire. Dakpo included districts on both north and south banks of the Tsangpo to the east of Tsetang. Today it includes only the districts of Gyatsa, on the north bank of the Tsangpo, and Lang, on the south bank, both to the east of the *Potang La. With its walnut and apricot trees and beautiful flowering shrubs, Gyatsa District gives intimation of the prolific variety and abundance of flora that is to be found in more eastern and southern regions of Tibet. Three important power-places are located in this district: Chokorgyel gompa, Lhamo Latso – the Oracle Lake, and Daklha Gampo gompa.

The once glorious Yellow Hat gompa of Chokorgyel, located in the upper part of the Metoktang Valley, lies at the geomantically powerful confluence of three rivers. Built by the second Dalai Lama, this monastery is associated with Lhamo Latso and its functions. Lhamo Latso derives its importance from the principal Protectress of Tibet, Pelden Lhamo, whose spirit is said to reside in the lake. It provided oracular visions for the Dalai Lamas and their Regents and it is still a very significant power-place, the destination of many contemporary pilgrims. Daklha Gampo, located to the north of the Tsangpo east of Gyatsa Qu, was founded by Milarepa's great scholar-disciple, Je Gampopa, the root-guru of several Kagyu lineages.

Access

Since no road penetrates the deep gorge through which the Tsangpo flows for about 50 km from Sangri to Gyatsa, the pilgrim must take the Tsetang-Chamdo highway that crosses the 5,000 m *Potang La on the south side of the Tsangpo. A side road at km 314 crosses the Tsangpo bridge for access to Gyatsa Qu. At Gyatsa Qu the Metoktang Chu, debouching from the gorge to the north, waters a fertile oasis. A 35 km jeep-road up the Metoktang Valley now links Gyatsa Qu with Chokorgyel. This distance can be covered on foot in two days. A half day's walk to the north-east of Chokorgyel, Lhamo Latso is viewed from the Dalai Lamas' throne on a ridge above the lake. Lhamo Latso drains into the *Nye Valley, which runs parallel to the Metoktang Valley and down to the Tsangpo. Towards the foot of the *Nye Valley Daklha Gampo is accessible high on the western side.

An alternative route to Chokorgyel follows the now decaying paved path from Sangri. The pavement was laid for the succession of Dalai Lamas and Regents bound for the Oracle lake. The path follows the Woka Valley (pp.248-254) over the Gyelong La and down into Metoktang from the north. This is a five-day walk.

Chokorgyel Gompa (Chos 'khor rgyal dgon pa): The Triune Gompa

Chokorgyel Gompa was built on the flatland in the elbow formed by the river flowing down from the Gyelong La in the north and the effluent joining it from the north-west. A third river, forming a confluence of three valleys, flows in from the north-east. The walled monastery compound is of triangular shape to reflect the triadic geomantic symbolism of this power-place where three valleys and three rivers meet, where three mountains dominate, where the elements air, water and earth are present in equal proportion, and where the female principle in the form of Pelden Lhamo, represented by an inverted triangle, is pre-eminent.

The mountain immediately behind the gompa to the north is

[17.] [above] CHOKORGYEL: the ruined triangular gompa looking down Metoktang (photograph by K. Dowman) [below] LHAMO LATSO: the Oracle Lake from the Dalai Lama's Throne (photograph by *Stone Routes*)

the "white" residence of the Shidak, the ancient Bonpo protector of the earth; to the south is the "blue" mountain residence of the Protectress Pelden Lhamo upon which the *dundro* site is located, and where the trees originated from the Goddess' locks; and to the east is the "red" mountain residence of Chamsing, better known as the Protector Begtse, a Yellow Hat import from Mongolia. On the east-facing slope of Chamsing Mountain is the old Red Hat gompa called simply Nyingsaka (*Nying*ma, *Sa*kya, *Ka*gyu) because it was shared by all three Red Hat schools. To the north of this, on the path, is a square rock in which lies the key to the treasure that will liberate the faithful when external conditions become insupportable. At that time the three mountains will close in, forming a hidden valley, a paradise of Guru Rimpoche.

The massive walls of Chokorgyel, protected by bastions and pierced by four towering gateways, confine all the monastic buildings cheek by jowl. During the Cultural Revolution every scrap of wood was removed from the buildings, leaving an impressive set of barren, roofless ruins. At the centre of the compound is a small courtyard with a pillar engraved with *sutra* and the Buddhist swastika. On the western side of this area is the old red-coloured Lukang, the temple of the Serpent Protectors. This temple was built over the hermitage of the second Dalai Lama, a cellar that is now filled in. The building was said to have been constructed by red eagles (*kyungka*, Garudas). On the north side is the principal red-coloured lhakang, called the Tsuklakang, in which murals can still be discerned. This was the Jampa Lhakang that housed a large image of Mipam Gompo dating from the monastery's foundation. The walls of Chokorgyel also protected two *dratsangs* of Geluk monks.

Outside the gompa walls are several sites of interest. Immediately to the south is the so-called Shinje Melong, the Mirror of the Lord of Death, a grey, polished granite stone in which horoscopes may be read as in a crystal ball, and which assists in rain-making rites. At the foot of the slope of Shidak Mountain is the Dalai Lamas' residence, a ruin of superior quality. Higher up the slope is the site of a demolished temple where the footprint of Damchen Choje, the Dharma Protector Bound to Service, is to be found. Higher still is the site of the second Dalai Lama's meditation cave, now obliterated. His footprint in stone has been preserved, although a contemporary inscription claims that the footprint belonged to the Emperor Songtsen Gampo.

In the old days Chokorgyel boasted 500 monks. Today no one lives within the monastery compound, but two Lamas and three monks living in villages down the valley act as caretakers. Before the road from Gyatsa was constructed rebuilding of the gompa was not feasible. Plans for reconstruction are now under way.

History
Although the geomantic merits of the site of Chokorgyel were recognized in ancient times, and a small community of Red Hat monks lived there, it was left to the second Dalai Lama, Gendun Gyatso, to endow it with the recognition it deserved. This Dalai Lama made retreat here and founded the monastery in 1509. Like most of the gompas in this area, Chokorgyel suffered severely from the depredations of the Dzungar Mongols in 1718. Although it was immediately rebuilt by the Regent Kangchene, nothing of antiquity would have remained in 1959. The last Dalai Lama to visit the gompa was the Thirteenth, and the Reteng Regent visited it after the death of the Thirteenth while on his way to Lhamo Latso to seek signs of the whereabouts of the Omniscient Lord's reincarnation.

Lhamo Latso (Lha mo bla mtsho): The Oracle Lake

It is Tibetan belief older than Buddhism that every individual, every family, and an entire country, possesses a "life-spirit", called a *la*. This *la* is embodied in natural phenomena, such as mountains, lakes, trees, and so on. When the place of residence of the *la* is damaged, the individual, family or nation suffers directly. Thus when a lake that is the home of a *la* dries up, this omen of death or disaster can inflict the terrible result that is presaged. The "life-spirit" of Tibet is identified with Lhamo Latso,[1] "The Life-Spirit-Lake of the Goddess", and the Goddess is Pelden Lhamo, the Protectress of Tibet.

The specific form of Pelden Lhamo at the sacred lake is Gyelmo Maksorma, "The Victorious One who Turns Back Enemies". The lake is also known as Pelden Lhamo Kalidevi, indicating that Pelden Lhamo is none other than the Indian goddess Kali, the *sakti* of Siva Mahadeva's destructive mode. She is also known as Remati.

Lhamo Latso is also the "life-spirit lake" (*latso*) of the Dalai Lamas. Most of the Dalai Lamas made at least one pilgrimage here, usually after completing their *geshe* examination and before assuming their functions in the political sphere, in order to foresee the events of their careers and the manner of their deaths. The powers of the lake also provide detailed knowledge of the place and nature of the Dalai Lama's reincarnation, and Lhamo Latso was visited therefore by the Regent whose task it was to search for the infant reincarnation. Further, even today pilgrims from all over Tibet visit the lake to gain intimation of the future of their country and of their personal fortunes.

The path to Lhamo Latso leaves Chokorgyel on the northern side of the Chamsing mountain, turning north at the base of the red mountain called *Lhamonying, which remains as a pregnant vision behind the pilgrim as he walks for three or four hours up the valley to the north. Half way along the route is Yoni Lake, a diamond shaped pond fed by glaciers. At the top of the valley is a sharp cragged ridge upon which is built the Dalai Lama's throne, and from this eminence the divine rulers of Tibet once sat to gaze into the lake 150 m below, and a kilometre in front, to divine the future. There was a temple dedicated to Maksorma at the eastern end of the lake, its site now marked by prayer-flags and pilgrims' offerings.

The ridge upon which the throne is built is at a height of about 5,300 m, above the snowline for most of the year. However a *korra* path skirting the lake does exist. The stream that drains the lake is an effluent of the *Nye Chu. The *Nye Valley, passing Daklha Gampo, descends to the Tsangpo, which can be reached in three days from Lhamo Latso.

A six- to eight-day *korra* in Dakpo, beginning and ending at Daklha Gampo, includes Lhamo Latso, a lake sacred to Demchok called Demchok Tso, and twenty-one peaks and lakes belonging to the twenty-one forms of Drolma. One of these lakes lies just below the Gyelong La on its western side.

Metoktang (Me tog thang): Meadows of Flowers

Strictly, the name Metoktang refers only to the upper part of the valley south of Chokorgyel. Around the gompa are alpine pastures ideal for grazing yak, where many tented *drokpas* live in the summer, but a short distance below Chokorgyel the valley is covered by a bewildering profusion of vegetation. Juniper, poplar, willow, cherry, silver birch, larch, rhododendron, walnut and apricot trees are found in this valley, together with miniature rhododendron, dog-rose, pussy willow, and a wide variety of flowers and other flowering shrubs. The plant from which is obtained the medicinal root Yatsagambu, "summer grass winter worm", also grows profusely in this valley.

Daklha Gampo (Dwags lha sgam po): Residence of Je Gampopa

The most renowned of the Red Hat power-places in Dakpo, Daklha Gampo,[2] lies in the elbow formed by the Tsangpo and *Nye Valleys to the east of Gyatsa Qu. Separated from the *Nye Valley by a ridge it nestles in the lee of Daklha Gampo Ri, from which it derived its name, and on the east side of the Daklha Chu. There is now a jeep-road from Gyatsa Qu that follows the Tsangpo for 12 km before climbing up to Daklha Gampo Ri, and another jeep road ascending from the *Nye Valley.

Restoration of the monastery, totally destroyed after 1959, is now under way. We have no contemporary description of the site.

History

Daklha Gampo was established in 1121 by Je Gampopa, Dakpo Lhaje Lodro Drak (1079-1153), the master of meditation who was the scholarly disciple of Jetsun Milarepa. After his wife died when he was twenty-seven years old, the medical student Gampopa was ordained as a monk and became learned in the tradition of the Kadampas in Penyul. Initiated by Milarepa he became particularly adept at controlling his internal energies (*tsalung*), and also in the practice of *mahamudra*. Amongst many other tomes he was the author of the famous meditation manual called the *Targyen*, which deals with practice of the first stages of the *mahamudra* path. Gampopa established his seat at Daklha Gampo in his forty-second year, after Milarepa had died. Drogon Pakmodrupa (the founder of Densatil), the first Karmapa Dusum Kyempa, and Gampopa's nephew Gompa (the teacher of Lama Shang who founded the Tsepa Kagyu), were Je Gampopa's most important disciples.

Like many monasteries in this district Daklha Gampo was destroyed in 1718 by the Dzungar Mongols on one of their punitive raids against the Red Hat sects, but it was rebuilt soon thereafter. Daklha Gampo never obtained the political power or wealth of Gampopa's disciples' foundations.

Dakpo Dratsang (Dwags po grwa gtsang)

Also known as Dakpo Shedrubling this famous Yellow Hat academy is located in what is now Gyatsa Xian. The principal lhakang has been preserved, the courtyard for debate is now restored, and the school of dialectics reconvened. In the 16th century Dakpo Shedrubling was governed by the Shamarpas. The sixth Shamarpa was enthroned here in 1589. Dorje Shukden protects this gompa.

Lhagyari (Lha gya ri)

The Lhagyari Valley extends from the village of *Rong up to the *Potang La. At Rong, 35 km from Tsetang, the motor ferry crosses the Tsangpo to Sangri. Lhagyari is included in this section because it formed part of the old province of Dakpo. Until 1959 the valley belonged to descendants of the Emperor Songtsen Gampo. The village of Lhagyari lies in the middle of a dusty plain from which the road begins to ascend steeply to the *Potang La. At *Rong are the ruins of Lhagyari *dzong* and below them Chagar Gompa. 200 m to the west of the gompa is the Jowo Lhakang.

Chagar Gompa was built by the third Dalai Lama, Sonam Gyatso, in the 16th century. During the Cultural Revolution the gompa was used as a Party building and thus preserved. It is built in an old style with access to the portico and dukang gained by stairs. Some good murals in Central Tibetan style in the dukang and lhakang still remain. But in 1986 only an aging *gelong* lived there, and a painter was in residence restoring the murals.

East of Dakpo

To the south-east of Dakpo, near the Indian border, is Tsari, reckoned by the Indians as one of the Twenty-four Power-places of the Mother-*tantras*. In Kongpo to the east, where the Nyang Chu joins the Tsangpo, is Kongpo Bon Ri, the sacred mountain of the Bonpos.

18

ACROSS TSANG TO THE NEPAL BORDER

Western Tibet is divided into two provinces, Tsang and Ngari Korsum. Ngari Korsum includes the upper Indus Valley and the vast spaces of the Changtang, which is the rolling plateau north of Mt Kailash. Tsang stretches from Mt Kailash to Yamdrok Tso in the east. The capital of Tsang was, and still is, Tibet's second city, Shigatse, although Gyangtse was Tsang's principal city in earlier centuries. To the west of Yamdrok Tso and the Karo La the change in topography from narrow valleys divided by high ridges to wide valleys between mountainous massifs and high plateau, marks the passage from Central Tibet to Tsang, and the landscape grows more broad and vast towards the west. The southern border of the province is the watershed of the High Himalayas, while the Tsangpo and its tributary the Raga Tsangpo runs to the south of its northern border.

The highway from Chaksam to *Shammo (Nepali = Khasa) was built in the mid-1960s, and the connection from Kathmandu, the Aniko highway, was completed with Chinese assistance by 1970. Within Tibet the new highway was built to link the valleys to the south of the Tsangpo and it follows the ancient trade route from Lhasa to Kathmandu only for short stretches. But Tsang was criss-crossed with old routes linking the chief monasteries and there was no single caravan route across the province.

Although Central Tibet has always been the heartland of the country, Tsang has played an important role in Tibetan political and religious history. After the collapse of the Tibetan empire and the resurgence and decline of Tibetan culture in the Kingdom of Guge in Ngari, during the 13th and 14th centuries Sakya Gompa was the centre of the country. Tsang did not lose its independence and its ambition to rule all Tibet until the Princes of Tsang with their seat at Shigatse were defeated by the Mongols supporting the Great Fifth Dalai Lama in the 17th century. Thereafter the great monastery of Tashi Lhumpo has represented Yellow Hat interests in Tsang, although until 1959 the rivalry between the Panchen Lamas and the Dalai Lamas can be seen as an extension of the old rivalry between Tsang and Central Tibet.

Until the 17th century the principal monasteries of Tsang were Red Hat establishments. The chief Sakya gompas were Pel Sakya, Ngor, and Gyangtse, while the Kagyupas were represented at a string of smaller, independent gompas across Tsang, many of which were important institutions in their day. In the Tsangpo Valley, below Lhatse, the heterodox Jonangpas established an important gompa at Puntsoling; the Butonpas were located at Shalu; while Nartang retained its Kadampa independence. The area from Jomolungma (Mt Everest) west to Kyirong is associated with Milarepa, and his caves are still to be found in the region, mostly in mountain fastnesses. Guru Rimpoche travelled across Tsang from Kathmandu on his mission to Tibet, and his caves can be found in many valleys. The 12th-century Indian yogin Padampa Sangye is connected chiefly with the Tingri area and his important disciple Machik Labdron was born at Labchi to the north-west of Tingri. Labchi became a centre of pilgrimage and retreat that gave it the same prestige as Mt Kailash and Tsari.

The Vicinity of Yamdrok Tso

From Chaksam to Nangkatse
From Chaksam and Chuwo Ri (km 60) the road ascends steeply to the Kampa La (4,794 m), and from the *lhabtse* on top of the pass (km 94) the turquoise water of the Yamdrok Tso (Lake Balti) is visible. Pede Dzong (km 130) is located by the lake at the foot of the pass. Yamdrok Tso is one of the four large sacred lakes of

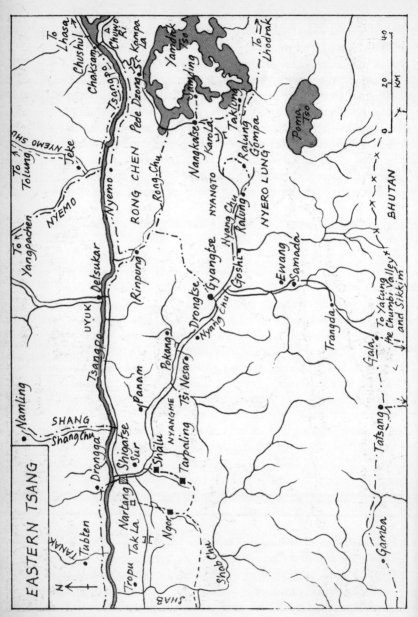

Map 17 Eastern Tsang

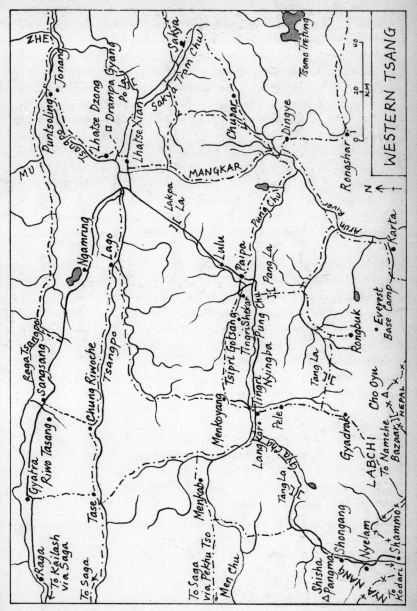

Map 18 Western Tsang

Tibet that are the residences of wrathful deities. Further south, under a sheltering cliff, is Nangkatse Xian (km 163) dominated by the inhabited remnants of its *dzong*.

Samding Dorje Pakmo (bSam lding rDo rje phag mo)

Some 10 km to the east of Nangkatse, situated on a 100 m hill on the isthmus of a peninsula jutting into the Yamdrok Tso, is the Samding or Samten Ling gompa. This Ani Gompa (some monks also lived here) was the seat of Tibet's highest female incarnation, known as Dorje Pakmo (Demchok's consort), or Sera Kandro. An abbess of this Geluk establishment achieved renown when she transformed herself and her nuns into sows (*pakmo*) to thwart a Mongol raid on her nunnery. Samding was destroyed after 1959, but it is now in process of restoration. The incarnation of Dorje Pakmo lives in Lhasa.

Lho Taklung (Lho sTag lung)

The Taklung Kagyu school is represented in Tsang at the Lho Taklung gompa located close to the road that skirts Yamdrok Tso to the south-west of Nangkatse. We have no contemporary information about this gompa.

Karo La (Kha ru la)

The high range between Yamdrok Tso and Nyero Lung is crossed at the Karo La (5,045 m) (km 180), which lies beneath spectacular glaciers. In 1904 the Tibetans chose to block the advance of Major Younghusband's British military expedition at the Karo La. In the major action that followed, during which 700 Tibetans were killed, the Tibetans were astonished at the failure of their amulets to ward off bullets and amazed by the British field hospital's attempts to save their wounded.

Nyangto and Nyangme

Ralung (Rwa lung): Seat of the Drukpa Kagyu

In the lee of the snow peaks to the south of the Karo La, and a

7 km walk from the village of Ralung[1] (km 200), is the Drukpa Kagyu seat of Ralung. This important gompa was founded in 1180 by Drogon Tsangpa Gyare, a disciple of Drogon Pakmodrupa. The Drukpa Kagyu school, increasingly assimilating Nyingma elements, became an important political force in Bhutan after the Great Fifth Dalai Lama's failed invasion. Bhutan, or Druk, takes its name from the Drukpa Kagyu school. This school has always retained its emphasis on the Milarepa tradition of solitary meditation, although its monks are frequently married in the *ngakpa* style. At Ralung the vast walls of the Lhakang Chempo still stand to the north of the site, but only a small lhakang and the monks' quarters have been restored. In the valleys behind Ralung's magnificent site are many hermitages and caves.

Goshi Retang (sGo bzhi re thang)
Below Ralung in the Nyang Chu valley is the village of Goshi, which was the birthplace of Yutokpa Yonten Gompo, the court physician of the Emperor Trisong Detsen. He is renowned as the founder of Tibetan medicine.

Gyangtse (rGyal rtse)
Gyangtse[2] dominates a broad, fertile stretch of the Nyang Chu valley where the major southern trade route from the Chumbi Valley, Yatung[3] and Sikkim divides, one road going downstream to Shigatse and the other upstream and over the Karo La to Central Tibet. The small town is dominated by the Gyangtse Dzong, the former seat of the Governors of Tsang, which was shelled and heavily damaged during its capture by the British in 1904, but restored afterwards. It was partially demolished after 1959 and again recently restored. The Dzong's lhakang has been preserved and refurbished.

The Gyangtse PELKOR CHODE (also known as Shekar Gyangtse) was built beneath and on the side of a semicircular ridge to the west of the Dzong and surrounded by a high wall. It was founded by the second Prince of Gyangtse, Rabten Kunsang Pakpa, in 1418. This independent prince was inspired by Lamas of the Sakya school, but he was also a devotee of Kedrub Je, Tsongkapa's disciple. Thus Pelkor Chode, consisting of sixteen *dratsangs*, most belonging to the Sakya (some Ngorpa Sakya) and others to the Butonpa, Geluk and Kagyu schools, was always an eclectic academy. Its early domination by the Sakyas was later lost to the Geluk Kempo whose authority then rivalled that of the Dzong.

All the *dratsang* buildings have been destroyed, leaving large empty spaces within the walls. But together with a large *labrang* (above the Tsokang), the *tanka*-display building (at the top of the compound) and a small lhakang (to the left of the Tsokang), the important Tsokang of Pelkor Chode was preserved with its remarkable 15th-century images and murals. The most sacred image in the Tsokang is the Jowo Sakyamuni in the main lhakang. The gomkang and lhakang, entered from the left side of the dukang, contain notable symbols of the Buddhas, but the first-storey Drubtob and Neten Chodruk Lhakangs, containing murals and images of the Mahasiddhas and Sixteen Arhats respectively, and dating from the 15th century, are rooms of immense power. The walls of the Utse Lhakang, the top chamber, are covered from ceiling to floor with large mandalas of the Sakya tradition done in the famous Ngor style, also dating from the 15th century.

The GYANGTSE KUMBUM, the great *gomang* (many-doored) chorten of Pelkor Chode, is now unique in the Buddhist world. It was built after 1418 by the founder of Pelkor Chode. Its many lhakangs were painted by masters of a Tsangpa school of painting derived from the Newari tradition of Nepal. The clay images in the lhakangs are mostly poor, new, substitute statues, but most of the original murals are in good condition. The lhakangs of the nine levels of the Kumbum, decreasing in number at each level, are structured according to the compendium of Sakya *tantras* called the *Drubtab Kuntu*. Thus each lhakang and each level creates a mandala, and the entire Kumbum represents a three-dimensional path to the Buddha's enlightenment in terms of increasingly subtle tantric mandalas. With attentive fidelity to the varying rites of *tantra* for which the Sakya school is renowned, *sadhana* and *puja* of all classes of *tantra* were practised here.

Drongtse ('Brong rtse)
Built on the side of a ridge just to the south side of the highway

some 20 km (km 71) from Gyangtse, Drongtse was one of the more important Yellow Hat gompas in Tsang. It is presently being restored.

Tsi Nesar (rTsis gnas gsar): An Emperor Songtsen Gampo Temple

To the west of Drongtse (km 60), in a side-valley 3 km south of the road, is the site of two small empire-period temples. Both the Runo Tsuklakang built by the Emperor Songtsen Gampo, and the Yumchen lhakang built by the Emperor Trisong Detsen with its image of Yumchenmo consecrated by Guru Rimpoche, have been destroyed. Some of the revered ancient timbers have been incorporated into the new country-style temple. Included in some lists of Songtsen Gampo's missionary temples, Tsi Nesar is also a *terne* (see p.294).

Shalu (Zhwa lu): Buton Rimpoche's Residence

In the history of Tibetan Buddhism, and also in Tibetan art history, Shalu is one of the most important gompas in Tibet. Located in a village some 5 km south of the highway and 19 km from Shigatse, the chief buildings of Shalu have been preserved, although their condition is precarious. Shalu was founded by Chetsun Sherab Jungne in 1040, and its dukang erected by the Sakya hierarch Drakpa Gyeltsen at the beginning of the 14th century, when the Mongol influence in Tibet was at its height. This explains its Chinese architectural influences seen particularly in the roofs decorated with turquoise-coloured glazed tiles and mouldings. The religious renown of Shalu was also achieved in the 14th century when it became the residence of Buton Rinchen Drub (1290-1364), the great scholar who compiled the Tibetan Buddhist canon, the Tenjur and Kanjur. Thereafter it became the seat of the Butonpa, a school based on the lineage of Buton, derived from both Kadampa and Sakya teachers. Most of the treasures of Shalu have vanished, including the library of Sanskrit palm-leaf manuscripts; but fine murals from the 14th century still remain, though in a decayed state, and there are several remarkable images of both Tibetan and Newar provenance dating from the 12th and 13th centuries.

The NYANGME GYENGONG shrine of Rabtenma, a form

of the Protector Pelden Lhamo, 150 m north of Shalu, was destroyed but has been rebuilt recently. It was founded by Loton Dorje Wangchuk of Tsang in 973. It was the place of Sakya Pandita's ordination – the vessel in which he washed his hair is now kept at Shalu gompa. The RIBUK hermitage in the mountains to the south-west of Shalu was also destroyed, and its chief relic, a vase (*bumpa*) of the Indian progenitor of the Sakya lineages, the *mahasiddha* Birwapa, is now preserved at Shalu. Another hermitage site is situated in the mountains to the east of Shalu.

Tarpaling (Thar pa ling)
An old route from Shalu to Ngor crosses the mountains to the south-west of Shalu. To the south lies the site of Tarpaling gompa. It was founded in the 14th century by Tarpa Lotsawa, a teacher of Buton and a translator of renown. Restored in the 17th century after the Mongol invasions, it was the British envoy Samuel Turner's residence during his visit to the fourth Panchen Lama in the winter of 1783. Its present condition is unknown.

Sur Sangak Ling (Zur gSang sngags gling)
The village of Sur is located in the lee of the ridge on the eastern side of the Nyang Chu valley to the south-east of Shigatse. Its religious importance is historical. As the ancient home of the Sur clan, in the 11th and 12th centuries the principal centre of the Nyingma Kama tradition was located here.

Shigatse (gZhis ka tse)
Shigatse[4] is located just above the confluence of the Nyang Chu with the Tsangpo in the district previously known as Samdrub Tse. Its position astride the major route from Gyangtse to the West is supported by roads that follow both north and south banks of the Tsangpo to Chaksam, and another road reaching Lhasa by way of the "Northern Route" via Yangpachen. The ruins of the immense Samdrub Tse Dzong that dominates Tibet's second largest town was the seat of the Princes of Tsang until their overthrow by Gusri Khan in 1642.

One of the four great Geluk gompas, TASHI LHUMPO, was founded in 1447 by Tsongkapa's nephew and disciple Gendun Drub (retrospectively designated the first Dalai Lama), who was interred in a chorten here. Gendun Drub's successor moved to Drepung, which became the chief seat of Geluk power, but as the principal Geluk gompa in Tsang Tashi Lhumpo regained its prestige when the Great Fifth recognized his tutor as the fourth incarnation of Wopame (Amitabha) in the line of Panchen Lamas and abbots of Tashi Lhumpo. Since Wopame is the spiritual source of Chenresik, who incarnates as the Dalai Lamas, the Panchen Lamas are often considered spiritually superior to the Dalai Lamas. As representatives of Tsang the Panchen Lamas sustained the political rivalry with the Dalai Lamas of Lhasa, a relationship that was to be exploited by the Chinese. The tenth Panchen Lama remained in Tibet after the Lhasa Uprising of 1959, and even after spending a decade in a re-education camp he has returned to the political arena using his influence to benefit Tibet and the Buddha-*dharma*.

The extent of Tashi Lhumpo has been reduced by two-thirds, the buildings razed consisting chiefly of the 4,000 monks' quarters. The fine examples of 17th- and 18th-century construction that remain form the splendid nucleus of this monastic museum. The Labrang contains the fourth Panchen's magnificent reliquary chorten (*kudung*). The reliquary chorten of Gendun Drub, the first Dalai Lama, is found in the Tsokang. The Tsokang also contains several galleries where small images are exhibited. However there is little of great age at Tashi Lhumpo due to its sack by the Gorkhalis in 1792. The Ngakpa Dratsang and the Tsenyi Dratsang (the College of Debate comprising the three original *dratsangs* – Shartse, Kyilkang and Tosamling) are the two surviving colleges at Tashi Lhumpo. The most amazing image at Tashi Lhumpo is the Jampa Chempo (Maitreya) erected in its own lhakang by the ninth Panchen in 1914, standing 26 m high and covered with 279 kg of gold.

The Lingkor that circumambulates the site outside the walls is perhaps the most rewarding activity for the pilgrim at Tashi Lhumpo.

From Shigatse to Sakya

Nartang (sNar thang): Tsang's Kadampa Gompa
Located west of Shigatse (km 266) in a village north of the highway, Nartang is known as the place of origin of the Kadampa school in Tsang. It was founded in 1153 by Tumton Lodro Drakpa, a disciple of Sharapa. It retained its independence as a Kadampa school, but its size and importance was much reduced. Today the 240 m by 240 m site consists of hillocks of clay and rock contained within high walls, and in the centre is a small country-style lhakang, the residence of a single monk. The priceless relics of Nartang have all disappeared: the woodblocks from which the authoritative Nartang Kanjur and Tenjur were printed (carved 1730-42); the Kadampa *tankas* of the Sixteen Arhats; Dromton's crystal staff and the images of Kadampa incarnations of Indian arhats – all have vanished.

At JANGCHEN RITRO, located in the mountains behind Nartang, accessible by foot, are the *drubkangs* of Kadampa lamas and particularly of Nartang Sangye Gompa. Some of these hermitages have been preserved and are now occupied. The chief power-place is the residence of the Protector Pel Gomshel.

Ngor Ewam Choden (Ngor EVAM chos ldan): Origin of the
  Ngor School of Painting
The Sakya school's second most important gompa is Ngor EWAM Choden. Ngor is located half a day's walk to the south of Nartang, and the old road is visible vanishing into the mountains up the river valley to the south. It is also accessible by foot directly from Shalu to the east, and also from Sakya. Ngor was founded in 1429 by Ngorchen Kunga Sangpo (1382-1444), who was born and educated at Sakya. *Lamdre* is the tantric practice for which the gompa was renowned, and the Throne-holder would give this instruction annually to Ngor's 500 monks and visiting students from all over Tibet. Ngor was known for its library including a rich collection of Sanskrit manuscripts and also for the Newar-derived school of painting that flourished in the 15th century. Of its eighteen colleges, and Upper and Lower Tsokangs, only a single restored lhakang survives.

Pel Sakya (dPal Sa skya): "White Earth", Seat of the Sakya
   School

The road to Sakya[5] leaves the highway at Sakya Bridge, west of
the *Po La, 127 km west of Shigatse. The Glorious Sakya Gompa
is located 25 km to the south-east of the Bridge up the *Sakya
Trom Chu valley, and it is situated against the valley's north
side. It is also accessible on a rough jeep-road from Tingri
Shekar, and there is an old path from the Mangkar Valley. Sakya
is the principal seat of the Sakya school, and as such it played a
dominant role in both the political and religious history of Tibet
in the 13th and 14th centuries. Konchok Gyelpo, a scion of a
local noble family, founded Sakya in 1073, and the rise of Sakya's
fortunes coincided with the Mongol conquest of Central Asia.
Sakya Pandita and Pakpa, successors to Konchok Gyelpo in the
uncle-nephew succession, were given political control of Tibet by
the Khans, and thus Sakya Gompa became the principal recipient
of Mongol, and later Chinese Yuan Dynasty, patronage and
cultural influence. Sakya's great temples were built during this
early period, but warfare, time, 16th-century restoration, and
finally the Red Guards, destroyed the greater part of the Sakya-
Mongol legacy.

The oldest and principal buildings of Sakya Gompa were
located on the northern side of the river. The Utse Nyingba, Utse
Sarma, the Gorum Lhakang, the Shitok Labrang, and the
Labrang Shar were the most significant of the temples in the
monastic-town that climbed the valley-side. Now only part of the
monks' quarters converted into commune housing remain. The
one surviving ancient building, on the western side of the river,
is the Lhakang Chempo, also known as the Sibgon Trulpa. It is
surrounded by a high fortified wall with the enormous bulk of the
Lhakang protruding above it.

The Lhakang Chempo was built in 1268 during the lifetime of
Pakpa by Ponchen Sakya Sangpo, and restored in the 16th
century. In 1985 the buildings outside the central Lhakang
Chempo structure were unrestored. Within the Shung Go, the
Main Door, on the north side of the *kyamra* courtyard, the
Nguldung chamber had been restored, and inside the Lhakang
Jangma the notable mandala murals were in process of
restoration. On the south side of the courtyard the Purdung

lhakang was virtually empty but the murals were undamaged. The Lhakang Chempo itself had survived unscathed but the altars were stacked with artefacts from other temples.

The Lhakang Chempo contains an extraordinary wealth of symbols of the Buddha's Body, Speech and Mind, by which the history of Buddhist art in Tibet and surrounding countries can be traced. However, the sacred objects in this temple-museum represent only a fraction of the artefacts that had been assembled from Pala Bengal, Kashmir, Nepal and China during the period of Sakya's greatness. There is no space here to describe even the chief relics and great images standing on the front altar of the Lhakang Chempo. Suffice to list the four most sacred objects that Kyentse Rimpoche mentions: the image of Jamyang called Siwo Barba, a large Kashmiri image that was Sakya Pandita's heart-commitment and still Sakya's most treasured relic; the Chamgon statue made of the skin of an Indian king (thus also known as Sebak Nakpo), one of four Protectors of the Gorum, which belonged to *mahasiddha* Birwapa and was brought from Bodh Gaya; a statue of Jetsun Drolma that was Pakpa's heart-commitment; and the Namgyel Chorten containing the previous Buddha Kasyapa's relics and robe, constructed by Baripa, now a small, damaged chorten of clay.

On the north side of the river the pilgrim will be shown a cave where a spring rises in the rubble and where Sakya Pandita meditated under Baripa's tutelage. The old Labrang Shar was built on this spot. On the same level a small chorten and a small lhakang have been rebuilt. In the vicinity of Sakya is Sakya Pandita's birthplace called Truma (up-river); a shrine of Pelgon Shelshipa (to the east); the *drubkang* of Jetsun Drakpa Gyeltsen; and a shrine of Maksorma called Samling.

The Lhatse District

Lhatse Dzong (Lha rtse rdong) or Drampa Lhatse (Gram pa Lha rtse)

The new town of Lhatse Xian[6] (km 402), 151 km west of Shigatse, is situated on the south side of a high, broad, fertile

[18.] [above] SAKYA: the forbidding walled 12th century Lhakang Chempo (photograph by R. Demandre) [below] GYANGTSE: yak and rider before races at the annual June festival (photograph by *Stone Routes*)

plain crossed by the Tsangpo. A strong local culture was formed here during a very early period and historically the district was called Drampa. Lhatse Dzong, the old administrative centre and fort, is located where the Tsangpo enters a deep gorge that cuts through the range on the northern side of the plain. A jeep-road, turning off the highway at km 400, links Lhatse Xian (Lhatse Sarpa) with Lhatse Dzong (Lhatse Nyingba).

Lhatse Dzong was built on a rock 150 m high at the entrance to the Tsangpo gorge. The old residence of the district governor was totally destroyed, but on the north side of the rock is a chamber 3 m square carved out of the living rock. This cave, filled with symbols of the Buddha's Body, Speech and Mind, was the residence of Drokmi Lotsawa, who was the link between the Indian lineage of the *mahasiddha* Birwapa and the founding Sakya master, Konchok Gyelpo. Drokmi was an important translator, a master of *lamdre* and a teacher of Marpa Lotsawa. He met the Kashmiri Pandita Gayadhara in this cave. Below the rock to the east is Lhatse Chode, a Yellow Hat gompa miraculously preserved from the Red Guards by the flooding of a Tsangpo tributary. The dukang has survived, but years of neglect have left it in a sorry state. It is presently being restored.

Drampa Gyang (Gram pa rgyangs): An Emperor Songtsen Gampo Temple

The 7th-century Drampa Gyang Lhakang, one of the Emperor Songtsen Gampo's twelve missionary temples, pinions the left hip of the Tibetan Demoness (p.287). It lies in ruins on the eastern side of the Lhatse plain. It was here in the 14th century that the treasure-finder Sangpo Drakpa discovered the popular Nyingma text called the *Leu Dunma*, a compilation of prayers and devotions given by Guru Rimpoche. To the north of the ancient temple is the great ruined pile of the GYANG BUMOCHE, an immense *gomang* (many-doored) chorten built in the style of the Gyangtse Kumbum at the end of the period of Sakya ascendancy by Sakya Sonam Tashi (1352-1417) assisted by the great bridge builder Tangton Gyelpo. East of the Kumbum are the ruins of the monastery attached to it. Further to the east of the Kumbum a stream waters a delightful miniature valley with trees and meadows on its slopes. Here, above the ruins of a Nyingma gompa and a number of hermitages, is the Guru Rimpoche cave of GYANG LOMPO LUNG. The large cave contains a shrine, but in 1985 the valley was deserted.

Puntsoling and Jonang (Phun tshogs gling dang Jo nang)

A jeep-road winds north for some 30 km through the Tsangpo gorge from Lhatse Dzong to the confluence of the Tsangpo with the Raga Tsangpo. On the south side of the river where a new bridge has replaced one of Tangton Gyelpo's famous iron bridges, the gompa of Ganden Puntsoling, also known as Jonang Gompa, is situated. At the head of the valley to the south is the ruined Jonang Kumbum and the hermitages of the Jonangpa school, particularly the hermitage of the founder Dolbupa Sherab Gyeltsen (1292-1361). Puntsoling and Jonang are associated primarily with Taranatha Kunga Nyingpo, the historian and chief expositor of the Jonangpa, a small heterodox but influential Kagyu school. Taranatha restored Puntsoling and the Jonang Kumbum early in the 17th century, but the Great Fifth Dalai Lama suppressed the Jonangpas and converted Puntsoling to the Geluk school after Taranatha's death. The Jonang Kumbum, called Tongdrol Chempo, the Great Chorten that Gives Liberation by Setting Eyes upon It, constructed in the *kumbum* style of Drampa Gyang and Gyangtse, was built by Dolbupa. It has been severely damaged, its murals beyond restoration.

Close to Puntsoling stood a powerful shrine of the protecting deity Begtse, established in the 12th century by Bodongpa Rinchen Tsemo.

Mangkar Valley (Mang mkhar lung)

The Mangkar Valley enters the Lhatse plain just south of Lhatse Xian. A few hours' walk to the south the valley divides, the chief arm running to the south. This is known as the valley of Thirteen Caves. The Dragur Lotsa Puk, where the first translators of Sanskrit texts worked, is probably the most important. Ma Rinchen Chok, one of the great translators and one of Guru Rimpoche's Twenty-four Disciples, lived in Mangkar. Other caves of importance are Sungak Lamdre Puk where Padampa Sangye granted *lamdre* instruction; Woser Dawa Puk was Drokmi Lotsawa's retreat cave, close to his residence at Nyugu Lung; and

Tsalung Dorjedrak Dzong, where Jetsun Drakpa Gyeltsen and also Tsarchen Losel Gyatso meditated. In the lower part of Mangkar were two important Sakya gompas: at Dar Drongmoche, Tsarchen Losel Gyatso (1502-67), the founder of the Sakya Tsarpa school, established the Tsarpa seat; and the Sem Karchung gompa, also known as Ngok Karchung, was founded in 1064 by Drubchen Se Karchungwa, a Sakya master of *lamdre*. We have no knowledge of the present condition of these places.

The Tingri Valley

From Lhatse the highway turns south and crosses the *Lakpa La (5,220 m) from the Tsangpo Valley system and into the Tingri basin. The rivers of the Tingri valley system drain into the Pung Chu, which becomes the Arun River in Nepal. The Arun predates the Great Himalayan Range, keeping pace in its downward cutting power with the mountains' constant uplift. Its longest, northern-most tributary rises north-west of Tingri less than 30 km south of the Tsangpo itself.

Tingri Shekar (Ding ri Shel dkar)
Before the police check-point at Paipa (km 484), which marks the 50 km limit beyond which Nepalis may not travel without visas, is the turning to Tingri Shekar,[7] the district Xian. The old *dzong* that dominates the new town, climbing the peak behind it, was called Shekar Dorje Dzong, and within these walls lay the Yellow Hat monastery complex of Shekar Chode. The Shekar gompa was completely destroyed but is now in process of restoration.

Tsipri Gotsang (rTsib ri rGod tshang)
To the west of Shekar Dzong is the sacred Tsipri massif encircled by a *korra*. The most significant power-place on this circumambulation is Tsipri Gotsang, situated on a sheer cliff to the south-east of the range. This Drukpa Kagyu "eagle's nest" was founded by the great yogin Gotsangpa Gompo Pel (1189-1258), a disciple of Tsangpa Gyare. We are informed that this hermitage gompa is in process of restoration.

Tingri Dzong (Ding ri rdzong)

Tingri Dzong (km 542) lies in the middle of the Tingri plain (or Tingri Maidan), which is a long, wide plain at 4,500 m extending some 80 km from east to west. The Everest massif is visible in the south and the jeep-road to Rombuk and the North Face Base Camp turns off the highway at Tingri (the new road to Rombuk leaves the highway at km 494). Two days on foot to the south-west of Tingri lies the Nangpa La which crosses into the Sherpa homeland of Kumbu. The caravan route to the west is marked by frequent ruined caravanserais that evoke the desert forts of Persia.

The hill that shelters the small community at Tingri Dzong (also Tingri Nyingba or Old Tingri), which lies south of the highway, is now shorn of the *dzong* and gompa that dominated the village. In the past Tingri's importance was derived more from its status as a commercial centre than from any religious significance.

Tingri Lankor (Ding ri glang 'khor): Padampa's Residence

Tingri Lankor lies west of Tingri Dzong on the south-west side of a medial ridge on the Tingri Maidan, to the south of the highway, and accessible from the village at km 554. Tingri Lankor was established in 1097 by the extraordinary South Indian adept, Padampa Sangye. During the latter part of the 11th and the beginning of the 12th century Padampa Sangye (d.1117), a disciple of the Bengali *mahasiddha* Maitripa, made five visits to Tibet, and he was a significant figure in the re-establishment of the Buddha-*dharma* in Tibet, particularly in the Tingri area. He established lineages bearing the esoteric yogas of *chod* (gcod) and *shije* (zhi byed), the first a means of purification by offering the body-mind aggregates as food for demonic spirits of the *dundros*, and the second a method of concentration meditation. His consort was the renowned Tibetan Kandroma Machik Labdron (p.248). The Lankor gompa, now in process of restoration, which was built about the cave in which Padampa Sangye meditated, became the seat of the so-called Dampapa school.

Tang La (Thang la)

To the west of Tingri the highway again turns south, climbing to the high plateau. Although the pass on the divide between the

Tingri and Sun Koshi basins at 5,214 m is now called Tang La (km 636), the original Tang La on the old Nepal-Lhasa trade route is located further to the east. The pass is marked by many *lhabtse*, prayer-flags and pilgrims' offerings. From this vantage point the peaks of the high Himalayas are clearly visible including Jomolungma (Everest; Nepali – Sagarmatha), *Cho Oyu and *Shishapangma (Gosainthan).

Mila Puk (Mila phug)

10 km before Nyelam, near the village of *Shongang (km 684), is a cave excavated from the river bank where Tibet's greatest yogin, Jetsun Milarepa (1040-1123), meditated. A shrine containing a new statue of Milarepa has been built in front of the recess in the bank which was the cave. The Pelgyeling Gompa that stood adjacent to it was destroyed and has now been rebuilt and decorated by Nepali artisans. This is one of the many caves associated with Milarepa that are located on both sides of the Himalayas between Langtang and Jomolungma.

Nyelam to Shammo

Nyelam (km 694) is an important trading town, once belonging to Nepal, situated at 3,750 m at the north end of the deep Po Chu gorge that cuts through the High Himalayan range to *Shammo[8] (km 730). The Po Chu is a tributary of the Nepali Sun Koshi river. A Tibetan neolithic site has been excavated by Chinese archeologists at Nyelam. Nyelam means "The Path to Hell", referring to the tortuous passage down the Po Chu gorge to *Shammo before the highway was built. Located above the actual border with Nepal, above the Friendship Bridge, as the first town in China the small Nepali village of Khasa at 2,300 m has been enlarged into the boom-town of *Shammo. There are no power-places in this town.

To the West of Tsang

To the west of Tsang is the province of Ngari Korsum. Its present extent approximates the boundaries of the ancient Bonpo kingdom of Shang Shung, which had its capital at Kunlung to the west of Mt Kailash. In the 10th century the kingdom of Guge, with its capital at Tsaparang, was established in the upper Sutlej and Indus Valleys. The kings of Guge were largely responsible for the re-establishment of Buddhism in Tibet in the 11th century, and although the kingdom had disappeared by the 12th century, temples from that period have been preserved in the thin air and cold climate at Tsaparang.

The "southern route" to Mt Kailash leaves the highway between Nyelam and Tingri Dzong and follows the Tsangpo Valley to Kailash; the "northern route" turn-off is at Lhatse, and from Raga this route makes a wide northern detour into the Changtang, to turn south at Shiquanhe (also Chinese Ali, Tibetan Ngari). The highway to Kashgar in Xinjiang, and to Pakistan over the Khunjerab Pass, runs north from Shiquanhe.

Mt Kailash, which the Tibetans call Gang Rimpoche, Precious Mountain, is known by all Buddhists and Hindus as the centre, the *axis mundi*, of the world. The four major rivers of the Indian sub-continent rise in its vicinity: the Brahmaputra (Tsangpo), Ganga, Sutlej and Indus. In *tantra* the Kailash mountain is the universal male principle, while the Manasarovar Lake (Mapam Yumtso), that lies to the south of the mountain, is the female principle. For Hindus, Kailash is the paradise of Siva Mahadeva; for Tibetans, it is asociated with Milarepa, who meditated there. It has always been the chief destination of Hindu pilgrims in Tibet, and one of the three Himalayan peaks (with Labchi and Tsari) that attract Tibetan pilgrims.

APPENDICES

I Tibet and the Supine Demoness: Songtsen Gampo's Temples

An awareness of natural forces, the relationship between them, and their interaction with man, was an integral part of shaman and animist consciousness. When Buddhism was first introduced into Tibet from India the indigenous Tibetan Bonpos and the Hindus possessed a sophisticated awareness of natural powers; but at this time in China geomancy, with its allied arts of divination and astrology, was considered to be a science. When in the year 640 one of the Chinese Tang emperor's daughters, Wencheng, was married to the Tibetan Emperor Songtsen Gampo, she brought as dowry a precious Indian image of Sakyamuni Buddha to Tibet. In Lhasa it happened that the Princess Wencheng's chariot that carried the image became intractably stuck, whereupon she resorted to divination to discover the cause of this ill-omen and the solution to her difficulties. The result of her calculations was the discovery that the whole of Tibet was "like a Demoness (*srinmo, yaksi*) fallen on her back", that the lake in the Plain of Milk in Lhasa was the heart-blood of the Demoness, and that the three hills rising out of the plain (Marpo Ri, Chakpo Ri and Bompo Ri, now sacred to Chenresik, Jamyang and Chakna Dorje respectively) were the breasts and *mons veneris* of the Demoness. The Plain of Milk was the palace of the *lu*, the naga-serpents, who together with the *dre* demons, the *mamo* elemental goddesses, the *tsen* nature spirits, and the hostile *sadra* earth-spirits, together with the *sinmo* Demoness herself, were the cause of all evil and obstructive forces in Tibet. Wencheng's solution was to build a palace for the king, a temple for her Buddha, a monastery for monks and a park for the common people. The cairn of the *dre* demons was to be destroyed and the lake in the Plain of Milk was to be filled in.

The Tibetans' geomancy, synthesizing indigenous wisdom with elements of the Indian and Chinese science, may have been adequate to the task, but both the Emperor Songtsen Gampo and his queen from Nepal, Bhrikuti, accepted Wencheng's Chinese divination. However, the fulfilment of Wencheng's prescription was hindered and delayed by Bhrikuti's insistence that construction of the projected temple was her prerogative and that the merit generated should accrue to her. The Emperor allowed that Bhrikuti should oversee the work; but at each stage whenever obstacles arose, usually because Bhrikuti failed to follow Wencheng's stipulated procedure, the Nepalese princess deferred to her Chinese sister, obtaining instruction on how to overcome demonic interference. Finally the lake was drained and the foundation of the temple, the Lhasa Tsuklakang, or Jokang, was laid, but by this time the Emperor himself had become involved and conceived a grand design to secure the Tibetan Demoness for ever and simultaneously to convert the Tibetan people to Buddhism.

In ideal design the Lhasa Tsuklakang would lie at the centre of three constellations of temples forming concentric squares. The temples at the corners of each square would tether the Demoness at increasingly greater distances from her heart, which lay in the Lhasa Jokang, and civilize tribes increasingly far distant from Lhasa. The four temples at the corners of the inner square pinioned the Demoness' shoulders and hips and civilized the "Four Horns" (see below) of Central Tibet and Tsang. The four temples at the corners of the intermediate square pinned the Demoness' elbows and knees and subdued the provinces of Tibet. The four temples at the corners of the outer square pinned the Demoness' hands and feet and subjected the border areas of Tibet. The Demoness is lying with her head in the east and her feet in the west with her limbs spread-eagled towards the intermediate directions. The inner square linked the Four Runo Lhakangs (*ru* gnon chen po bzhi), "the four great temples subduing the horns"; the intermediate square linked the Four Tandul Lhakangs (mtha' 'dul lha khang bzhi), "the four temples subjecting the provinces"; and the outer square linked the Four Yangdul Lhakangs (yang mtha'dul lha khang bzhi), "the four temples subjecting the border areas". In practice, in spacial reality, this ideal design was only partially achieved, as only the Runo temples form a quadrilateral.

The four "horns" or "wings" (ru bzhi) were administrative areas responsible for recruitment to the four parts of the Emperor's army. Uru, the Kyichu Valley, formed the Tibetan army's centre; Yeru, eastern Tsang, formed the right wing; Yoru, Yarlung and Dakpo, formed the left wing; and Rulak, western Tsang, formed the reserves. This system was instituted only after Songtsen Gampo's conquests; the "four horn" system was initiated in the 7th century.

The source of the legend of the founding of the Lhasa Jokang and Songtsen Gampo's so-called "missionary temples", summarized above, is the Mani Kabum, a compilation of semi-historical treasure-texts concerning Songtsen Gampo, discovered and compiled into a single volume in the 13th century. It describes what has become popular Tibetan belief. It is also Tibetan belief that Songtsen Gampo was a thorough-going Buddhist. There is little doubt that he built a number of Buddhist temples throughout Tibet, the thirteen missionary temples amongst them; he may also have spent time in retreat performing Buddhist meditation, as tradition has it; and he may have also have propagated the Buddhist moral code of the ten virtues. But all the emperors before Trisong Detsen were deeply involved in pre-Buddhist shamanism and the "black arts" of astrology, geomancy and divination and so on. The key-word in this shamanistic religion, and maybe descriptive of it, was tsuklak, which meant "religious science". The name of the great temple of Lhasa (the Jokang [Jo bo'i lha khang] the Temple of the Jowo) is still called Tsuklakang, which means the House of Science in the term's old meaning. The religion of which tsuklak formed a part also included Iranian Manichean elements and elements derived from the oldest Tibetan religion, which was a form of animism. Bon is the umbrella term used here for all elements of pre-Buddhist Tibetan religion.

Songtsen Gampo's Missionary Temples

Name	District	Direction from Lhasa	Part of Demoness Confined
Central Temple			
Lhasa Jokang (p.41)	Uru	Centre	heart-blood
Runo Temples			
Trandruk (p.177)	Yarlung, Yoru	S.E.	left shoulder
Katse (p.108)	Medro, Uru	E.	right shoulder
Drampa Gyang (p.278)	Lhatse, Rulak	E.S.E.	left hip
Tsang Dram	N.Tsang, Yeru	W.N.W.	right hip
Tandul Temples			
Koting (p.287)	Lhodrak	S.	left elbow
Buchu	Kongpo	E.	right elbow
Bumtang (p.287)	Mon (Bhutan)	S.	left knee
Pradun Tse	Jang, Guge	W.	right knee
Yangdul Temples			
Lungno	Jang Tsangpa	E.	left hand
Langtang Dronma	Dokam	E.N.E.	right hand
Kyerchu	Paro, Bhutan	S.	left foot
Jamtin	Mangyul	W.S.W	right foot

Other Temples in Central Tibet and Tsang built by Emperor Songtsen Gampo or his Wives

Ramoche (p.59) in Lhasa built by Wencheng Kongjo.

Pabongka (p.65), north of Lhasa near Sera, founded by Songtsen Gampo.

Tangkya (p.109) near Medro Kongkar, included amongst the Runo temples according to Buton (p.184).

Tsi Nesar (p.271) in Nyangro, west of Shigatse, considered locally to be a Runo temple, built by Songtsen Gampo (see *Gyelpo Katang*).

II Guru Rimpoche's Cave Power-places

The principal caves in which Guru Rimpoche meditated are called the Five Power-places of the Guru. Three additional power-places are included in the list of the Eight Solitary Places of Realization[1] (*lung bstan dben pa'i gnas brgyad*). Four of these eight caves are located in Central Tibet within a radius of 40 km from Samye, and the remaining four are located in Lhodrak and Mon (Bhutan). All these cave-hermitages are places of extraordinary geomantic significance, and they are all places where Guru Rimpoche concealed important treasure troves. They all have prophecies associated with treasure that predict the coming of treasure-finders who would meditate there and discover the treasures that the Guru concealed. Also, they are power-places that induce dream and vision, and to that extent they are places where Guru Rimpoche had prophecies revealed to him and where he asserted that yogins would attain realization. The Guru's consort, Yeshe Tsogyel, stayed for some time in all of these caves and concealed treasure-texts therein. Some of the Guru's Twenty-four Disciples meditated in these caves after their final initiation, and attained *siddhi* there. Since the 8th century these caves have been the residence of many important Dzokchempas.

As these Eight Solitary Places, without exception, are located at extraordinary sites, it is most probable that they were discovered by the Bonpos before the Buddha-*dharma* was known in Tibet, although only Chimpu amongst them is mentioned in Bonpo documents. Knowledge of nature, and of the natural powers and spirits that exist in natural phenomena, was the special province of the Bonpos. Although the Bonpos had no formal science of geomancy like the Chinese, by intuition they found the natural places where combinations of the elements resulted in peculiarly auspicious conditions, or where a specific element manifested in an intense form, resulting in physical conditions that sensitive human receptors responded to in ways conducive to accomplishment of their *sadhana*. Later, when religious institutions built large monasteries, temples and hermitages around the original caves and rocks, the geomantic import was frequently ignored, the original reason for the site's importance forgotten, and even the physical conditions for its efficacy destroyed. The vistas that gave light and space and vision of the cave's macrocosmic *yantra* may have become obscured; the fire element provided by the sun may then have become obstructed; over-population may have destroyed the proximity of *drubchu* or a spring; or movement of rock and stone may have changed the forms of rock-faces and, indeed, entire hill sides. Thus the destruction of monastery buildings during the Cultural Revolution has sometimes opened up a site that had been rendered less a place of power by human interference and manipulation of nature. The silence imperative in hermitages has now been restored and the extraordinary tameness of birds and animals has once again become a feature of these power-places.

Although we have no means of authenticating the historicity of the stories associated with the Eight Caves, there is every reason to believe that Guru Rimpoche himself did inhabit them. However, it is useful to remember the story of the dog's tooth. On his return from India a Tibetan pilgrim to Bodh Gaya recalled that his mother had asked him for a relic of the Buddha. Wishing not to disappoint her, he picked up the tooth of a dog he found on the road and presented it to his mother as the tooth of the Buddha. The woman worshipped it and was rewarded by a series of miracles. Further, there is the story of the simple yogin slightly hard of hearing who heard OM MONEY PEME HUM when his Guru transmitted Chenresik's mantra to him. Nevertheless he attained perfect Buddhahood through faithful, thought-free recitation of it.

The Five Guru Rimpoche Power-places
1 Drak Yongdzong (p.210), Power-place of the Guru's Body (*sKu'i dben gnas sGrags yongs rdzong*)
2 Samye Chimpu (p.226), Power-place of the Guru's Speech (*gSung gi dben gnas mChims phu*)
3 Lhodrak Karchu (p.289), Power-place of the Guru's Mind (*Thugs kyi dben gnas Lho brag mkhar chu*)
4 Yarlung Shetak (p.191), Power-place of the Guru's Qualities (*Yon tan dben gnas Yar klung shel brag*)
5 Monka Nering Senge Dzong (p.204), Power-place of the Guru's Action (*Phrin las dben gnas Mon kha ne ring*)

The Eight Solitary Places of Realization
To the above five power-places of the Guru three are added:
6 Drakmar Yamalung (p.233) (Brag dmar gYa' ma lung)
7 Monka Sridzong (Mon kha Sri rdzong)
8 Paro Taktsang Puk (sPa gro sTag tshang phug)

Other Guru Rimpoche Caves in Central Tibet

In the developed Nyingma school doctrine of revealed texts, it is said that wherever a realized yogin meditates that spot is blessed by Guru Rimpoche. Thus in so far as enlightened yogins are emanations of Guru Rimpoche, the caves in which they meditated are called Guru Rimpoche Caves. Most valleys in Central Tibet have their Guru Rimpoche cave and it is usually an important power-place and site of pilgrimage.

Yonpu Taktsang in Won (p.241) (one of the three Taktsangs)
Kiri Yongdzong Kandro Tsokang in Shoto Tidro in Drigung
   (p.119)
Yugang Drak, behind Dingboche in Dranang (p.168)
Wokar Drak, in Jing (p.161)
Namkading, on top of Pel Chuwori (p.138)
Namka Dzong Sangyak Drak, on the Riwo Tsenga *korra* (p.145)
Garpuk, in Woka (p.253)
Dawa Puk, at Drak Yerpa (p.75)
Dralha Lupuk, on Chakpo Ri in Lhasa (p.49)

III Power-Places with Treasure Troves

There is very little in the Tibetan tradition of Buddhism that lacks an Indian antecedent. As a typical facet of Tibetan Buddhism, the *tulku* tradition of reincarnate Bodhisattvas returning to preside in the monastery of their lineage is a practical elaboration of a metaphysical principle enunciated in India. Likewise, the tradition of revealed texts also has its roots in

India, although the reformed school prefers to see this as a heterodox belief. The beliefs surrounding the origin of the *prajnaparamita sutras*, which Nagarjuna discovered in a *naga* cave deep under the earth, are commensurable with the Nyingma tradition of revealed texts called *terma*. The chief difference is that Nagarjuna's finds were hidden by the first Buddha, Sakyamuni, while the Nyingma texts were concealed by the second Buddha, Guru Rimpoche, whose name was Padma Sambhava.

In short, before Guru Rimpoche left Tibet for Ngayab in the South-west he dictated his entire body of discourses to his Tibetan consort, Yeshe Tsogyel, who then supervised their transcription into various languages. Those texts written in Tibetan, Sanskrit or the language of Orgyen (Oddiyana), which was the Guru's native tongue, were to be hidden and revealed in a literal manner. Those texts written in the language of the Dakinis, in concise hieroglyphics, were to remain in the sphere of the Dakinis, and their discoverers would be dependent upon the Dakinis as mediums of transmission and interpretation. Several other lineages of transmission evolved, some functioning in the mystical sphere and others in the human realm. Besides the many treasure-texts, Guru Rimpoche and Yeshe Tsogyel hid images made of different substances, ritual artefacts such as *dorjes* ("thunderbolts") and *purbas* (ritual "daggers"), and small chortens and so on, and also mantras inscribed in various ways. Lists of the treasure-texts and artefacts that they concealed were then compiled and hidden in or near the treasure lode. Thus the *terton*, the treasure-finder, must first obtain a list of *terma*-treasures, in order to locate the *terne*, the power-place with treasure trove, where the *terka*, the treasure cache, was hidden.

In a mystical light it is certainly true that every single power-place in Tibet, even the most obscure and minor spot, is blessed by the Guru and, therefore, has connection with the Guru's Mind, which is the source of visionary treasure. *Gongter*, mind-treasure, and *daknangiter* (*dag snang gi gter*), vision-treasure, are accessible everywhere, more dependent upon the state of mind that allows access than upon any external condition. However, in the chief power-places in the human realm geomantic conditions and the Guru's blessings have created a special conjunction in which the existence of treasure-trove is palpably felt. One facet of the "Guru's blessing" is the accretion of vibrations of aspiration, perseverance and fulfilment of successive generations of the Guru's incarnations, that have impregnated the very rock. But it was the geomantic conditions that attracted the Guru in the first place and determined the places where he hid rock-treasures and earth-treasures, treasure-texts and treasure-icons and so on. Nevertheless the texts aver that Guru Rimpoche hid treasures in 108 major power-places and 1008 minor power-places. The same prophecies promise that 22,000 treasure-finder incarnations of the Guru will appear to recover his caches.

The twenty-five power-places listed below are all given the special status of mention in the Guru's biographies. About sixty-five *terne*, power-places with treasure-trove, are listed in the chapter of the *Padma Katang* that gives indications of the type of treasure-texts, images or ritual artefacts that are to be discovered there, and also in the chapter that gives the temporal conditions that will augur the appearance of a particular treasure-finder who will reveal the treasures of a given power-place. Since Guru Rimpoche spent most of his time in Tibet in the Tsangpo and Kyichu Valleys, and also en route to the Nepal border, it is to be expected that most of these power-places are to be found in Central Tibet and Tsang. The Samye area, particularly the temples within the walls of the Samye Chokor and the Yarlung Valley, were positively loaded with his caches. The great caves of the Guru (p.289) were very important *ternes*: Yarlung Shetak, Samye Chimpu, Drakmar Yamalung and Drak Yongdzong. Since Guru Rimpoche visited the Demoness-suppressing temples built by Songtsen Gampo (p.287), caches were also concealed there: in Yarlung Trandruk, Drampa Gyang, Tsang Dram and Tsang Tsi Nesar and the Lhasa Tsuklakang. Thus the caves in the eagles' nests and the temples in the valley bottoms were both places of concealment. The third column in the table below indicates the nature of the treasure or the *terton*'s name.

Terne in the Samya Area

In Samye Chokor treasures were concealed in the Utse Rigsum and in all the Four Lings and Eight Lingtrens, in the Nyima and Dawa Lhakangs, in the Four Gates, the Four Chortens and the Jomo Ling Sum.

Gegye	Hepo Ri	Terton Sha mi rDo rje rgyal
Yangwen	Chimpu	Heart terma (*Thugs gter*)
Lompo Gul	Chimpu	Alchemical terma (*bCud len*)
Koting	Chimpu	Terton Ra shag
Yamalung	Drakmar	Long-life terma (*tshe grub*): Minling Terchen
Koro Drak	Drakmar Drinsang	Terton Ratna gling pa

In the Yarlung Valley

Trandruk		Sacred artefacts (*rDzas gter*)
Chorten Gonga	Trandruk	Profound terma, sacred artefacts (*Zab, rdzas gter*)
Pema Shepuk	Shetak	Ra mo shel sman
Puk	Shetak	Secret Kadu terma (*gSang gter bKa' 'dus*)
Yambu Lhakang	(*'khor la*)	Secret terma (*gSang gter*)
Yambu Lhakang		Terton Orgyen rig rje gling pa
Yui Lhakang	Tsentang	Five important caches (*gTer chen lnga*)
Drak Ri	Tsentang	
Bangso Marpo	Chongye	Terma of wealth and *dharma* (*Nor gter chos gter*)
Shampo Gang	(Gangri)	Secret and "Crazy" terma (*gSang gter smyon gter*)
Taktse Chingwa	Chongye	Mind terma (*dGongs gter*)

In Other Side-Valleys of the Tsangpo

Drakpoche	Drachi	"Tibetan" terma (*Bod gter*)
Yugang Drak	Dranang	"Crazy" terma (*gTer smyon*)
Taktsang	Yonpu	Sutra and Tantra (*bStan gnyis*)

| Garpuk | Woka | |
| Yongdzong | Drak | The Dorje Purba Cycle (*Phur ba*) |

In the Kyichu Valley System

Peme Gepel	Ushangdo	Terton Lha btsun sngon mo
Sangyak Drak	Riwo Tsenga	Secret and Tangyik terma; Terton Guru Jo rtse
Dawa Puk	Drak Yerpa	Profound treasure (*Zab gter*)
Tidro	Shoto	The Kandroma Cycle (*mKha' 'gro skor*)
Shai Lhakang		Vimala Nyingtik; Terton lDang ma lhun rgyal

Important Terne without Prophecy in Central Tibet

| Wokar Drak | Jing | Terton gTer bdag gling pa |
| Namkading | Pel Chuwori | |

Terne in Tsang

Drampa Gyang	Rulak	Terton dBon gsas kyung thob
Tsang Dram	Yeru	Terton mDo sngags gling pa; sacred artefacts
Tsi Nesar	Nyangro	Orgyen bstan gnyis gling pa; exoteric terma
Shinje Dongka	Gyangtse Dum	108 major terma and 1072 minor terma
Simpo Dzong	Lato	"Pacifying" terma (*Zhi byed*)
Dingchung	Lato Tingri	Yoga terma
Riwoche	Tsang	"The *siddhas*' powers" (*sGrub thob dngos grub*)
Shang Drak	Nyingdrung Nyemo Shu	Terton sNye mo Zhu yas
Yakde	Wuyuk	Terton gYag phyar sngon mo

IV THE LUME TEMPLES

The *gelong* Lume was the most important of ten Central Tibetans to travel to Kham and obtain ordination from Khampa *gelongs* who had sustained the tradition of Buddhist ordination during the period of suppression of Buddhism in Central Tibet in the 9th century. The following five temples built by Lume or his disciples during the late 10th or early 11th century are considered the oldest foundations of the second period of propagation of the *dharma* in Tibet.

Neten Lhakang at Drak Yerpa (p.77)

Lamo, in the Kyichu Valley, built 1009 (p.103)

Dratang, or Dranang, in Dranang (p.158)

Tsongdu Tsokpa in Drachi (p.161)

Sonak Tang, in Chongye, built 1017 (p.197)

V SOME PRINCIPAL KADAMPA GOMPAS

Drolma Lhakang at Netang: probably founded by Dromton between 1045 and 1054); adopted by Gelukpas (p.134).

Yerpa Drubde: converted to Kadampa after Atisha's visit c.1047; adopted by the Gelukpas (p.79).

Reteng: founded in 1056 by Dromton; adopted by Gelukpas (p.91).

Sonak Tang: founded in 1017 by Drumer Tsultrim Jungne, becoming Kadampa later in the century; adopted by Gelukpas (p.197).

Rinchen Gang: founded by Geshe Gyar Gomchempo Shonnu Drakpa (1090-1171) and rebuilt in 1181 by Sangye Wonton; adopted by Sakyapas (p. 104).

Sangpu Neutok: founded in 1073 by Ngok Lekpai Sherab; adopted by Sakyapas then Gelukpas (p.140).

Langtang: founded in 1093 by Langtangpa; adopted by Sakyapas (p.83).

Lo: founded in 1095 by Chenga Tsultrim Bar (1038-1103); adopted by Gelukpas (p.82).

Nalendra: founded in 1435 by Rongtonpa; adopted by Sakyapas (p.84).

VI THE ORIGINAL KAGYU GOMPAS

Daklha Gampo, the gompa of Je Gampopa established in 1121 (p.261).

Densatil: seat of Pakdru Kagyu established 1158 by Drogon Dorje Gyelpo (p.242).

Tse Gungtang: seat of the Tsepa Kagyu established 1175 by Lama Shang (p.96).

Drigung Til: seat of the Drigung Kagyu established 1179 by Drigung Kyapgon (p.113).

Tsurpu: seat of the Karma Kagyu established 1185 by first Karmapa Dusum Kyempa (p.122).

Taklung: seat of the Taklung Kagyu established 1185 by Taklung Tangpa (p.87).

Ralung: seat of the Drukpa Kagyu established 1180 by Tsangpa Gyare, in Tsang (p.268).

NOTES TO THE TEXT

1 *Lhasa*

1 This silver jar was identified by Heather Stoddard-Karmay in 1985.

2 Also Meru, Maru and Moru.

3 Also Chokpori.

4 Also Balalugu. Chinese: Palalubu.

5 Also Bomburi (Bong ba ri, Bong bu ri) and Parmari (sPar ma ri), and Bamari, Bamori.

6 Also Dargye Ling.

7 Also Tatipu Ri(?).

8 Also Depung.

9 Wylie(1), p.79.

2 *Drak Yerpa*

1 Also Dagyeba, Dayerpa and Trayerpa.

2 Tucci(1), p.107.

3 Roerich, p.44.

4 Wylie(1), p.84.

5 Dowman, p.115.

3 North of Lhasa

1 Also Damjung. Chinese: Damxung and Tang-hsiung.

2 Also Dromto and Bomte.

3 Also Langdong.

4 Chinese: Lunzhub.

5 Also Talung.

6 Perhaps gSer gling rgod tshang, the Hermitage of Serlingpa.

7 Also Chiomo Lhakhang (bCom mdo lha khang).

8 Also Phongdo, Phondu (Phu mdo), and Chomdo (bCom mdo).

9 Also Reting.

4 To Ganden and Beyond

1 Chinese: Maizhokunggar.

2 Also Khungtang.

3 Also Tshal Gung thang Chos 'khor gling and mTshal Gung thang;
   later also dGe 'dun tshal pa.

4 bLa ma Zhang (bLa ma Zhang brtson grags) is also known as Zhang
   mtshal pa, Zhang Rimpoche and Zhang 'gro ba'i mgon po.

5 Chinese: Dagze.

6 Also Gaden, Galdan, and Kenda.

7 Also rGya ma khri 'og.

8 Also rGya ma Rin sgang and sTag tse'i rGya ma Rin sgang.

9 Also Gyar ra and dGyer.

10 Also Tumbiri.

5 Drigung Mandala

1 Medro (Mal gro, Mal dro or Mas dro) Kongkar (dGon dkar) is the
   Chinese Maizhokunggar and also K'o-shih-ssu.

2 Chinese: Zhigung and Chih-kung.

3 Also Drigong ('Bri gong) and Drikung ('Bri khung).

4 Also Tangyab (Thang gyab).

5 Also known as Uru Sha Lhakhang (dbU ru zhwa lha khang).

6 Also Yangri Gar (Yang ri sgar).

7 Also 'Bri gung thil or -thel.

8 "Terdrom" (gTer sgrom) approximates contemporary local pronunciation, but early texts give Tidro, or Shoto Tidro. Roerich has gZho Ti sgro, and the *Padma bKa thang* has gZho stod Te sgro.

9 Amongst them 'Bri gung rGyal sras Nyin byed 'od zer who was the son of Kun mkhyen 'Jig med gling ba (p. 202).

6 *Tolung*

1 Also Tulung Churbu Gompa.

2 Also Angchen Gompa, and Hyangpachen; Chinese: Yangbajain and Yang-pa-ching.

7 *The Highway from Lhasa to Chaksam Bridge*

1 Also Gawa Dong (dGa' ba gdong).

2 Also Kimulung and Minchuling(?).

8 *Below Lhasa to Simpo Ri*

1 Also On. Historically 'U shang rdo. 'On ljang rdo, or 'On cang rdo, appears to have been the name of the former royal palace at 'On.

2 Wylie(1), p. 147; *La dwags rgyal rabs* f. 20b.

3 Tucci(1), p. 117.

4 Also Semori.

5 Chinese: Ch'u-shui.

9 *The South Bank of the Tsangpo*

1 Chinese: Kung-ka.

2 Also Gongkar Chodra and Kongka Chode.

3 From Chaksam to Gongkar Airport the milestones show distances from Lhasa; from Gongkar to the east they show distances from Chaksam.

4 *Khyentse's Guide* (p. 55) has the order of the valleys and their gompas west of Dranang confused. The order of Nam rab, Ra ba smad, and gDung phud chos 'khor should be reversed.

5 Also Ramedh and Ravame.

6 Tucci(1), p. 149.

7 Also Kyitisho and Kitisho. Chinese: Che-t'i-sha.

8 Also Dumbui Chokhor.

9 Tucci(1), p. 148.

10 gDol gSung rab gling; also Toi Suduling.

11 Also Tathang (Grwa thang) and Grwa mda'. Chinese: Cha nang.

12 Tucci(1), p. 147-8.

13 Also Champaling and Jiambaling.

14 Also Tshong dui gya ling, Tucci's Guru Tsokpa. In *Khyentse's Guide* spelt brGyad gling tshogs pa.

15 Also Drachinang.

16 Also Chinduchoka, Tsongdu Tatsang, Chongduchog, and on the OS map, in error, Danang.

17 Also Chin; the names Chincholing (Bying Chos gling) and Bying bSam gtan gling may be the names of a gompa that once stood near the village.

18 Also 'O dkar brag.

19 Also Yar klungs Bya sa lha khang.

20 Tucci(1), p. 144.

10 The Upper Dranang and Drachi Valleys

1 Derong (sTod rong) is the local diction. Thondup gives Tra Tong tod (Grwa stong stod) and Wylie(1) gives gYu ru Grwa'i phu sTong grong.

2 Also Targye; and Dar rgyas chos sding.

11 Yarlung: The Heart of Tibet

1 Wylie(10), p.90.

2 S.C. Das, *Tibetan English Dictionary*, p.1130.

3 Also Yumbu Lankhar (Yum bu bla mkhar), Yumbu Lagang (gla sgang), Umbu Dzangkhar (rdzangs mkhar), Ombu Lankhar ('Om bu bla mkhar). The name 'Om bu is probably derived from the Tibetan for tamarisk, since these trees once grew below the palace. bLa mkhar, means "palace residence of the (valley's) spirit".

4 Also Lharu Mengye (Lha ru sman brgyad).

5 Hugh Richardson: *Khyentse's Guide*, n.248.

6 Wylie(1), p.54, & p.115 n.15.

7 Also Lha ri yol ba.

8 Obermiller, p.182-3.

9 *Khyentse's Guide* describes its location "at the mouth of the Chaktsel La" (*phyag rtsal la khar*), which we failed to identify.

10 Also Tsegyel Bumpa (Tshe rgyal 'bum pa).

12 Chongye and the Royal Tombs

1 Also Chongye Dzong.

2 Also Riudechen.

3 Also Chongyechenyag.

13 Drakyul

1 Also Dorjetra.

2 Das, p. 220.

3 *Khyentse's Guide* (p. 46) notes the chief meditation caves as Upper (steng), Lower (shod), and the cave called (gNas sgo sar pa), the New Door to the Power-place. An interlinear note mentions Rig 'dzin Padma 'phrin las's cave as gNas sgo phye. There is uncertainty regarding the identification of gNas sgo sar pa and gNas sgo phye as my informant was a Khampa ill-acquainted with the place.

4 Also pronounced locally Dzong Kumbu, perhaps rDzong sku 'bum.

14 Samye Chokor

1 Das, p. 220.

2 *Ke'u tshang* is derived from a Chinese word meaning "store-house" or "treasury"; Tibetan: *mdzod;* Sanskrit: *kosha*.

3 Das, p. 223.

4 Also 'Brin bzangs.

5 Also Ningong, Namgo or Nyengo.

6 Also Yemalung or Emalung.

15 The Valley of Yon

1 Also Won or On.

2 *Khyentse's Guide* (p. 47) has mNga' ri Dwags po Grwa tshang, which is probably an error derived from a contraction of Ngari Dratsang and Dakpo Dratsang, the latter being a Yellow Hat college in Gyatsa (p. 262).

3 Tucci(1), p. 125.

4 Wylie(1), p. 170.

5 Also Yon Lhakhang Geru ('On lha khang ge ru).

6 Also Phamu bub and Phagmodu.

16 *Sangri and the Woka Valley*

1 Also Oka and Oga ('Ol kha, 'Ol dga or 'Od kha).

2 Also Sangri Khangmar (Zangs ri khang dmar).

3 Also Wode Pugyel ('Od lde pu rgyal) and 'O de gung rgyal.

4 Tucci(1), p.130.

5 Wylie(1), p.91-2.

6 Chinese: Chen-ch'i-kung-pa.

7 Also Gephuk ('Gal phug) and mKhar phug or 'Gar phug.

8 Also Samling (bSam gling).

9 Wylie(1), p.91 & n.525.

17 *Dakpo and Lhamo Latso*

1 Also Tso Lhamo (mTsho Lha mo), Chokhorgyelgi Namtso (Chos 'khor rgyal gyi gnam mtsho) and Makzorma (dMag zor ma). Also Cholamo of the old maps.

2 Also Dala Kampa, Talha Kampo, etc.; also Dwags la sgam po.

18 *Across Tsang to the Nepal Border*

1 Chinese: La-lung.

2 Also Gyangkartse. Chinese: Chiang-tzu.

3 Chinese: Ya-dong.

4 Chinese: Jih-k'a-tse, Xigatse.

5 Chinese: Sacha.

6 Chinese: Lhaze Xian.

7 Chinese: Xegar.

8 Chinese: Zhangmu; also Drammu.

Appendixes

1 See *bKa' thang sdus ba*, *Le'u bdun ma* and also the *Padma bKa' thang*.

GLOSSARY OF TIBETAN TERMS

ani (*a ni*): a nun

ani gompa (*a ni dgon pa*): nunnery

bumpa (*bum ba*): vase

chakje (*phyag rjes*): hand or foot print

chikor (*spyi 'khor*): outer circumambulation

chiwa (*phyi ba*), gomchen (*sgom chen*), chili (*phyi li*): marmot

chokang (*mchod khang*): offering hall

chorten (*mchod rten*): a *stupa* or *caitya*: a symbolic, three-dimensional representation of the Buddha's mind; sometimes a reliquary; appears in eight different forms

damaru: the two-faced "monkey" drum kept in a case slung over the ngakpa's back

depa (*sde pa*): Regent or ruler

doring (*rdo ring*): stone pillar, often inscribed

dorje (*rdo rje*) *vajra*: a common ritual instrument; a stylized thunderbolt symbolizing indestructibility

drakpuk (*brag phug*): a walled in overhanging rock forming a hermitage

dratsang (*grwa tshang*): monastic college

dre (*dre*): pre-Buddhist demons

drilbu (*dril bu*): a hand bell usually wielded with the *dorje* in tantric rites and symbolizing the feminine principle

drokpa (*'brog pa*): nomadic pastoralists herding yaks or goats on the high plateau and living in black yak-hair tents

drubchu (*sgrub chu*): a spring supplying water for hermits

drubdra (*sgrub grwa*): school of meditation

drubkang (*sgrub khang*): hermitage

drupuk (*sgrub phug*): meditation cave

duchen (*'du khang chen po*): great assembly hall

dukang (*'du khang*): a gompa's assembly hall

dulwa (*gdul ba*): monastic discipline

dundro (*dur 'khrod*): sky burial site

dzokchen (*rdzogs chen*): the summum bonum of Nyingma attainment

dzong (*rdzong*): fort; administrative district
dzongpon (*rdzong dpon*): lord of the *dzong*

gelong/gelongma (*dge slong*); bhiksu/bhiksuni: a fully ordained monk or nun, shaven headed, wearing the red or yellow shirt of Red-hat or Yellow-hat schools

geshe (*dge shes*): title indicating success in highest Geluk examination

gomkang (*mgon khang*): the lhakang where the Protectors are worshipped

gompa (*dgon pa*): a monastery or vihara

gonyipa (*mgo gnyis pa*): "two headed", collaborator

gotsang (*rgod tshang*): "eagle nest"; mountain hermitage

gyapip (*rgya phibs*): ornate, copper gilt roof

kashak (*bka' shag*): national assembly

katak (*bka' brtag*): formal offering scarf

konyer (*sgo nyer*): door-keeper

korra (*'khor ba*): circumambulation; a devotional exercise

korsa (*'khor sa*): path or passageway for korra

kuten (*sku rten*): a Buddha image

la (*bla*): life-spirit

lashing (*bla shing*): "life-spirit tree"

lari (*bla ri*): "life-spirit mountain"

lam (*lam*): path

Lama (*bla ma*): a Guru, or highly respected religious elder

lamdre (*lam 'bras*): tantric Sakya meditation

lhabtse (*lha rtse*): a cairn or chorten on a pass

lhakang (*lha khang*): "residence of the deity", temple, or inner sanctuary

losar (*lo gsar*): the Tibetan lunar new year in February or March

lu (*klu*): *naga*, Serpent Protectors of water and the treasures of the earth

lukang (*klu khang*): residence of the Serpent-Protector

lungta (*rlung rta*): "wind horse", prayer-flag

nangpa (*nang pa*): an insider or Buddhist

ne 1.(*gnas*): any place of pilgrimage or power-place; 2.(*nas*): barley

nechen (*gnas chen*): an important power-place

nekor (*gnas 'khor*): pilgrimage or circuit of power-places

nekorpa (*gnas 'khor pa*): a pilgrim

neljorpa or **neljorma** (*rnal byor palma*); yogin or yogini

neyik (*gnas yig*): guide-book

ngakpa (*sngags pa*): a long-haired, wandering *tantrika* and yogin who performs rituals for villagers; usually Nyingmapa or Kagyupa

nyerpa (*nyer pa*): monastery steward

puk (*phug*): a cave

purba or **purbu** (*phur bu*): a ritual dagger

rangjon (*rang byon*): self-manifest

ringsel (*ring bsrel*): pearl-like relics

ritro (*ri khrod*): mountain hermitage

rogyapa (*ro rgyab pa*): outcast corpse-worker

rongpa (*rong pa*) or shingpa (*shing pa*): a farmer, valley-dweller

sang (*bsang*): offering of scented wood

sangkang (*bsang khang*): hearth and chimney for juniper incense offering

shidak (*gzhi bdag*): "Lord of the Site", protecting spirit

shukpa (*shugs pa*): juniper

simkang (*gzim khang*): hermitage

simpuk (*gzim phug*): "sleeping-cave", residential cave

sungjonma (*gsung byon ma*): "Talking Deity"

sungkang (*bsrung khang*): residence of a Guardian-protector

tengwa or **tenga** (*phreng ba*); *mala*: rosary counted by the left hand held at the heart centre

terma (*gter ma*): texts and artefacts hidden as treasure by Guru Rimpoche

terne (*gter gnas*): power-places where treasure troves have been found or remain to be found

terton (*gter ston*): the discoverers of Guru Rimpoche's terma

togel (*thod rgal*): Dzokchen Atiyoga

trapa (*sgra pa*): a novice or student monk

trawa (*bra ba*), dza (*rdza*), awara (*a ba ra*), dzabra (*rdzab ra*): the tailless rodent *lagomys*

trekcho (*khreg chod*): Dzokchen Atiyoga

tsamkang (*mtshams khang*): hermitage

tsampa 1. (*mtsham pa*): a hermit or ascetic in constant retreat; 2. (*tsham pa*): roasted barley flour

tsatsa (*tsa tsa*): small clay icon of a deity, found in caves, in open chortens

tsechu (*tshe chu*): water of immortality

tsenpo (*btsan po*): epithet of early kings

tsokang (*tshogs khang*): assembly hall

tsokchen (*tshogs chen*): a great assembly hall

tulku (*sprul sku*): an incarnation of a Buddha-lama; the spiritual head of a gompa

yatsagambu (*dbyar rtsa dgun bu*): "summer grass winter worm", medicinal tonic

yidam (*yi dam*): a personal Buddha-deity

yishinorbu (*yid bzhin nor bu*): wish-fulfilling gem

A VISUAL GLOSSARY OF BUDDHAS

If a Buddha is a fully-enlightened being, then all four classes of Tibetan tantric deities – Lamas, Yidams, Kandromas (Dakinis) and Protectors (Chokyong, Dharmapalas) – can be called Buddhas. The Lama has attained Buddhahood as the fruit of his meditation; the Yidam, a personal deity, represents the enlightened mind and a means of attaining it; Kandromas are female Buddhas similar to the Yidam; and the Protectors are Buddha-deities charged with the specific duty of guarding the yogin's personal mandala and the greater circle of tantric precepts.

In the context of meditation the Lama represents the enlightened mind (*dharmakaya*); the Yidam represents the Buddha's speech and vibration (*sambhogakaya*); and the Kandroma represents the Buddha's Body of Transformation (*nirmanakaya*). The pure awareness of the Buddha's mind is in constant equanimity and the Lamas are depicted in peaceful forms. In so far as the mind's manifestation as sound, energy and light-form can be either passive or active, the Yidams and Kandromas have both peaceful and wrathful aspects, although the yogin more commonly concentrates upon the dynamic energy-forms that invoke the wrathful manifestations. These forms, like those of the Protectors, will appear demonic to the layman who has no knowledge of the essential purity of his own mind and its manifestations. A great sculptor or painter is able to show the essential compassion behind the wrathful mask.

The canon of Tibetan art decrees a standard form and colour for each deity, and the relative size of the four classes of Buddha. The visions described in the root *tantras* are the origin of a deity's iconography but the variant visionary inspiration of the four principal schools of Tibetan Buddhism and their many lineages, has resulted in a wide diversity of iconographical form. Thus depictions of the same deity may vary from gompa to gompa – even though the gompas belong to the same school. Different schools of Tibetan art have modified representation in terms of form, but they have not changed iconographical standards. The styles of these schools of art have generally been determined by a predominant foreign influence – Kashmiri, Central Asian, Nepali, Indian or Chinese. The *tankas* and murals now to be seen in Central Tibet are done mostly in the Central Tibetan style (Menri and Kyenri).

Although this glossary includes the most commonly depicted Buddha-icons it is not inclusive, and reference to a particular school's iconography may be necessary for identification purposes. The line-drawings represented here have been taken from the *Three-hundred Icons of Tibet* (Lokesh Chandra, New Delhi), which is a Geluk compendium, and from the *Nyingma Icons* (Diamond Sow, Kathmandu). They may be broken down into the following categories: 1-2 Present and Future Buddhas; 3-4 *arhats*; 5-6 Indian *panditas*; 7-8 Indian *Siddhas*; 9-12 Tibetan Kings; 13-18 Nyingma Lamas; 19-24 Tertons; 25-30 Kagyu Lamas; 31-32 Padampa and Machik; 33-34 Buton and Sapan; 35-42 Geluk Lamas; 43-49 Bodhisattvas; 50-54 Dhyani Buddhas; 55-63 Yidams (55-58 Gelukpa *tantras*); 64-66 Dakinis; 67-80 Protectors (67-69 Dzokchen Protectors); 81-84 Guardian Kings and Door-Protectors.

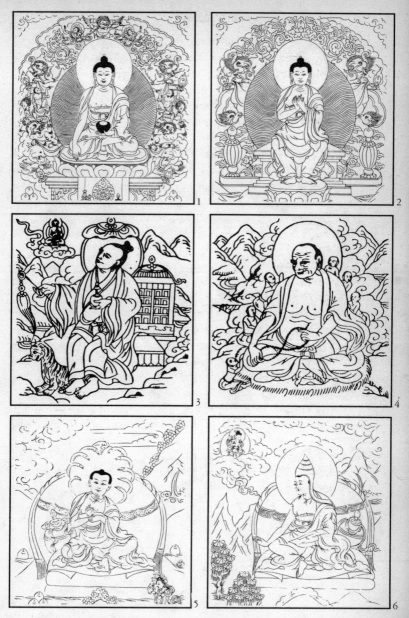

I   *1* Sakyatubpa, Sakyamuni, the Buddha Gautama   *2* Jampa,
Namdren Mapam, Maitreya, the Immanent Buddha of Love
3 Dharmatala, Indian *arhat*   *4* Hwashang Mahayana, Chinese *arhat*
5 Ludrub, Nagarjuna, founder of *madhyamika* school   *6* Tokme,
Asanga, founder of *yogacara* school

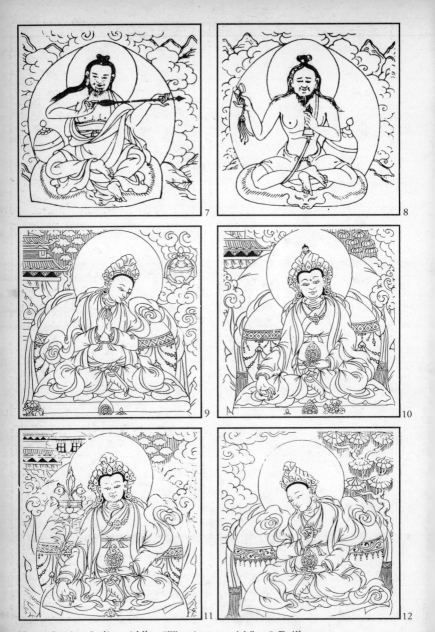

II *7* Saraha, Indian *siddha*, "The Arrowsmith" *8* Drilbupa,
Vajraghanta, Indian *siddha* *9* Lhatotori, 3rd C. King of Tibet, *see*
Yambu Lhakang *10* Songtsen Gampo, first Tibetan Emperor, *see*
Gyelpo Kang *11* Trisong Detsen, 8th C. Buddhist Emperor, *see*
Drakmar Drinsang *12* Repachen, last Buddhist Emperor, *see* Chongye

III   *13* Kunzang Yabyum, Samantabhadra, Nyingma *adi-buddha*
14 Shiwaitso, Santaraksita, first abbot of Samye, *see* Samye   *15* Guru
Rimpoche, Pema Jungne, Padma Sambhava   *16* Yeshe Tsogyel, the
Guru's Kandroma, *see* Tsogyel Latso   *17* Vimalamitra, Indian
Dzokchen *siddha*   *18* Bairotsana, Vairocana, *see* Bairo Puk

IV *19* Longchempa (Longchen Rabjampa), Dzokchempa, *see* Derong
20 Jigme Lingpa, *nyingtik terton*, *see* Tsering Jong *21* Godemchen,
Rigdzin Ngodrub Gyeltsen, *jangter terton*, *see* Dorje Drak *22* Gyurme
Dorje, Minling Terchen, *nyingtik terton*, *see* Mindroling *23* Tangton
Gyelpo, bridge-building *terton*, *see* Chaksam *24* Jamyang Kyentse
Wangpo, *rimepa*, author of *Kyentse's Guide*

V   25 Tilopa, Kagyu root-guru   26 Naropa, *mahasiddha*   27 Marpa
Lotsawa, "The Translator", *see* South of Chongye   28 Milarepa,
"The Cotton-clad", *see* Mila Puk   29 Gampopa, yogin and *pandita*, *see*
Daklha Gampo   30 Rangjung Dorje, third Karmapa and *terton*, *see*
Tsurpu

VI   *31* Padampa Sangye, Indian *siddha*, *see* Tingri Lankor
32 Machik Labdron, Padampa's Kandroma, *see* Sangri Karmar
33 Buton, *mahapandita*, see Shalu   *34* Sakya Pandita Kunga
Gyeltsen, *see* Sakya   *35* Dorjechang Yabyum, Vajradhara, Kadampa
adibuddha   *36* Jowo Je Pelden Atisha, Kadampa root-guru, see Netang

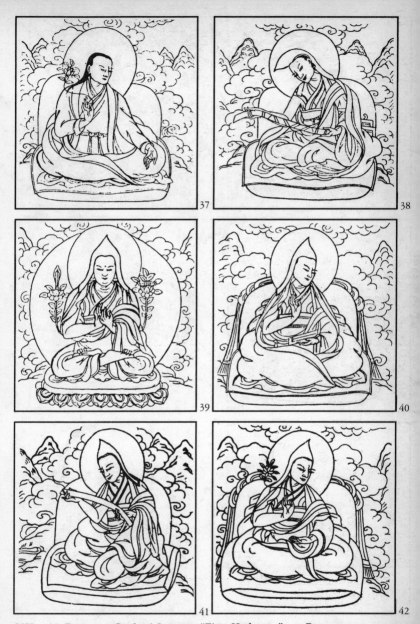

VII *37* Dromton Gyelwai Jungne, "First Kadampa", *see* Reteng
38 Ngokton Lekpai Sherab, *see* Sangpu   *39* Je Rimpoche Tsongkapa,
Geluk root-guru, see Ganden   *40* Gyeltseb Je Dharma Rinchen
(Kedrub Je with *mudra* reversed)   *41* Gendun Drub, first Dalai Lama,
see Tashi Lumpo   *42* Gyelwa Ngapa, Great Fifth Dalai Lama, *see*
Potala

VIII *43* Chenresik Chakshipa, Avalokitesvara, Protector of Tibet and
Speech *44* Tujechempo Chuchikshe, Mahakarunika, Eleven-faced
Bodhisattva of Compassion *45* Jamyang, Manjugosha, Bodhisattva-
Protector of Mind *46* Chagna Dorje, Vajrapani, Bodhisattva-Protector
of Body *47* Yangchen, Sarasvati, Goddess of Learning and
Music *48* Drolkar, Sitatara, Goddess of Service and Devotion

IX *49* Tsepame, Amitayus, Buddha of Long-life   *50* Namnang, Vairocana, Dhyani Buddha of Vast Space   *51* Miyowa, Aksobhya, Dhyani Buddha of Unshakeable Union   *52* Rinchen Jungne, Ratnasambhava, Dhyani Buddha of Abundance and Happiness
53 Wopame, Amitabha, Dhyani Buddha of Boundless Light
54 Dondrub, Amoghasiddhi, Dhyani Buddha of Successful Action

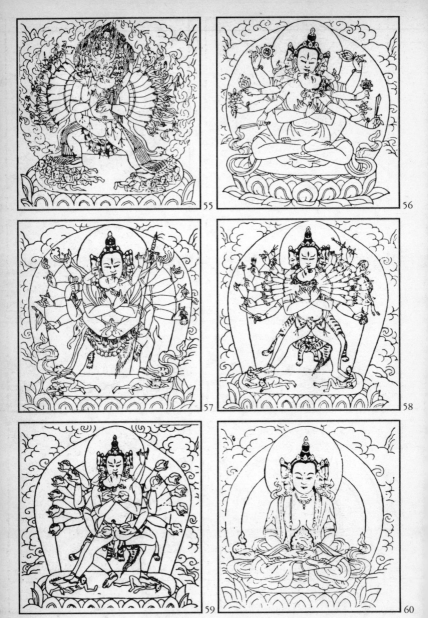

X 55 Dorje Jigche, Vajra Bhairava, Yamantaka, "The Fearsome One" 56 Sangwa Dupa (Sangdu), Guhyasamaja, "The Secret Community" 57 Korlo Dompa (Demchok), Cakrasmavara, "Circle of Bliss" 58 Dukyi Korlo (Dukor), Kalacakra, "Wheel of Time" 59 Kye Dorje, Hevajra 60 Kunrik, Sarvavid, "Omniscience"

XI *61* Dorje Purba (Dorje Shonnu), Vajrakilaya *62* Tamdrin, Hayagriva, "Horse-neck" *63* Dorje Drolo, "Adamantine Sagging-belly" *64* Dorje Pakmo, Vajra Varahi Dakini, "Diamond Sow" *65* Kurukulle (Wangdze Dakini), "Bestower of power" *66* Senge Dongma, "Lion-headed Dakini"

XII 67 Dorje Lekpa, Vajrasadhu 68 Rechikma, Ekajati, Queen of
the Mamo 69 Rahula, Kyabjuk Chempo, Lord of the
Nagas 70 Pelden Lhamo, Remati (Kalidevi), Protectress of Tibet
71 Nakpo Chempo Chakshipa, "Four-armed Great Black One"
72 Tseringma, "Long-life Protectress"

XIII 73 Dzambhala, Jambhala (Kubera), Giver of Wealth
74 Namse Serchen, Mahasuvarna Vaisravana, Victorious Protector
and Giver of Wealth   75 Bramze Sukchen, Brahmanarupadhara,
"Sadhu-Protector"   76 Dundro Dakpo, Citipati, Lord of the Dundro
77 Gurgon, Panyjarnath, "Lord of the Tent"   78 Maksorma,
Kamadhatvisvari Parvati, the Lady of Lhamo Latso

XIV 79 Pehar, the State Oracle and Protector of Nechung and Tibet
80 Tseumar, Protector of the Buddha-*dharma*   81 Virudaka (Pakyewo)
82 Vaisravana (Namtose)   83 Virupaksa (Mikmizang)   84 Dhrtarastra
(Yolkhor Sung)

SELECTED BIBLIOGRAPHY

A Record of Nyingma Monasteries in Tibet (Dalhousie, India).
Avedon, John F., *In Exile from the Land of Snows* (London 1985).

Dargyay, Eva, *The Rise of Esoteric Buddhism in Central Tibet* (Delhi 1977).
Das, Sarat Chandra, *Journey To Lhasa and Central Tibet* (Delhi 1970).
Dowman, Keith, *Sky Dancer* (London 1984).

Essais Sur L'Art Du Tibet (Paris 1977).
Ferrari, Alphonsa, *mK'yen brtse's Guide to the Holy Places of Central Tibet* (Roma 1958).

Richardson, H.E., *A Corpus of Early Tibetan Inscriptions* (London 1985).
Roerich, George N., *The Blue Annals* (Delhi 1976).
Sangpo, Khetsun, *Biographical Dictionary of Tibet and Tibetan Buddhism* (Dharamsala 1973).
Snellgrove, David, & Richardson, Hugh, *A Cultural History of Tibet* (Boulder 1968).
Stoddard, Heather, *Le Mendiant De L'Amdo* (Paris 1985).

Thondup, Tulku, *The Tantric Tradition of the Nyingmas* (Marion, MA. 1980).
Trichen, Chogay, *The History of the Sakya Sect* (Bristol 1983).
Tucci(1), Giuseppe, *To Lhasa and Beyond* (Roma 1956).
Tucci(2), Giuseppe, *Tibetan Painted Scrolls* (Kyoto 1980).
Tucci, Giuseppe, *Tibet: Land of Snows* (London 1967).

Wylie(1), Turrell V., *The Geography of Tibet According to the 'Dzam-gling-rgyas-bshad* (Roma 1962).
Wylie(2), Turrell V., *A Place Name Index to George N. Roerich's Translation of The Blue Annals* (Roma 1957).

I INDEX OF PLACE–NAMES

II INDEX OF LAMAS AND SCHOOLS

III LIST OF DEITIES WITH TIBETAN TRANSLITERATION

[Figures refer to the Visual Glossary]

Apchi (A phyir)
Begtse (Beg tse)
Bernakchen (Ber nag can)
Bramze, Brahma 75
Chagna Dorje, Chakdor, (Phyag na rdo rje) Vajrapani 46
Chakdrukpa (Phyag drug pa) Mahakala
Chaktong Chentong (Phyag stong spyan stong)
Chaktong Chuchikshel (Phyag stong bcu gcig shal) 34
Chamgon ('Cham mgon)
Chamsing (lCam sing)
Chenresik (sPyan ras gzigs) Avalokitesvara
Chenresik Senge Drak (sPyan ras gzigs Seng ge grags)
Chingkarwa ('Phying dkar ba)
Chogyel Chaktakma (Chos rgyal lcags thag ma)
Chokorma (Chos 'khor ma)
Chorten Gye (mChod rten brgyad) Astacaitya
Darlenma (Dar len ma)
Demchok (bDe mchog) Samvara 57
Dorje Chodron (rDo rje chos sgron)
Dorje Jigche (rDo rje 'Jigs byed) Vajrabhairava 55
Dorje Lekpa (rDo rje legs pa) Vajrasadhu 67

Dorje Pakmo (rDo rje phag mo) Vajravarahi 64
Dorje Purba (rDo rje phur ba) Vajrakila 61
Dorje Shonnu (rDo rje gZhon nu) Vajrakumara
Dorje Trollo (rDo rje gro lod) 63
Dorje Yudronma (rDo rje gyu sgron ma)
Dorjechang Yabyum (rDo rje chang yab yum) 35
Droljang (sGrol ljang) Shyamatara
Drolkar (sGrol dkar) Sitatara 48
Drolma (sGrol ma) Tara
Drolma Shesema (sGrol ma zhal zas ma)
Drolma Sungjonma (sGrol ma gSung byon ma)
Drupa Kabgye (sGrub ba bka' brgyad)
Dsetoma (mDse thod ma)
Dudtsi Men (bDud rtsi sman)
Dukor (Dus 'khor) Kalacakra 58
Dutsi Kyilwa (bDud rtsi dkyil ba)
Dzambhala, Kubera 73
Dzamling Gyen (rDzam gling rgyan)
Dzamling Gyenchik (rDzam gling rgyan gcig)
Ekajati (Relchikma) 68
Gompo (mGom po) Mahakala
Gompo Gur, Gurgon, (mGon po Gur) 77
Guru Tsengye (Guru mtshan brgyad)